D0949939

FRIENDLY FIRE

Losing Friends and Making Enemies in the Anti-American Century

JULIA E. SWEIG

A Council on Foreign Relations Book

PublicAffairs

NEW YORK

Founded in 1921, the Council on Foreign Relations is an independent, national membership organization and a nonpartisan center for scholars dedicated to producing and dis-
seminating ideas so that individual and corporate members, as well as policymakers,
journalists, students, and interested citizens in the United States and other countries, can
better understand the world and the foreign policy choices facing the United States and
other governments. The Council does this by convening meetings; conducting a wide-
ranging Studies program; publishing *Foreign Affairs*, the preeminent journal covering international affairs and U.S. foreign policy; maintaining a diverse membership; sponsoring
Independent Task Forces; and providing up-to-date information about the world and
U.S. foreign policy on the Council's website, www.cfr.org.

THE COUNCIL TAKES NO INSITUTIONAL POSITION ON POLICY ISSUES AND HAS NO AFFILIATION
WITH THE U.S. GOVERNMENT. ALL STATEMENTS OF FACT AND EXPRESSIONS OF OPINION CON-
TAINED IN ITS PUBLICATIONS ARE THE SOLE RESPONSIBILITY OF THE AUTHOR OR AUTHORS.

BOOK DESIGN AND COMPOSITION BY JENNY DOSSIN. TEXT SET IN JANSON TEXT.

Library of Congress Cataloging-in-Publication Data
Sweig, Julia
Friendly fire : losing friends and making enemies in the anti-American century / Julia E.
Sweig.—1st ed.
p.   cm.
A Council on Foreign Relations Book.
Includes bibliographical references and index.
ISBN-13: 978-1-58648-300-5
ISBN-10: 1-58648-300-5
1. Anti-Americanism. 2. Anti-Americanism—History—20th century. 3. United States—
Relations—Foreign countries. 4. United States—Foreign relations—Latin America. 5.
Latin America—Foreign relations—United States. 6. United States—Foreign public
opinion. 7. United States—Foreign relations.—2001- I. Council on Foreign Relations.
II. Title.
E840.S94 2006
327.73009'0511—dc22
2005056686

FIRST EDITION

10 9 8 7 6 5 4 3 2 1

FOR REED, ISABEL, AND ALEXANDER

CONTENTS

INTRODUCTION

Are We All Anti-Americans Now?

Anti-Americanism, anti-American, anti-Americans: mouth-fuls that roll off the tongue with a kind of poetry that just doesn't have a match in the (as yet) nonexistent "anti-Chinaism," "anti-EUism," "anti-Russianism." The syncopated assonance alone makes the words friendly in the mouths of pundits, analysts, and government officials—convenient to describe a seemingly ubiquitous, increasingly visceral phenomenon. Today's anti-Americanism is a far cry from the eighteenth-, nineteenth-, or early twentieth-century garden variety, and even from the Cold War type, when knee-jerk America-bashing was part of the ideological canvas of the fashionable European left or nationalist right. But as long as a dystopian alternative universe loomed in the Soviet bloc, posited as the attitude was against the far more noble cause of anticommunism, anti-Americanism remained a manageable if annoying feature of America's strategy of containment and ascent to power in the twentieth century.

The twenty-first century's anti-American backlash now extends well beyond the anti-Western worldview of radical Islamic *jihadistas*, well beyond the violent fundamentalist fringe. Anti-Americanism is going global, stretching from within America's own borders, across continents, classes, ideologies, religions, gender, and generations. That giant "thing" out there, ready to ensnare America's and the international community's designs for peace, war, prosperity, or security, has morphed from a nagging, marginal ideology into a new international state of mind better expressed by the idea of "Anti-America," the proper noun.

Two events in the fall of 2005 crystallized the phenomenon of Anti-America. The Nobel Prize Committee of Sweden gave its annual award for peace to the United Nations–sponsored International Atomic Energy Agency (IAEA) and its head, Mohamad ElBaradei. An Algerian lawyer and diplomat, ElBaradei had opposed the 2003 Iraq war, disagreeing with the U.S. contention that Iraq was in the process of reconstituting its nuclear weapons program. Apparently out of retribution for his insistence that IAEA inspectors be given more time before a U.S.-led military intervention, the United States stopped sharing intelligence with the agency, tried to have ElBaradei removed from his post, and tapped his telephones in an attempt to marginalize him. The Nobel award was not only a signal of disapproval of the war in Iraq and a rebuke of the United States but also a warning against future U.S. attempts to bypass the United Nations, whether over Iran or other nuclear proliferation crises.[1]

Fair enough. The United States had thumbed its nose at the international community over Iraq, and the symbolism of awarding the Nobel to ElBaradei and his agency reflected the conventional global wisdom that the United States could use a humbling slap on the wrist for its unilateralism. But a few days later, the Nobel committee delivered a punch in the face when it announced that its 2005 Nobel Prize for Literature would go to Harold Pinter, British playwright, director, and poet, for his lifetime of creativity stretching back to the 1950s. More than his theatrical contributions, though, was it Pinter's odes reviling Tony Blair, George Bush, and their war on Iraq and vision of democracy that the Nobel committee sought to highlight? Though their vulgarity gives them an air of dark humor, read as straight antiwar poetry, Pinter's "God Bless America," "The Special Relationship," and "Democracy" take vicious and graphic aim at the U.S. and British motives in Iraq and helped galvanize and color the British public's opposition to the war. Awarding Pinter the Nobel, while surely intended to recognize the entire oeuvre of a man suffering from throat cancer, reflected the deep disdain and contempt with which America is viewed, at least by the Swedish committee, and was, as one British editorial noted, "just about the biggest and sharpest stick with which the Nobel committee can poke America in the eye."[2]

Hurricane Katrina likewise proved an opportunity for the expression of international disillusion with America's failures—this time for its neglect of its most vulnerable citizens. In the Czech Republic, no hamlet of Anti-America, a local newspaper described Katrina as "the last point in a long process of degradation of American public life. American state power doesn't have any conscience anymore."[3] In the two weeks following Katrina's devastation, hundreds of foreign press stories from dozens of countries around the world registered similar dismay, sometimes with a perverse tone of delight, over America's failure to make manifest government's fundamental commitment to protect its citizens. Between 2001 and 2005, Iraq and Katrina exposed a significant rift between the United States and much of the international community, whether over America's motives in war and peace, or its ability to protect the environment, combat terrorism, drive growth, fight poverty, or promote democracy. Polls in Europe, Latin America, the Middle East, and parts of Asia showed negative, declining, entrenched, or barely improving opinion of the United States, the American president, American foreign policy, even of the American people, year after year.[4]

But prizes, punditry, and polls alone cannot tell the whole story behind this wave of disillusion with the United States. The foundations of Anti-America are held together by a shifting mix of related elements: history, power and powerlessness, economic globalization, and national identity—what we do, who we are, who they are, and what they do. Anti-America is expansive and diverse, deep and shallow; its intensity varies and is difficult to measure.[5] In some countries or whole regions of the world, only one or two of these elements combine to explain the antipathy toward America. Elsewhere, all of the elements feed the dynamics of anti-Americanism, as does the cumulative legacy of past policy failures. Often, there is an undertow or a more overt anti-Semitic hostility that accompanies the new anti-Americanism, as it did the old, and vice versa. Although seldom the burden of any single U.S. administration or political party, these structural, often latent sources of Anti-America can be exacerbated by specific policies and styles of diplomacy, making the poisonous atmosphere impossible to ignore.

After the September 11, 2001, terrorist attacks but before the war in Iraq, the conventional wisdom in the United States held that it was principally the last two elements—who they are and what they do—that best explained the growing backlash. Anti-Americanism in the Arab world, one observer noted, "is largely the product of self-interested manipulation by various groups within Arab society, groups that use anti-Americanism as a foil to distract public attention from other, far more serious problems within those societies."[6] Taking anti-Americanism at face value, it was argued, vastly underappreciated the extent to which local media, clerics, elites, intellectuals, and politicians exploited easy anti-American answers as a way to distract from their own shortcomings or bury their own history. "They," the conventional wisdom went, might say they hate us because we are too pro-Israel or because we have designs on their power, sovereignty, culture, markets, or oil, but such hot air deflected attention from their own self-loathing, their own societies' failures or historical neuroses. The United States could be faulted for having propped up autocratic dictators in the twentieth century, but America's stability-for-democracy trade-offs or its policies toward Israel were no excuse, many persuasively argued, for decades of corruption, stagnant economies, political exclusion, or inflammatory fundamentalist bile that had snowballed into a wave of terrorist attacks worldwide that began in earnest in the 1990s.[7] Americans might accept constructive criticism of certain policy-specific complaints, even recognize the importance of engaging in the pursuit of a just settlement to the Israel-Palestine conflict, but the "blame-America" industry was understood by America's political class largely as a cynical dodge by those abroad unwilling or incapable of taking responsibility for their own failures.

By making regime change in Iraq the center of the war on terror, botching the diplomacy leading up to the war, and because of the abuses and torture now associated with both the war in Iraq and the war on terror, the United States single-handedly rejiggered the mix of elements supporting the foundations of Anti-America. It could no longer be persuasively argued that only "their" failures, self-loathing, or power designs bore the lion's share of responsibility for inflaming anti-Americanism. Instead, America's own choices and policies, often an expression of the country's internal political and cultural divide, upended the conventional wisdom. By 2003, Anti-America was no longer "their" creation—it was ours as well.

This book is not primarily about radical Islamic Anti-America. The reader can consult a vast bibliography that has flowered on that subject. Indeed, the threat posed by most of America's nuclear or terrorist-supporting adversaries is mostly knowable.

The United States is now attuned to expect opposition or hostility from their ranks. Now, at least, it comes as no surprise. But the overt enmity of governments and overwhelmingly negative public opinion in countries as culturally diverse and geographically distant as Great Britain, Germany, Turkey, and South Korea, where the United States historically assumed that an attitude of deference would ultimately overcome the usual resentment of power, has taken America aback. It is Anti-America among traditional U.S. allies where we must come to grips with the sources, internal and external, of the extraordinary wave of bitterness and distrust now entrenched among governments, elites, and broad sectors of public opinion. Without the consent and support of U.S. allies on a complex constellation of international issues that by their nature require global cooperation, Anti-America may turn out to be more than an ephemeral anomaly with negligible consequences. Instead, if allowed to settle into an acceptable global reflex, the new anti-Americanism will undermine the international community's political will to give the United States the benefit of the doubt on a range of foreign policy goals and thus hamper the prospect for cooperative initiatives to confront global challenges. By sowing the seeds of suspicion and anger among young generations who have no memory of America as a credible, trustworthy partner, Anti-America will sabotage even the best-intentioned U.S. leadership or well-designed policy and will weaken national and international security for decades to come.

This book is about the past, present, and future. In the first part, I explore the foundations of contemporary Anti-America. Particularly during the Cold War, the twentieth century registered notable moments of anti-American animus. But whether over the Cuban Missile Crisis, the Vietnam War, or Euromissiles, Anti-America never got in America's way. Still, the cumulative effect of many elements of the Cold War—interventionist policies in the developing world, and how the United States later understood and explained the causes and implications of the Cold War's demise—did lay the groundwork for a good deal of the backlash the United States encountered after the 1989 fall of the Berlin Wall. Beyond the Cold War and its ambivalent legacy, four elements explain and may well sustain the new anti-American impulse: power and powerlessness, economic globalization, and American national identity—what we do, and who we are.

In Part Two, I depart from the made-in-America features of anti-Americanism to look at how the domestic politics and national identities of America's longtime partners or dependents in Europe, Asia, and Latin America shape their response to the United States: Several countries long part of the U.S. sphere of influence, spurred by historic and domestic dynamics and inflamed by a clear rejection of U.S. policies, in recent years have moved away from their traditional deference toward the United States. Latin America, a region that can be viewed as the geographic and historic birthplace of Anti-America, is an especially prominent pocket of visceral anti-Americanism. Because of America's historic hegemony in Latin America, a past and present of bad policy, and the failures of economic globalization and of governments and elites to deliver better lives to more people, Latin America has become a proving ground for many of the sources of anti-Americanism among U.S. allies beyond the Western Hemisphere. Much of the world is just beginning to contend with America's undiluted power, but Latin America has done so for well over a century. That region, with its experience as a laboratory for U.S. power and policies, plus its own raft of internal quirks and idiosyncrasies, offers considerable insights into the backlash the United States is now experiencing across the globe.

Our security and well-being depend on understanding the sources of anti-Americanism among U.S. friends, allies, and dependents. Gaining that awareness without engaging in defensive chauvinism will give us a clear idea about how to avoid similar pitfalls in the decades ahead. In the short and medium term, the United States will wrestle with major strategic choices about how to manage its power in an unstable and unsettling international climate of stateless and state-sponsored terrorists, nuclear proliferation, failed and failing states, pervasive poverty, worsening inequality, epidemic disease, natural disasters and environmental decay, and personal insecurity for the vast majority of the world's population. The capacity of the United States and of the international community to contend with such issues of truly global dimension will be severely undermined until the United States can draw lessons from the past and present and recover for the future the trust that has been lost in recent years.

But how can the United States make such a recovery when underlying the dynamics that fan the friendly fire of Anti-America is a critical quality of human nature: Perception seldom squares with reality. Global (and for that matter American) perceptions of the intentions behind U.S. actions seldom coincide precisely with U.S. motives. For example, the current White House, as articulated in George W. Bush's 2004 inaugural address and the rhetoric of his deputies, embraces the ideals of spreading freedom and democracy as the driving motive for its foreign policies, aspirations embraced by presidents of both parties for a century or more. Yet for America's traditional allies, and for majorities of populations in countries that are the object of U.S. policies, there is a strong perception that the U.S. administration's contention is often not borne out by the policies adopted to advance such lofty goals. The gap between perception and reality is not itself a new feature of international life. But in today's 24/7 media environment, the perception gap is a principal reason the traditional tools of public diplomacy offer little solace for redressing the new anti-American impulse.

There is no easy fix to what has become, as a result of the confluence of structurally driven resentments and provocative foreign policies, a fundamentally altered international environment for the United States. Yet by drawing upon the very foundations of Anti-America, the United States, with thoughtful leadership, still has a chance to manage, if not solve, a chronic and, I would argue, debilitating perception problem. Thus, in the last section of the book, I offer a set of proposals—modest compared with the scope of the damage—for both the United States and those countries and populations most tempted by the perversely feel-good aspects of Anti-America, to prevent its permanent consolidation.

FRIENDLY FIRE

I

Cold War History and the Latin American Laboratory

"The past is never dead; it's not even past."
—Gavin Stevens in *Requiem for a Nun*,
William Faulkner, 1951

Henry Luce's description of the twentieth century as the "American Century" struck a chord because the phrase coined by the founder of the magazine empire Time Inc. captured the widespread recognition—within and beyond the nation's borders—that, on balance, the United States exercised more positive influence than not on the people, countries, and international institutions with which it engaged. The twentieth century is not generally regarded as one colored by expansive or even particularly threatening anti-Americanism. Still, to gloss over the century as a golden era of American wisdom and success in global projection would not only ignore the divisiveness of U.S. foreign policy debates at home but also miss the kernels of today's backlash. Planted especially during the Cold War, those seeds have come to blossom in the twenty-first century, a period that might, albeit prematurely, be termed the Anti-American Century.

In particular, such a glimmering patina would lose sight of the experience of Latin America, a part of the world where anti-Americanism ranging from ambivalent to virulent was the default political environment decades before it became a more global impulse. Indeed, precisely because the twentieth century brought the United States virtually uncontested hegemony in Latin America, the combination of physical proximity, domestic turmoil and politics, profound inequality, and intimate familiarity with and expectations of the United States by the region's governments and population, in addition to specific U.S. policies, made it a proving ground for inelegantly manifest U.S. power. For example, the U.S.-supported insurgency in El Salvador in the 1980s has become a positive reference point for advocates of counterinsurgency warfare's capacity to defeat the insurgents and bring democracy to Iraq. Likewise, just as Latin Americans rejected the U.S.-backed counterinsurgency campaign in El Salvador in the 1980s, and the United States routinely rebuffed the region's diplomatic initiatives to end armed conflict in Central America, so also did the United States in 2002 and early 2003 spurn efforts by the international community to allow the inspection process to play out fully before going to war in Iraq without a second resolution from the United Nations Security Council. This U.S. defiance caused a revolt against the United States that stretched beyond the more dependent powers of Latin America to America's principal allies. Whether because of the interventions of the early twentieth century, the Central American wars of the 1980s, or America's contempt for the region's views, Latin America's history with the United States makes the region a prophetic microcosm of what has now become an increasingly instinctive anti-American reflex well beyond the Western Hemisphere.

President William McKinley's self-described divine intervention in the Cuban war of independence against Spain in 1898 initiated the first era of twentieth-century anti-Americanism. Whether they invoked God, democracy, money, the protection of U.S. citizens, or the threat posed by outside powers, Teddy Roo-

sevelt, William Taft, and Woodrow Wilson continued the south-
ward expression of U.S. power with a total of twenty-eight interventions in Honduras, the Dominican Republic, Nicaragua,
Panama, Mexico, Haiti, Costa Rica, and Guatemala between
1900 and 1921. Among other effects, these events served as
demonstrations of American muscle for consumption by European powers. Indeed, France, Germany, Russia, Spain, and Great
Britain sustained their own minor or major bruises from run-ins
with emerging U.S. naval, industrial, financial, and geographic
power: By the early twentieth-century, anti-Americanism born of
French universalist jealousy, British contempt, Spanish pique,
Russian envy, or German spiritual decay had accumulated over
the centuries as the inevitable outcrop of America's successes.

The unilateralism and intervention that came to be thought
of by Latin Americans as the essence of the Monroe Doctrine
and the Roosevelt Corollary, and by American power thinkers
and practitioners as legitimate tools of statecraft, became part of
the lore of American exceptionalism: the notion that America
could throw its weight around—willy-nilly of international law
or the sovereignty of other states—because its goals were noble,
its values universal in their appeal. The countries of Latin America were among the first, but by no means the last, to experience
the impact of Alexander Hamilton's idea in the Federalist Papers
that America's security would be best protected by "extending
the sphere" of its interests.

What for the United States was the rightful and manifest ex-
ertion of power in the name of national interest, values, markets,
democracy, or nation-building became for Mexicans, Cubans,
Nicaraguans, Haitians, Hondurans, Costa Ricans, Dominicans,
and Filipinos trespasses of sovereignty by a colossus that dressed
up its raw power grab in the garb of divine duty and civilizational
light to tame the disorganized, fractious, nationalist upstarts of
its southern neighborhood. Although Latin American resistance

to U.S. power was not uniform, consistent, or unambiguous, it focused on the symbols of that power: company towns, sugar mills, banana plantations, military bases, rapacious client dictators, U.S. capital, marines, and diplomats.[1]

Anti-American sentiment in the hemisphere, whether from the left, the right, peasants, trade unionists, oligarchs, local business elites, or the armed forces, and whether driven by a genuine desire for independence or by designs on power, money, or justice, was born foremost of nationalism. Long before communism had made a name for itself, Latin American intellectuals from José Enrique Rodó in South America, for whom North America was Caliban to Latin America's Ariel, to José Martí in the Caribbean Basin, whose life's work was to protect not just Cuba but "our America" from the "monster of the north," wrestled with how the continent could develop an independent cultural, political, and economic identity growing up in the shadow of a power at once so attractive and repulsive.[2] By 1933, when Franklin Delano Roosevelt launched the Good Neighbor policy in an explicit attempt to reverse the damage of the interventionist period of the previous two decades, nationalism and sovereignty in the Americas had become thoroughly entwined with resistance to or manipulation of American power.

In establishing the right to preemptive military intervention in the Americas, by the middle of the twentieth century the United States had accomplished two objectives. First, it had clearly established a line the European powers no longer would cross, a move that would prepare the ground for the great-power horizons that lay ahead. Second, it had opened lines of investment, trade, markets, and influence for an experiment in nation-building beyond its borders that would establish the United States and its diplomatic, economic, and military representatives as the go-to powers at the center of local politics. In short, although Americans tend to favor the conceit that the United

States became the sole superpower only in 1989, in its own sphere it had primed the pump for this role long before the Soviet collapse. Until the late twentieth century, other than Vietnam, it was Latin America that registered the most direct and consistent experience with the good, the bad, and the ugly of U.S. power, making the region the cradle of Third World anti-Americanism long before radical Islamic terrorist groups would make their wrath felt.

Just as Franklin Delano Roosevelt's anticolonialist reputation, Good Neighbor policy, and commitment to harnessing the state and the market for the betterment of society inspired independence movements around the globe, Latin Americans looked to FDR's New Deal as the model for modernizing their own backward, corrupt, unequal, and impoverished societies. In the 1940s, for example, bright, educated, idealistic young men from Central America and the Caribbean, including Cuba, formed what they called the "Caribbean Legion," an armed enterprise aimed at dislodging dictators throughout the region. Their objective was not to install pro-Soviet politburos but to hold U.S.-style elections, modernize and purge their civil services of corruption, and get on with the business of creating democratic welfare states of the sort that seemed to be prospering north of the Rio Grande and that the United States would underwrite in Europe after World War II.

Not that there was no communist presence in Latin America—it just wasn't strongly anti-American in its earlier incarnations. From the 1920s through the end of the 1940s, right under America's nose, pro-Soviet communist parties thrived throughout South America, from Brazil to Mexico, El Salvador to Guatemala, and Cuba too. They accumulated membership rosters in the hundreds of thousands that represented a who's who of the region's cultural and intellectual stars together with the vastly more numerous and anonymous miners, peasants, and industrial workers who embraced the party's promise to make life better for the wretched of the earth. In Cuba, Guatemala, and Brazil in the 1930s, 1940s, and 1950s, respectively, communists held ministerial posts. During the interwar period, through World War II and the late 1940s, Washington tolerated the party's presence in Mexico and Latin America, much as the political culture of the United States still preserved some, albeit dwindling, space for the nation's branch of the Communist Party, the CPUSA.

It wasn't until 1947, as the Cold War ignited, that Latin Americans were put on notice: Good relations with the United States depended on a purge of local communists (and later noncommunist leftists), whose rhetoric had grown anti-American as Uncle Joe's fuzzy Russian bear morphed into Stalin's Soviet menace. An anti-American predisposition was not limited to communists in the hemisphere: Peronists in Argentina, indigenous miners in Bolivia, trade unionists in Mexico, anti-imperialists in Central America, protectionist oligarchs throughout South America, intellectuals, the military, and the Catholic Church—nationalists all—chafed under, even as they accommodated to, U.S. power. Just as the McCarthy era in the United States cast many noncommunists as guilty fellow travelers, a vast ideological and political rainbow of Latin Americans set on modernizing their countries became suspect and suspicious of American power.

The election in Guatemala of Jacobo Arbenz in 1950 represented a victory for the political ideals of the Caribbean Legion and was the first challenge to the United States of the post–World War II period. Arbenz was not a communist himself. But like many socially minded liberals of the era, he included in his kitchen cabinet communist intellectuals and labor leaders known to be good managers and free of corruption—a problem that plagued party and government bureaucrats throughout the hemisphere. In the nine years that Arbenz and his predecessor, Juan José Arévalo, were in power, they brought to Guatemala a new, modern, and liberal constitution, workers' rights, women's rights, the beginnings of a civil service, a progressive tax code, and land reform.

These last two steps especially tweaked the country's taxophobic oligarchs and awakened the genteel wrath of John Foster Dulles, the U.S. secretary of state, and his brother Allen, head of the Central Intelligence Agency (CIA) and whose law firm represented the United Fruit Company. Following a combination of psychological warfare and economic pressure, the CIA successfully deployed the Guatemalan military against the civilian president. Jacobo Arbenz was not anti-American. He was a democratically elected left-leaning nationalist. But he found that making Guatemala a modern, sovereign nation meant overturning the symbols and substance of U.S. power and challenging the purview within society of the landed oligarchs and local elites that had become America's allies. The 1954 coup inflamed extremist nationalism on the left and the right, permanently weakened Guatemala's moderate center, dashed the country's prospects for modern national development, and ushered in thirty years of civil war, repression, insurgency, counterinsurgency, and indigenous genocide.[3]

Thirty-five years later, in 1999, the United Nations and Catholic Church–supported truth commission that emerged after the peace process determined that some 200,000 Guatemalans, mostly civilians, were killed or disappeared during the war. The commission found the army responsible for 93 percent of the 42,000 civilian killings it investigated, and it reported that the "government of the United States, through various agencies including the CIA, provided direct and indirect support for some state operations."[4] The role of the United States was pronounced enough that President William Clinton issued an official apology for U.S. actions in Guatemala. There is almost no political actor in Guatemala today whose mouth does not carry a bitter anti-

American taste, while the overthrow of Arbenz dashed hopes in Latin America that the United States might become an active ally, whether in the pursuit of democratic politics or equal economic opportunity.

With its coup against Arbenz, the United States went on record that it would not tolerate in Latin America the core twentieth-century social policies that in Europe and Asia had begun to break the link between poverty and inequality and political exclusion. The concentration of land, wealth, and power in the hands of a tiny percentage of the country's population, for whom the idea of a social contract was anathema, came to be widely understood throughout Latin America as the root of political violence in the era. After World War II in Japan, Korea, and Western Europe, the United States thoroughly grasped the political significance of progressive taxes and land reform. In Guatemala it instead stood firmly on the side of the most politically regressive and financially irresponsible segment of society, and that stance came to be properly understood as a statement of U.S. preferences for the hemisphere as a whole and contributed to deepening anti-American animus on the ground. The democratically elected Arbenz offered a project to modernize Guatemala that collided head-on with what Henry Kissinger would later, in the context of Chile, characterize as the right of the United States to establish the "limits of diversity" in Latin America.[5] Latin Americans came to expect the draconian U.S. approach to friends and allies—you are either with us or with the enemy—fully sixty years before the European West tasted such fare.

Still, along with the gunboat diplomacy of the first half of the twentieth century and the polarizing effect of the Cold War, the United States helped organize the basic infrastructure of Latin countries: ports and customs houses, public security, a modicum of education and health, social services, and the Lord's word ministered by Catholic, Methodist, and Protestant evangelical missionaries. Latin Americans fought in World War II and the Korean War, trained in the American military, sent their children to prep school and college in the States, worked for U.S. companies, learned English, and reached for pieces of the American dream and its middle-class life in the boom years during and after the war. By the end of the 1950s, Latin Americans had developed a solidly ambivalent view of their neighbor to the north. And because U.S. government officials tended to get their information about Latin America from the generals they backed in power or the elites who benefited from such alignments, Americans remained largely oblivious to Latin America's souring view of the United States until angry crowds stoned Vice President Richard Nixon's convoy in Caracas in 1958.

The stoning and riots awakened Americans to the brewing nationalist anger at the United States for having kept the faith with military dictators, whether in Venezuela, Colombia, Cuba, Haiti, the Dominican Republic, or most of Central America, and for reverting to the turn-of-the-century disregard for national sovereignty. Having so aggressively sought to control Latin American politics and cultivated the perception of blanket control by aligning itself with the key pillars of power within the region's societies, the United States opened itself to blame for all that went wrong on the ground, a pattern that subsequently would emerge on a global scale.

Despite Vice President Nixon's wake-up call in Caracas, the administration of Dwight D. Eisenhower was almost completely blindsided by the extent of popular support for the Cuban Revolution. Within a few years of Fidel Castro's 1959 triumph, the revolution would rewrite the rules of the game for any Latin American hoping that electoral politics and democratic institutions could promise a viable path from authoritarian rule and poverty to democracy and prosperity. Initially, the revolution was not an anti-

American event. Fidel Castro arrived in Havana from the mountains of eastern Cuba on January 9, 1959, at the head of a broad political coalition that had coalesced against Fulgencio Batista in the 1950s. Of all the anti-Batista political parties, insurgent groups, underground militia, middle- and working-class activists, high school and university students, doctors, lawyers, architects, and other professionals, the only group with an expressly anti-American line was the local communist party. But despite its open anti-American hostility, the party was an extraordinarily minor player in the Cuban insurgency. Like the Soviets, party officials preached popular-front politics and thought the revolution in Cuba would come only with proletarian solidarity and elections— the first of which was woefully lacking and the latter either postponed, fraudulent, or otherwise manipulated repeatedly by Batista and overlooked by the United States throughout the 1950s.

Most of the young militant anti-Batista revolutionaries in Castro's Twenty-sixth of July movement and in other organizations had grown up in close contact with some aspect of the United States—whether in U.S.-owned company towns, working in the mob-infested tourist industry, studying in U.S. bilingual high schools, or attending graduate school in the States. They fully grasped the extent of Cuba's economic and political dependence on the United States and used their ties within the country to build financial, diplomatic, and public relations support. They needed the United States to rid Cuba of its dependence upon it. But they also looked to the United States, its meritocracy, low levels of corruption, and democracy as an inspiration for the kind of more equitable society many hoped their country could become.

The political platform of the revolutionaries was not far removed from the Arbenz agenda to modernize the economy, armed forces, bureaucracy, and political system. The revolutionaries said they wanted to restore the 1940 constitution, one of the most progressive of the hemisphere, and bring social justice to the country's poor and indigent. Above all, whether they were revolutionaries under arms or still sipping cocktails at the Havana Yacht Club, Cubans working to unseat Batista were nationalists—patriots who wanted Cuba for Cubans. They felt humiliated by their dependence on the United States and ashamed by the ease with which Batista and the corruption and division of an earlier generation of revolutionaries could sweep away the semblances of a republican government they had begun to create in the 1930s. They were acutely conscious of their failure to take control of the country when the United States snatched their independence victory from the Spanish at the tail end of the 1898 war.

Sixty years later, nationalism and revolution had become thoroughly intertwined. In that time, the cultures of Cuba and the United States had grown connected by everything from sugar to baseball, Ernest Hemingway to Cab Calloway. Those Cubans able to sustain a middle-class lifestyle—and they were few and declining in number by the late 1950s—pined for U.S. material culture. They wanted our stuff, but Cubans increasingly chafed under the weight of our political baggage. When the revolutionaries came to power, even before the Soviet flirtation became particularly passionate, it was clear that they could not find a way to draw a nationalist line without pointedly challenging the rules of the game the United States had established at the turn of the century. U.S. capital and power were simply too pervasive and bound up in too many pregnant symbols—sugar, electricity, telephones, the Guantánamo naval base, popular culture, the military, the dictatorship, the mob, drugs, and prostitution—for the revolutionaries and their professional, middle-class base to settle for a nonprovocative course of nation-building not on U.S. but on Cuban terms.

Before the first Soviet trade mission to the island in late 1960,

Cuban land reform and nationalization programs—crafted by attorneys well schooled in international law—had already been handily rejected by the Eisenhower administration. By early 1960, Eisenhower moved to punish Cuba with cuts in its sugar quota and authorized a covert-action program. By the time Fidel Castro declared the revolution to be socialist on the eve of the 1961 Bay of Pigs invasion, U.S. officials had made it impossible for a moderate nationalist path of development to succeed. And Fidel Castro came to believe that the revolution, which for most Cubans then represented the culmination of almost one hundred years of thwarted nationalist aspirations, could not succeed without extirpating America from Cuba.

Thus, the Cuban Revolution came to be an anti-American event once it became clear that neither Americans nor Cubans could find a way to escape the inherited inequalities that had both embroiled and alienated each country from the other in the twentieth century. Knowing of America's rejection of moderate reforms and attempts to overthrow the Castro government, Cubans grasped this truth and were even, incomprehensibly to the United States and to Soviet officials, willing to risk nuclear war to stake out their independence. The United States found it easier to dismiss Cuba's ferocity of focus mainly as a matter of geopolitics, largely dismissing its own responsibility for events that led to Cuba's extreme dependence before and radicalization after 1959. What began as a localized, nationalist antidictatorial movement in 1953 had become, a decade later, a direct challenge to the United States, not only in Cuba but in Latin America as a whole.

What lessons did the principal international, domestic, and regional actors derive from Cuba's successful defiance of the United States? Once chastened by the near-death experience of the 1962 missile crisis, the Soviet Union agreed to withdraw its nuclear warheads from Cuba in exchange for a verbal U.S. commitment not to invade the island. Though the Soviets stayed in

Cuba until 1991, they were careful in any subsequent regional dabbling not to trespass on the zone of U.S. hegemony established by a string of U.S. presidents. For example, although the Soviets had intelligence on the Chilean military's plans in 1973 to overthrow socialist president Salvador Allende, a physician by training, they chose not to share it with the good doctor, taking the position that Chile's troubles were none of their internationalist solidarity business. Détente with the U.S. administration of President Gerald Ford was a far greater priority.

The Cubans, on the other hand, believed they had no such American or Soviet doctrinal constraints to respect. The Cuban revolutionaries believed that in overthrowing Batista through force of arms, they had both overturned the yoke of American tutelage and defied Comintern doctrine, which held that revolution could never succeed against a country's standing armed forces. Cubans believed their revolution had succeeded not because of the Soviets or the local communists but in spite of them: Once Soviet Premier Nikita Khrushchev struck a deal with President John F. Kennedy to withdraw the missiles from Cuba without first consulting Castro or his emissaries, the humiliated Castro concluded that revolutionary Cuba would survive only by defying both the open hostility of one familiar great power and the treacherous and itinerant whims of another.

In this context, Cuba's decision in the 1960s to train and arm Dominicans, Venezuelans, Bolivians, Argentines, Colombians, and Nicaraguans was driven by three strategic motives. The first factor was immediate self-defense. Though the Soviets had extracted a pledge from the Kennedy administration not to invade Cuba, the United States—as senior officials in the Ronald Reagan administration would later remind the world—never signed anything to that effect, in essence keeping its fingers crossed behind its back in agreeing to such terms. After the Bay of Pigs and the missile crisis, the United States continued covert operations against Cuba, with all manner of schemes to assassinate Castro, destroy Cuban crops, and otherwise damage the economy, all with the express purpose of overthrowing the regime. As the United States grew more deeply involved in Vietnam, Castro and the revolutionaries around him came to believe that the best form of self-defense was to pin Gulliver down not only in Asia but also in various other global hot spots. If Latin America and Africa were burning, the United States would diffuse its energy trying to put out fires, and thus, the logic went, it would expend less energy on direct efforts to dislodge the Cuban Revolution.

Second, Cuba genuinely believed that a successful revolution in one part of the globe obliged the revolutionaries, out of international solidarity, to help brothers and sisters anywhere and everywhere. In the specific case of Latin America, Che Guevara and Fidel Castro saw the Americas as one large continent of misery, oppressed from within by corrupt elites and vicious U.S.-sponsored military regimes and ignored or exploited by the United States. If the revolutionaries could change those terms of reference in Cuba, why, the whole region could very well be their oyster. Over Khrushchev's and, later, Leonid Brezhnev's objection, they were happy to use Soviet resources to advance their survival strategy. Their third motive was domestic: Like Hamilton, the revolutionaries regarded extending Cuba's sphere abroad as a means to strengthen their legitimacy and suppress factionalism at home.

The left in Latin America drew several lessons from the Cuban Revolution and the U.S. and Soviet response to it. First, communist parties in the region had become too institutionalized bureaucratically and too Stalinist politically to plausibly deliver the huddled masses from oppression. Second, the Soviet Union was a superpower first; only second or third was it a source of revolutionary inspiration or support. Most important, if armed struggle could overturn the status quo in Cuba, then surely it could do so elsewhere in Latin America, where an anti-imperial, anticolonial critique of power and inequality placed the blame for the region's suffering and oppression squarely on the United States and the local institutions it supported.[6] By the 1960s, when most Latin Americans lived in dire poverty, with little hope and fewer prospects for democratic inclusion, Latin America was ripe for social and political upheaval.

Cuban strategies for survival and U.S. efforts to foil them inflamed but did not create Latin America's class and armed conflict of subsequent decades: The organic social, political, and economic material of the hemisphere sustained it. Without the Cuban Revolution—indeed, without the geopolitical contest with the Soviets—the United States still would have confronted significant social convulsion throughout the hemisphere. Having lost its bid to prevent a revolution in a country long regarded as a reliable and controllable ally, U.S. policies in the hemisphere for the remainder of the Cold War were largely shaped by the instinct to prevent a repeat of such a loss of face. As a result, stability prevailed over democracy, "rollback" or counterrevolution over revolution, and American unilateralism over regional diplomacy. Each new challenge to the existing order, whether from democratically elected leaders (for example, Salvador Allende in Chile or Michael Manley in Jamaica) or from armed revolutionaries (the Sandinistas in Nicaragua or the Farabundo Martí National Liberation Front [FMLN] in El Salvador), was viscerally rejected in Washington as a potential rerun of the Cuban loss.

The United States wanted to think that its answer to the Cuban Revolution was the Alliance for Progress program, which included a new emphasis on development, democracy, and political parties. Indeed, the revolution held appeal in the hemisphere, and given the region's devastating social conditions, U.S. officials did finally begin to see a connection between social conditions and political power, much as they had in Europe and

Japan after World War II. Even though it was Fidel Castro who first broached the idea of a Marshall Plan for Latin America in a speech at the Organization of American States (OAS) in Buenos Aires in 1959, the United States grabbed the proposal and ran with it. And over ten years, beginning in 1961, the United States devoted nearly $10 billion to the Alliance for Progress. But this was the Cold War in Latin America, not in Europe, and thus there was a dark side in the form of Green Berets and counterinsurgency, secret police training, military training, the School of the Americas, coups d'état, contra wars, more counterinsurgency, destabilization campaigns, and a handful of military interventions—all of which, even with the Alliance's soft side, and with the notable exception of Jimmy Carter's human rights policy and negotiations to return the Panama Canal, left much of Latin America by the end of the Cold War fundamentally distrusting and resentful of the United States.

Guatemala in 1954; Cuba in 1961; Dominican Republic in 1965; Chile from 1970 to 1989; the Southern Cone dictatorships in the 1970s and 1980s; the contras, counterinsurgency, and death squads in Central America; invasions in Grenada and Panama: Latin America's cumulative experience of the United States during the Cold War was, on balance, a negative one. Two secretaries of state and one American president have since apologized for U.S. trespasses in Latin America. Cuban revolutionaries relished their success in finally making the United States understand that the sun really did rise and set over their island. But the rest of the region, especially the democratic, nonviolent left, and eventually the United States itself, paid a steep price for the "Cubanization" of U.S. policy toward Latin America—just as it would later pay a price for the belief that regime change in Iraq was central to defeating al-Qaeda or bringing democracy to the Middle East.

CHAPTER TWO

The Cold War Beyond Latin America

Outside of Latin America, anti-Americanism surfaced with fits and starts and seldom, if ever, with the capacity to directly derail U.S. security or economic interests. The anti-American character of Soviet rivalry with the United States was a foregone conclusion. But the sheer scope of Soviet geopolitical power placed it in a class of its own, set apart from the kind of subordinate events, countries, leaders, or arguments that came to be readily understood as anti-American during the Cold War. Indeed, precisely because of the Cold War, anti-Americanism never took on the proportions of a widespread visceral impulse; the globe was divided and America could generally count on the alliance, complicity, or at least grudging consent of a solid bloc of nations and allies within them. Like Latin America during the New Deal and Good Neighbor period, ambivalence in the West toward the power of the United States was generally offset by admiration for its ingenuity, progress, innovation, and considerable military reassurance against a perceived Soviet threat. No less important were the ample financial contributions to the very societies that had been nearly destroyed during World War II, when the United States picked up the pieces of great-power folly and stood firmly, albeit with strings, on the side of independence for their former colonies.

Still, within the expanded international domain of the United States, what came to be known as the West, there were moments of stark and convulsive pique over U.S. policies during the Cold War. Three episodes stand out: European reaction to the 1962 Cuban Missile Crisis, European reaction to U.S. escalation in Vietnam in the late 1960s, and massive public protests over the placement of intermediate-range nuclear missiles on European soil in the 1980s. Popular clamor against and government derision toward the U.S. government or its presidents during these episodes was significant, to be sure. But opposition to specific U.S. policies stopped well short of the tenor of today's anti-Americanism: The American people were not the subject of anti-American animus, as they are today, especially after the 2004 elections. Moreover, such flare-ups registered little lasting impact on America's strategic success in containing the Soviet Union directly or indirectly.[7]

During the Cuban Missile Crisis, European differences with America were primarily over matters of diplomatic style. Europe felt snubbed by President Kennedy for his failure to consult across the Atlantic during the heady days of "ExComm" (the executive committee of senior officials Kennedy assembled to manage the crisis) and for his secret exchanges with Khrushchev. Walter Lippman quoted the pro-American French philosopher Raymond Aron, who said the United States had taken to treating the European allies as "protectorate nations," a sentiment reflected by Kennedy insiders who did not want to risk European "noise" during the crisis and considered European views peripheral to a settlement.[8] Although the perennially anti-American

Charles de Gaulle did laud the credibility of evidence from Secretary of State Dean Rusk that the Soviets had indeed installed missiles in Cuba, the French president ultimately determined from the standoff that the United States had marked its move toward strategic nuclear superiority and would thus require balancing by what he hoped would become an autonomous Franco-German defense alliance, independent of the United States. European publics were justifiably fearful of a nuclear confrontation, but they exerted little pressure on their governments to do more than protest the lack of consultation.

With the notable exception of Germany, European governments well-experienced in the pitfalls of colonial management opposed the Vietnam conflict and ridiculed the United States for confusing nationalism with communism, objecting not only to the war on policy grounds but concluding from the venture that the political culture of the United States had gone sour. Yet neither street protests against the war nor European government opposition to Vietnam ever translated into blocking cooperation with the United States on other political, economic, or security matters. In France, the exceptional levels of popular and government opposition to the U.S. war were intimately bound up with France's own colonial history in Algeria and Indochina itself. Late in the 1940s, and during and after the 1954 French defeat at Dien Bien Phu, the French had pleaded with the Truman and Eisenhower administrations for assistance there. As a good-faith gesture meant in part to garner French political support for the prospect of a newly rearmed Germany, the United States began sending arms and then advisers to Vietnam. Neither French official or popular opinion, nor the European left's opposition to the war, had hurt U.S. credibility or impeded solid government-to-government ties.

Anti-American sentiment reached its Cold War zenith when the United States decided to deploy new long-range nuclear missiles in response to the Soviet SS-20. Notably, when the Soviets began their own build-up beginning in the late 1970s, hardly a murmur of protest came from Europe. Despite hundreds of thousands of no-nuke protesters in the streets from Athens to Bonn and London to Rome, by 1983 the German, British, and Italian governments mustered the domestic political backing to accept America's "Euromissiles." To be sure, Ronald Reagan's saber rattling and politically incorrect Soviet empire–bashing raised hackles on both sides of the Atlantic over the drift to the right in the United States. And covert operations in Nicaragua and counterinsurgency in El Salvador horrified allies (and many Americans too). But even at the height of the Cold War tensions of the 1980s, indeed precisely because of the Cold War, neither popular protests nor legal judgments against the United States— the International Court of Justice in the Hague found it liable for mining Nicaragua's harbors—were able to shake the transatlantic relationship. But cumulatively, although European dissonance over the Cuban Missile Crisis, Vietnam, and the Euromissiles registered little substantive impact on these U.S. policies, the episodes left a deeply felt residue of suspicion of U.S. motives and doubts about America's belligerency among generations of Europeans who during the Cold War cut their teeth on political protest in the streets—and who decades later were governing in much of the Continent.

The unequal power dynamics within the West, "subordinate dependence" as one Japanese prime minister put it, remained a source of lingering discomfort throughout the Cold War. The United Kingdom clung to its special Anglo-Saxon relationship, even as its officials were privately repelled by America's adolescent good fortune and clumsy style. Impoverished and destroyed, the Germans and Japanese had no choice but to submit to the U.S. makeover, as guilt and shame for their own genocidal pasts suppressed nationalist impulses. In the early Cold War years, anti-

Americanism in both countries remained largely the province of the nationalist right, which feared that "Americanization's" emphasis on materialism and modern production would drain the spiritual essence of both cultures. By the early 1960s, the left in both countries joined in opposition to the United States.

French anti-Americanism, the most studied of the European brands, descends from the long-standing French tradition of defining France as not America. France cannot forgive the United States for challenging the French claim to represent the most universal, most civilized, most advanced nation. France's visceral trouble with the United States is utterly intrinsic to French identity. The two countries have competed for more than two hundred years. France's signal anti-American act of the Cold War, de Gaulle's withdrawal from NATO in 1966, became part of the strategic canon of the era. But the move was as much a declaration of French independence from the U.S. security umbrella as it was of French national identity writ large. And Americans calmly understood it as such.

Whereas French antipathy toward the United States has always played out at the civilizational stratosphere, anti-Americanism in Cold War Spain was born of that country's isolation within Europe, fascism, Catholicism, and a lingering macho resentment over the loss of its colonies to the United States at the turn of the century. On the left, the suppressed communist and socialist parties blamed the United States and the other European powers for the Republic's loss in the Spanish Civil War and the fascist rule that followed. U.S. military bases during the Cold War were seen by the nationalist left and right as a symbol of U.S. support for Franco, and the fascist Falange regarded Americans as too fast and loose with women, money, God, and politics. As Spain grew more integrated with the world and closer to the United States following its 1982 entry into NATO and the closing of U.S. bases south of Madrid, anti-Americanism did not disappear, but it receded as a factor in Spanish domestic politics until the government of former Prime Minister José María Aznar sought to align Spanish foreign policy closely with that of its former imperial rival.

Throughout the Cold War, European snottiness and disdain for the bad movies, bubble gum, or cultural coarseness of Americanization had made anti-American banter a fairly popular parlor game. Americans tended not to take much of it to heart: They had a higher calling and believed they had put their hearts, minds, blood, and treasure at the service of European reconstruction and security. It was no secret that although there was great cost involved in saving Europe from itself, presiding over the end of the colonial era, conquering Japan and its Asian imperial fantasies, and standing up to the Soviets, the United States reaped significant financial, diplomatic, and political gain from its Clark Kentish swoop onto the world stage. A bit of snickering from intellectuals, some healthy protest from the left and the right, not-so-muted scorn from U.S. friends and allies, even de Gaulle's defiance—these were a small price to pay for American primacy. Even at low points in the transatlantic relationship, U.S. brands from Marlboro to Coca Cola, Kodak, and Kleenex, from McDonald's to Disney, Sikorsky, and Boeing, prospered so long as buying American could still be construed as buying a piece of the American dream.

The challenge of anti-Americanism in the Third World was of a decidedly different scope and intensity than in the zones of U.S. reconstruction in the postwar period. After its own depression and the success of the New Deal, the United States instinctively understood that social democracy was the best political and economic antidote to the appeal of communism in countries facing destroyed economies, poverty, and ruined physical infrastructures. George Marshall, Douglas Dillon, and John McCloy were among the architects of European reconstruction for whom John Maynard Keynes's model of capitalism properly, and politically, included a role for the state not only in catalyzing economic growth through subsidies and other forms of industrial policy but also in providing a social safety net for those unable to survive exclusively through the free market.[9] With the exception of the McCarthy period, the United States eventually grudgingly came to tolerate the communist and noncommunist left in Europe, even more so than within America's own borders.

But in the Third World, the political sophistication the United States demonstrated in postwar Europe and Japan fell away. To be sure, until late 1946 into early 1947, the United States did adopt a decidedly positive stance toward the anticolonial nationalist movements of Asia and Africa, many of which took inspiration from a hybrid of revolutionary projects—the French, the American, the Russian. Even into the 1950s the Arab world saw America as an anti-imperial counterweight to British and French colonial rule, regarding Eisenhower's interruption of the French-British and Israeli move to retake the Suez Canal from Egypt as a boon to pan-Arabism. But despite this exception, once the Truman Doctrine established the United States as the world's policeman, America, over the next fifteen years, seemed steadily to lose the capacity to take the temperature of local nationalist movements or to apply the lessons of European reconstruction—particularly the political value of social democracy. The conflict with the Soviets, whose economic model bore no resemblance to Western Europe's Keynesian social democracies, nevertheless plainly began to crowd out such thinking.

With China's entry into the game and Soviet and Chinese backing of North Korea's invasion of South Korea, the Korean War significantly dampened the U.S. instinct to give space to leftish, nationalist Third World forces. By the middle of the 1950s, the anticolonial spirit of the United States had yielded to a coarser calculus of power. Nor did anticolonial movements function in an ideological or geopolitical vacuum. Just as the Americans, Soviets, and Chinese quickly learned to maneuver their client states and movements for tactical gain, so also did these clients make the most of the great-powers' contest, for their own internal and international benefit. As much as the United States may have been inclined in the abstract by political savvy and its historical instincts to support independence movements bent on taking power in an independent and unified Vietnam, Angola, or Cuba, for example, the geopolitical contest with the Soviets and the Chinese established priorities that elevated strategic gain and stability over the more noble republican objectives of the anticolonial nationalists.[10]

Seeing conflict in the developing world first and foremost as a product of Soviet or Chinese meddling caused the United States to adopt policies that weakened moderate political forces within nationalist movements or governments, whether in Vietnam, Angola, Indonesia, or Chile. Multiple tactics—covert actions, assassinations, proxy invasions, direct interventions, police repression, torture training, secret weapons programs, coups, puppet regimes to freeze out the left (the right was scarcely ever the object of U.S. wrath)—became part of the U.S. playbook for confronting social and political upheaval in the Third World, even where the Soviet or Chinese footprint was faint.

Of course, during the Cold War there was never a shortage of local players whose ambitions and interests America could tether to its own. Local elites throughout the developing world, good or ill-intentioned, found ways to make common cause with U.S. power, assuming the U.S. agenda and interests necessarily coincided with their own or those of their country. The story of U.S. power in the developing world has never been an unequivocal case of the big American boot crushing helpless and otherwise noble forces, as a common caricature would have us think, but rather of local forces gambling that aligning with U.S. power, whether willingly or out of coercion or a combination of both, was the best, if also sometimes the bloodiest, way to survive.

Nor was an alliance with the United States all the stuff of coups and covert operations. The U.S. seal of approval brought direct foreign aid, loans, development assistance, markets, technology, missionaries, doctors, weapons, education, visas, military training, and membership in the West. The club membership didn't benefit everyone and came at the price of lost autonomy, but compared with the alternative, for local elites the U.S. benefits package far outstripped the Soviet or Chinese appeal, as in South Korea, Turkey, Japan, or later, Egypt. But in Asia, Africa, Latin America, and the Middle East, the United States over time came to be seen more as the purveyor of a status quo colored by authoritarian rule, avaricious elites, and political repression than as the ticket to the political freedoms and middle-class advancement that prospered within U.S. borders. Neither the Soviets nor the Chinese could be accused of offering their clients such a study in contrasts. The gap in American credibility over time caused significant resentment and suspicion of U.S. motives.

America's moral authority was further undermined by the black marks of its Cold War exploits that came to pepper the globe. The United States overthrew Iran's Mohammad Mossadegh and installed the Shah and his Savak secret police in 1953, betrayed Hungarian freedom fighters in 1956, approved the assassination of the Belgian Congo's Patrice Lumumba in 1961, looked the other way during a coup and subsequent slaughter of communists in Indonesia in 1965, supported authoritarian governments in South Korea until the early 1980s, worked closely with Philippine autocrat Ferdinand Marcos during his twenty years in power, fought a counterinsurgency war in Vietnam, bombed Cambodia, waged proxy wars in Angola and Mozambique, embraced the apartheid regime in South Africa, and enabled dictators across Africa.

These episodes have receded from America's collective memory. In the standard story line of recent U.S. history, the Vietnam War was the only misstep—virtually an aberration in an otherwise noble U.S. trajectory of pioneering and reconstructing for freedom and democracy. After Vietnam came shuttle diplomacy, the Middle East peace process, the fall of the Berlin Wall, China's opening, the end of apartheid—these were the stories that captured Americans' attention. From the Cold War to the Gulf War—with the notable exception of the Iranian revolution—there was no discernible, and certainly no insurmountable, anti-American component to any of these episodes, not even to Saddam Hussein's invasion of Kuwait. The dramas that contained the seeds of today's rebellion played out in obscurity, as yet imperceptible to the naked American eye.

The United States has yet to collectively face a good century of evidence that when the tactics of grand geopolitical strategy, often considered by practitioners of the moment as the best policies for advancing the U.S. national interest, actually touch the ground, these can inflame often virulent anti-American nationalism. Never mind the crushing loss in Vietnam, the awakening of Islamic jihad in Afghanistan, or the insurgency in Iraq. For all of its billions spent on weapons, intelligence, warriors, and diplomacy, the United States does not appear to ask itself at liftoff what kind of response its policies might inspire at the landing. Instead, it nostalgically regards the Cold War as a sustained and deft combination of soft and hard power that brought about the defeat of communism and ushered in democracy where once there was only despotism. Yes, the United States stood for a set of values that were intrinsically coveted by citizens around the world, especially so because the alternatives offered by the Soviet Union and China held, in the end, so little appeal. But the U.S. public and political class has anchored its identity in an understanding of the Cold War's positive highlights that are drawn mainly from the experience of the European continent. In the rare instances that America's darker Cold War associations in the periphery are revisited outside of university classrooms, their sordid nature has been downplayed or treated as the unfortunate but necessary cost of doing business. That many countries once the object of U.S. mischief have since emerged with some measure of democracy, capitalism, or both seems even to suggest that the polarizing policies of an earlier era might very well have contributed to such felicitous outcomes. Yet it is precisely the reluctance of the United States to acknowledge the disconnect between its stated values and the full story, not just the happy ending, of what the country did during the Cold War (or does now) that feeds distrust and foments anti-Americanism, especially in the absence of an alternative to America's status as the globe's single superpower.

When the Cold War ended, Third World disappointment, distrust, and suspicion of the United States for its Cold War misdeeds did not immediately become manifest as hard-core anti-Americanism. There are many countries that at first glance might be lead candidates for Cold War–related anti-Americanism—Iran, Cuba, Chile, Angola, and Vietnam. Yet in Iran, the United States is admired at the popular level even as the government continues to seek its legitimacy from rivalry with the Great Satan: The bomb, and the attempt by the United States to thwart Iran's possession of it, represents one of the few sources of nationalist unity between government and population. Cubans by and large harbor great fondness for U.S. culture and society, despite Washington's unending genius in helping the Castro government inflame anti-American nationalism. The Chilean elite that inherited the country from Augusto Pinochet in 1989 sought social harmony and political healing; cultivating the United States as a source of trade and investment took priority over confronting it about Cold War destabilization campaigns despite the legacy of distrust. Vietnam and Angola combined lost more than two million citizens to wars in which the United States had a major hand. Both countries now actively seek U.S. investment and take pains to leave the past behind. Like Chile, Latin America largely attempted to move on after the Cold War, only to find itself now in open revolt against the United States. If that region's experience of the United States is any guide, the cumulative resentments born of Cold War trade-offs have to be seen as forming part of the parchment on which the new anti-American animus is expressed among populations and governments of historically friendly countries beyond the hemisphere that are now bumping up against American power.

After Vietnam, many Americans thought the United States had learned a thing or two about playing with the fire of nationalism. Congress passed laws—for example, the War Powers Resolution of 1973, enacted over Nixon's veto; the 1974 Hughes-Ryan amendment to the Foreign Assistance Act; and the Clark amendment to the International Security Assistance and Arms Export Control Act of 1976—intended in some fashion to constrain the executive branch's capacity to practice the dark arts; covert operations and counterinsurgency had become dirty words.[11] As the domestic and international divisiveness of the Vietnam War began to fade from the daily life of America's body politic, and especially in the years between the collapse of the Berlin Wall and the attacks of September 11, Americans came to think of their victory against the Soviets as a result of a battle of ideas, played out largely among Northern white people in Europe, not in the Third World, where Vietnam, Central America, and Angola, for example, were more casualties of containment than successes in promoting a positive model of democratic or social justice. Also, Americans came to believe that it was U.S. policies aimed at containing the Soviet Union in the periphery, more than what the communists called their own "internal contradictions," that deserved the lion's share of credit for slaying the bear. Just as the

Cold War drew comparatively less blood on European territory than in the periphery, so too in its wake the United States could quickly ratify the success of market democracy in Europe, whether in Poland, Hungary, Bulgaria, Romania, or the Czech Republic.

In addition, NATO enlargement reinforced America's celebration of its Cold War victory and the presumed universal appeal of the U.S. model, as did the monumental undertaking of reunifying Germany. Even Russia seemed to be joining the team. In the 1990s, armies of capitalist technocrats and businesspeople flooded Moscow to advise the country on how best and most quickly to privatize state companies and convert to the free market. The International Monetary Fund (IMF) and World Bank loaned Russia $22 billion in the course of the decade, making the one-time U.S. adversary among the West's largest post–Cold War beneficiaries. Success in making Western capitalism thrive in the birthplace of twentieth-century communism and the geographic heart of the Eurasian continent, Washington's foreign policy culture at the time seemed to suggest, would be the ultimate and uncontestable vindication that the Cold War was really "ours" to win through the appeal of U.S. ideas—primarily the free market—rather than "theirs" to lose. And the Western interventions in Bosnia and Kosovo—also European events—appeared to cure the United States of its Vietnam syndrome with the perfect opportunity to deploy U.S. force for noble humanitarian rather than crass geopolitical ends.

On the other hand, Somalia and Rwanda, the blights of the first post–Cold War decade, unfolded in the periphery: the South. Juxtaposed to what the United States regarded as its successes in Europe after the Cold War, its failures to tame warlords in Somalia or even attempt to stop genocide in Rwanda had the effect of truncating the collective discussion about what did and did not happen in the South during the Cold War itself. Perpetual bad news from the developing world made a predominantly Eurocentric post–Cold War discourse in Washington all the more reassuringly attractive and contributed to a reluctance to engage openly in what polite society calls a "lessons learned" exercise about the impact of U.S. Cold War policy in the periphery. That discussion would have revealed myriad effects: inflaming nationalism, weakening moderate forces, condoning human rights abuses, polarizing society, fueling insurgent violence, deepening anti-Americanism, and isolating the United States internationally. In the United States, such discussions stayed within the realm of the academy. But their lessons were hardly academic.

When the United States went to war in Iraq the second time, the argument that U.S. power could be deployed to bring democracy to Iraq (or elsewhere) was bolstered in America's collective memory by the recent example of the former Soviet satellites in Europe that had left the dark side for the market and freedom, with varying degrees of U.S. assistance. If democracy reached the former Soviet bloc in Europe, the logic went, why not Iraq? The Iraq debate was full of historical analogies. Yet one was hard pressed to find an accurate reference to a Third World state, highly suffused with secular, ethnic, or religious nationalism, to support the case for Iraq. Advocates of the Iraq invasion suggested that counterinsurgency against proindependence forces in the Philippines in the early twentieth century might serve as a viable model for defeating the Iraqi insurgencies, but there was no mention of the decades of U.S.-backed authoritarian rule that followed or the communist, Islamic, and nationalist insurgencies that burned in the ensuing decades. Memories of German and Japanese local populations willingly submitting to the mutually reinforcing structures of enlightened U.S. self-interest and beneficence encouraged the idea. But neither analogy held up; the messianic nationalism of both countries had sown the seeds of their own destruction before U.S. occupation and reconstruction began. It was one thing to reconstruct two countries that had self-destructed; it was quite another to occupy a country, as in Iraq, that neither in word nor, as the absence of weapons of mass destruction demonstrated, in deed had "invited" the foreign occupants.

Confirming Latin America's utility as a lab for U.S. power and a harbinger of the now widespread distrust of the United States, Vice President Richard Cheney embraced El Salvador as a model for Iraq during the 2004 presidential debates, in the process affirming the region's place on the short list of viable historical analogies to justify how to bring democracy to Iraq.[12] In El Salvador in the 1980s, the United States spent $1.2 billion to arm and train the Salvadoran military to carry out counterinsurgency operations against the FMLN, only putting its weight behind a negotiated settlement after 75,000 deaths, military stalemate, and significantly, the collapse of the Soviet Union. In subsequent years, the Salvadoran political and armed left joined democratic politics, and death squads (though not criminal violence and organized crime) largely disappeared. Like Cheney, advocates of U.S. support for counterinsurgency in El Salvador credit the hard line of the 1980s with the eventual political settlement that brought democracy to the country.

In suggesting that the sequence of events explains El Salvador's electoral democracy today, the logic goes that despite the enormous differences in scale and political cultures of the two countries, Iraq might follow the same path, which would vindicate not only the U.S. strategy of preemption in the Middle East but also of containment in Latin America. But this line of argument skips over both the cost to Salvadorans, who might, with U.S. support, have achieved democracy earlier in the century, the price paid in the region at the time, and the criminal, gang, and drug violence that today plagues the country. Latin America was polarized by the Central American wars. U.S. legitimacy suffered as well, as the United States rebuffed Latin American and European efforts to bring the war to a conclusion well before 1990 when the United States finally cut off military aid and backed the peace talks. Shorn of political, historical, or international context, counterinsurgency tactics applied in El Salvador (or, for that matter, anywhere) may very well weaken anti-American forces on the ground in Iraq. But without a political and diplomatic strategy—something the United States lacked in Latin America during the 1980s and has only just begun to recover in Iraq and the Middle East—such tactics only reinforce the impulse of the international community to see the United States humbled by the miscalculations of its own hubris.

Americans have not taken well to anti-American views or actions from the contested or Western-camp countries of the Cold War, feeling that gratitude for our leadership in the defeat of fascism and collective defense of the West against communism merits a far longer shelf life. Still more damaging to collective U.S. pride over World War II and the Cold War, continued conflicts and failing states have now made the periphery central: Parts of the world long neglected or treated mainly as proxies in the big-ticket fight with the Soviets now pose the greatest threat to our security. We thus managed to emerge from the Cold War as both uniquely powerful and probably more vulnerable than ever before in our recent history. With so much of the world fundamentally uneasy about U.S. power, the United States finds itself hard pressed to regain the trust of governments or populations now rallied around an unexpected and, for many in the United States, bewildering anti-American agenda.

CHAPTER THREE

Power, Powerlessness, and the 80/20 Divide

The U.S. inclination toward a Eurocentric view of the Cold War and the habit of quietly brushing under the rug the legacy of interventions in the developing world, best exemplified but not limited to Latin America, are grounded in the near inability of the United States to see its power from the perspective of the powerless. A corollary to history, the dynamic of power and powerlessness represents the second structural foundation of Anti-America.

In almost any way it is measured, other than population and energy resources, the United States today has more economic and military power than it has ever had and than any other country now has. That fact alone understandably inspires a complicated mix of envy, resentment, desire, jealousy, love, hate, and fear. Unlike Rome or Great Britain or France or Spain before us, in addition to the traditional measures of power such as land mass, guns, naval power, or money, the United States of America designs and markets desirable, high-quality goods that consumers worldwide love to love but increasingly love to hate. It stands to reason, then, that a certain tangible, even sizable portion of the current anti-American backlash derives from the very fact of U.S. power. No matter how carefully the United States tends to the care and feeding of its global constituents, unhappiness is part of the burden with which a world power must contend.

Without U.S. power, and in the absence of an alternative, the world, it was argued after 9/11, risked slipping into a dark age of chaos, fanaticism, and pillage much as U.S. presidents argued would be Latin America's fate without U.S. intervention over the past two centuries. Worried about the brittle state of the transatlantic relationship, others warned that if the "Euro-Gaullists" prevailed over the "Euro-atlanticists" and the European Union came to identify itself mainly in opposition to, rather than in partnership with, the United States, balance-of-power dynamics would return, threatening the signal achievement of the twentieth century: peace among the world's liberal democracies.

American power in the international system was compared with Adam Smith's "invisible hand" guiding the market: Just as individuals could trust the hand to lift all boats in the end, only the United States had the power to guide a resolution to the major global issues of the day. Resisting U.S. power was ultimately futile and self-defeating: A world tempted by anti-Americanism would be "less peaceful, less cooperative, less prosperous, less open, less stable." The United States had become the "crucial organizer of collective goods." U.S. leadership, even against the failure in Iraq, remained "indispensable."[13] There was no room to contemplate the prospect that subordinating American power, even ceding some of it, might help diminish anti-Americanism.

The very preponderance of that power obliges the United States to involve itself in the major challenges of the twenty-first century. But by confusing power with legitimacy or leadership, the United States has lent its own quite visible hand to the new anti-American consensus. American credibility is not at a low point because the United States has a lot of power.[14] The problem lies in how the nation uses that power. There is nothing magical, organic, God-given, or uncontrollable about American power. Americans have choices about how they use their power. And in large measure, until very recently, most of the world, with some obvious exceptions, was prepared to give America the benefit of the doubt.

Power thinkers—people who contemplate lofty-sounding concepts like America's "grand strategy"—may still, after Iraq, regard the United States as the centrifugal force of world stability, cooperation, and peace, and there may be many voices in the West who grudgingly or even readily agree, but the rise of Anti-America forces the question of whether U.S. power has itself caused instability, discord, and conflict. Of course, there are many other sources of global instability that have nothing to do with U.S. actions. But anti-Americanism's strength today is now tethered to the nation's collective mistake of having confused its power with leadership and legitimacy in a bloody, costly war of painful human toll. As it turns out, though, for all of the power, we do not possess a corresponding amount of leverage or influence—not with our allies, our dependents, the markets, the dollar, and certainly not with our enemies. Democrat and Republican White Houses long fueled the perception that the United States could be the world's panacea: the reality behind this myth—autocrats remain in power in the Middle East; Iraq is a mess; funding for democracy promotion has been cut; conflict, even genocide continues; poverty, disease, and misery define the lives of entire populations in Africa and Latin America that look to the United States for a lifeline—fueled anti-American resentment as it became clear that despite all of its power and high-minded rhetoric, the United States has yet to deliver on the expectations its 1989 triumphalism created.

If a central element of global antipathy toward the United

States is how it uses its power, the corollary element is powerlessness. This is not limited to the powerlessness that comes from the obvious fact that America's power means others have less of it. Rather, it also comes from the practice the United States has of garnering information about foreign lands largely from its elite counterparts, the powerful within societies, rather than from the powerless. I have called these blinders "America's 80/20 problem" in thinking about Latin America, but the concept, sadly, applies globally.

A few months before the 2002 coup in Venezuela, I asked a State Department official detailed from the CIA and fresh from four years in Venezuela about the extent of Cuban influence under the presidency of Hugo Chavez. Without access to or human intelligence about the 80 percent of the country's population that lived in poverty, with whom the Cubans were working, he was honest enough to reveal that he could hardly hazard a guess. U.S. diplomats understood that Chavez was a product of frustrations with the failure to spread Venezuela's oil wealth, and the political exclusion felt by those not graced by the patronage of the country's four-decade two-party system, the *partidadura*, or party dictatorship. But despite a sea change in Venezuelan politics in 1998, Americans had not appreciably diversified their contacts with Venezuelan society. Instead, the United States continued to get its information from the very interlocutors that had fed its understanding of Venezuela for the previous half-century—the top 20 percent in the private sector, the oil industry, politics, media, organized labor, the Catholic Church, and some academics. U.S. antipathy toward Hugo Chavez produced a willful ignorance of the needs, desires, preferences, and prejudices of those 80 percent whom Chavez claimed to represent.

By the spring of 2002, the perils of America's 80/20 blinders began to emerge. In a rush of wishful thinking, the Bush administration characterized a coup attempt in Venezuela as the expression of the Venezuelan people's will. In the early hours of the coup, the United States and Spain issued a joint statement that gave the impression they recognized the new interim government, which had issued an executive order eliminating the country's Supreme Court, Constitution, and National Assembly. Less than forty-eight hours later, army loyalists returned Chavez to office, and the leaders of the interim government and civilian opposition fled into exile.

In the years following the coup, the United States lost credibility, influence, and most leverage with a longtime ally and one of its largest sources of oil. From a few thousand in 2002, by 2005 there were closer to 20,000 Cuban advisers from barrios to barracks in Venezuela, engaged in the kind of comprehensive nation-building the United States likes to think of as its own preserve. Chavez has used a combination of oil revenues and "Bolivarian," anti-American rhetoric to strengthen and inflame his electoral base. The opposition, once doted upon with tea and sympathy by U.S. diplomats and democracy promoters, has taken aim at the United States and the impeccably credentialed Carter Center for endorsing the August 2004 referendum that left Chavez in office and free to run again in 2006. America had relied on the discredited but entrenched Venezuelan elite and owners of private media for its understanding of the politics and social forces that made the country tick. The consequence? The United States remained a player in Venezuela in only two ways: through oil and as a readily available foil for all factions.

Beyond Venezuela, the 80/20 dynamic feeds anti-Americanism in two ways. First, U.S. officials rely, to their peril, on the perspectives of local elites—the 20—to form the U.S. view of what is happening on the ground. Those 20, whether in Saudi Arabia, Indonesia, South Korea, or Colombia, have learned to speak in the shifting tongues of U.S. power, casting their interests as broadly consistent with those of the U.S. 20. When U.S. elites—

in government, media, and the private sector—get their information mainly from their counterparts in other societies, the United States becomes disconnected from the conditions, feelings, preferences, and experiences of those living on the margins of what Americans have incorrectly assumed to be a universal phenomenon of political, social, and economic progress promised by democracy and globalization.

The United States seemed to have learned this lesson in the case of Saudi Arabia, where the U.S. stake in oil and thus stability established so narrow a bilateral dialogue that officials missed the negative impact of U.S. association with the kingdom's own 80/20 problem until it literally hit home on 9/11. Similarly, the United States has missed the significance of anti-American sentiment even in fully democratic societies, such as Spain, where the 2004 reelection bid of Bush-friendly José María Aznar's party, the same that backed the Venezuelan coup, was thwarted by a terrorist attack that many Spaniards blamed on Aznar's hubris and willingness to risk the country's security by putting Spanish troops in Iraq. The United States misleads itself, and allows itself to be misled, when the information it collectively digests about societies both strange and familiar derives from sources whose interests are vested in keeping U.S. power on their side.

If one element feeding the 80/20 dynamic is the limited range of sources informing U.S. understanding of the world, the other element is how the United States explains itself. Anyone traveling abroad need only visit an American embassy to see the physical barriers that now separate diplomats from their host populations since 9/11. This is the case not only in Third World or Middle East hot spots but also in the capitals of America's most faithful allies, whether London or Canberra. Miles of cement barriers around Washington's monuments, federal buildings, and the White House reinforce the physicality and plain ugliness of fortress America. During the Cold War, U.S. tax dollars underwrote extensive programs that sent American books, magazines, newspapers, and writers around the world, while establishing U.S. Information Agency (USIA) libraries far afield from embassies in secondary and tertiary cities around the globe. To neutralize the appeal of communism, the United States funded extraordinarily creative books, magazines, and lectures generated by the Congress for Cultural Freedom, and underwrote world tours of American jazz musicians and abstract expressionists.[15] Now, we have become so insular and thin-skinned that the National Endowment for the Humanities won't even fund scholarship by tenured university professors that has the word "anti-Americanism" in the title. Most of the U.S.-sponsored libraries have been closed, and U.S. public diplomacy programs are widely and often correctly derided as too little, too late. Multimillion-dollar covert propaganda programs producing fake news have yet to turn public opinion in the Middle East. And out of an instinct to protect the country from further attack, the United States has thrown obstacles in the path of temporary and permanent visitors, whether among the working poor of the 80 or the professionals of the 20.

Once history purportedly came to an end with the collapse of the Berlin Wall, the United States decided it no longer needed to promote itself: The market would do the job, *sans* a boost from government. Nothing has replaced the vibrant public outreach programs of the Cold War, and underfunded public diplomacy efforts and faith in the market and mass media to tout continued U.S. scientific, cultural, and intellectual innovation have failed to compete with the relentless pulse of anti-American images and reporting in many of the world's hot spots. It isn't enough for the world's elites to learn about one another's politics and priorities from the *New York Times, Financial Times, Economist,* and *International Herald Tribune;* the 20 have to worry that the 80 are increasingly tuning in to outlets such as al-Jazeera and al-Arabiya, or even Fox News, where inflammatory distortion carries the day.

The United States may not be responsible for the balance of power within countries. But to the extent that elites are regarded as holding their power or wealth because of their association with their peers in the United States or their embrace of U.S. economic or security models that fail to deliver, the United States will necessarily become a target for anti-American hostility. In Latin America, for example, the early twenty-first century marked a simultaneous and precipitous slide in the public view of democracy and globalization, America's post–Cold War projects, and the politicians that are seen as their beneficiaries—all this magnified by the most negative view of the United States in the past fifty years.[16]

Beyond the hemisphere, anti-Americanism is intensifying in countries where the United States has had long-standing relationships with traditional elites who benefited from a status quo now in flux: This is true in countries as different from one another as Saudi Arabia, Germany, Turkey, South Korea, and Indonesia. In a sense, the 80/20 dynamic is born very much of the nineteenth century—the 20 among the great powers shall, by keeping their 80 in check, manage the world's affairs in concert—a belief that endured until the beginning of the twenty-first century. But democracies, driven by an increasingly globalized public, make the 20-20 pact, though still extremely powerful, increasingly unable to order the world, and they are vulnerable as a result.[17] Paradoxically, then, also courtesy of globalization, democracy, and the provocative, unifying effect of opposition to America's war in Iraq, elite and popular views of the United States have begun to fuse. This realignment has made governments less able to conduct affairs of state—especially on unpopular or unsavory matters involving cooperation with the United States—with the kind of insulation that existed between public opinion and government policy throughout the Cold War.

CHAPTER FOUR

Economic Globalization

In the years between the end of the Cold War and the 9/11 terrorist attacks, the United States embraced democratization and economic globalization as the organizing mission of American foreign policy. The Clinton administration saw these processes as mutually reinforcing and subscribed to the popular notion that more democracy in the world would mean less war: more democracy, more free markets, safer world, end of history. Many centrist and liberal democrats counted themselves among economic globalization's greatest champions in the 1990s and appeared to adopt a faith in the market that was reminiscent of the free-market theology of Ronald Reagan, Margaret Thatcher, Milton Friedman, and Augusto Pinochet. In government and the private sector, Americans were buzzing with excitement over the promise of globalization for lifting all economic boats. In hopeful speeches about bridges to the twenty-first century, the idea implied the chance for the entire world to progress to greater levels of prosperity through advances in technology and the disintegration of boundaries, whether of nations, markets, or ideologies. The collapse of the Soviet bloc helped in this respect, because with it the major competing ideology of the twentieth century vanished in all but a handful of countries. If the United States could extend its model to the globe, then conflict, the stuff of history, would finally be no more.

Globalization became a synonym for Americanization. By the end of the American Century, that pairing promised to play to U.S. strengths and reverberate globally. But in the twenty-first century, America's close association with globalization is becoming a liability in parts of the world where the hopes of more equitably distributed prosperity have been replaced by disillusion with the American recipe. In the 1990s, the Treasury Department and the International Monetary Fund preached the orthodox economic fundamentalism embodied in the reform prescriptions that came to be known as the "Washington Consensus," especially in Asia and Latin America. The basic bargain was that by privatizing state-owned industries and utilities, allowing foreign capital to enter and exit freely, eliminating trade barriers, and reducing state spending on domestic programs, developing countries could virtually guarantee themselves, with the help of a Treasury bailout here and an IMF loan there, the economic liftoff that had eluded many of them during the Cold War. Liberals, conservatives, and neoconservatives shared the belief that heavy communist or authoritarian state involvement in the economies of the South and the East had been an obstacle to growth. Therefore, by significantly pruning the deadwood of the state, the market unfettered would harvest greater returns.

The glee in Washington over the end of history was accompanied by an intellectual and rhetorical takeover by economists, whose jargon came to replace considerations of politics, history, or culture. Talk of budget deficits, haircuts, primary surpluses, current accounts, buying paper, and what the markets "think" often completely overshadowed discussions of what was really happening on the ground in, say, Thailand, Brazil, Argentina, or Indonesia. Washington seemed to be saying that a sound macroeconomic policy—open markets and free trade—was all a developing country needed to enter the posthistorical era. And because of its political and financial power within the institution, the United States and the IMF came to be seen as synonymous, not only in the eyes of antiglobalization protesters but also by governments on the receiving end of politically painful loan packages.[18]

In elevating the magic of the market and somehow forgetting the role the state had played in developing capitalist economies, whether right at home or in Asia in the 1970s and 1980s, the United States plainly threw the baby out with the bath water. In Latin America in particular, economic liftoff could not happen without state spending on physical infrastructure and developing human capital and a broad range of other services for which market economies need support. But the growing bias in the United States against the very kinds of government programs that had lifted it out of the depression or funded its domestic transportation network, built its electricity and energy infrastructure, educated its children, or otherwise supported the growth of a middle class augured poorly for a favorable view of such state-centered investments in the developing world after the Cold War. The economic homilies preached by Washington put no pressure on governments with highly skewed income inequality to institute progressive tax programs and tax the wealthy; instead, value-added or consumption taxes, which place the tax burden on the poor, carried the day. Throughout the 1990s, for example, the percentage of GDP from tax revenue hovered just around 15 percent on average in Latin America, half to one-third of most industrialized countries.[19] To be sure, the absence of a social contract in Latin America is fundamentally the responsibility of the region's own citizens, particularly those who hold the lion's share of its income and assets. But despite its historic influence in the region, the United States has seldom used its leverage to cajole the wealthy into adopting policies that recognize the political, economic, or security benefits of sharing the pie more equitably.

Despite the clear benefits of technology and information that are part of the broad forces of globalization, the perception grew among skeptics, many of them Americans with broad international audiences, that economic globalization primarily boosts the fortunes of the wealthy, whether in the United States and the advanced industrialized countries or in the developing world.[20] As one American critic put it:

> The policies of the WTO [World Trade Organization], the IMF, the World Bank, and other global regulators, represent the dominance of the investor class in the politics of the emerging global economy. . . . The questions of "who wins?" and "who loses?" from particular policies of the global institution cannot be answered on the basis of separate national identities alone because every country has an investor and a working class, i.e., there are rich people in poor countries and poor people in rich countries. . . . Accordingly, the fundamental purpose of the neo-liberal policies of the past 20 years has been to discipline labor in order to free capital from having to bargain with workers over the gains from rising productivity.[21]

Of course, the advocates of globalization seemed to genuinely believe that what was good for America was good for the world and good for the poor. Following the parable taught in all basic economics courses about comparative advantage between England and Portugal, they concluded that reducing barriers to trade and market entry would maximize the comparative advan-

tage of all players, large or small. President Clinton wholeheart-
edly embraced this view:

> Many people believe the forces of globalization are inherently
> divisive; that they can only widen the gap between rich and
> poor. That is a valid fear, but I believe wrong. As the distance
> between producers large and small, and customers near and far
> becomes less relevant, developing countries will have opportu-
> nities not only to succeed, but to lead in lifting more people
> out of poverty more quickly than at any time in human history.
> In the old economy, location was everything. In the new econ-
> omy, information, education and motivation are everything.[22]

But trade liberalization and privatization proved to be no universal remedy for profound inequality, poverty, corruption, or
the absence of a social contract. Two problems emerged as the
U.S. political class oversold the potential benefits of economic
globalization: Not everyone wanted a piece of the American
dream; and many of those who gave the benefit of the doubt to
American promises but have not reaped the payback came away
disillusioned and suspicious of U.S. intentions.

Two renowned cases of globalization's anti-American backlash arose from the financial and political crises in Indonesia,
1997–1998, and Argentina, 2000–2001, where positive indica-
tors of the United States dropped to the teens; they are climbing
back but extremely slowly.[23] In the 1990s, both countries loyally
adopted the prescriptions of the Washington Consensus and
were lauded as models for the developing world. But whether it
is Washington or Wall Street, or the governments and firms on
the ground that bear most of the blame, the United States is now
perceived as having led both countries down the primrose path
only to turn a frosty cheek when times got tough and debts grew
unsustainable.

The appearance that the United States was more interested in protecting its own corporate interests and prospecting for new opportunities, rather than in helping Indonesians survive the crash that followed a run on the rupiah, reinforced the sense of an American double standard. It was all well and good for the Clinton administration to demand anticorruption measures of Indonesia as part of the IMF package presented to clean up the mess, but this sudden awakening to Suharto and his cronies' corruption was perceived by the millions of protesters filling the streets in 1998 as too little and too late, and as motivated more by politics and the prospect of economic opportunity for U.S. capital than by a genuine surge of antiauthoritarian values.[24] In Argentina, which had sent troops to fight in the 1991 Gulf War and been granted the unique distinction of America's "major non-NATO ally," the prospect that the United States would simply walk away as presidents and ministers fell, the economy crashed, and millions were cast into poverty in a matter of days has left a deep well of resentment and profound distrust. Argentines have subsequently reoriented their foreign policy priorities, tethering their future more to Brazil, Venezuela, and China than to the United States. Both Indonesia and Argentina are rebounding politically and economically, but the United States gets little if any of the credit and has lost a once reliable ally in the Western Hemisphere and in international forums as a result.[25]

Outside of the halls of government, the globalization-antiglobalization debates had a "they are from Venus; we are from Mars" quality. The globalizers projected onto the antiglobalizers far more power than they actually possessed. Although the advocates of globalization embraced its potential market and political power, when confronted by opposition they seldom acknowledged how that very power might naturally generate resistance. The antiglobalizers often failed to articulate a positive agenda. Instead, they frequently appeared to those "inside the building" to be a dizzying array of hapless, disingenuous, and sometimes violent money-haters. Globalization's advocates argued that entrenched interests, such as U.S. labor, opposed free trade largely to protect their own members, and didn't genuinely care about Third World poverty. They argued that efforts by antiglobalizers, whom they called protectionists, to slow liberalization and allow time for local producers to adapt to the world market would ultimately hurt the very poor the activists purported to represent. Instead, they believed that increasing the volume, pace, and diversity of foreign investment and exports, even if the resulting jobs paid poorly and provided few social protections, offered the global underclass a real alternative to their garbage-picking fates.

In assessing global corporate conglomerates, many of them American, the antiglobalizers believed that yielding to unregulated market forces meant a race to the bottom and the Americanization of food, livelihood, culture, and politics.[26] Globalization's foes seemed to see only losers. Their serious and sustained attempts to make the rules regulating free trade and capital flows more equitable seldom got the kind of public hearing or media attention they merited, save from Bill Moyers or *The Nation* magazine, or perhaps an occasional fair piece in *Business Week*.[27] Instead, the negative agenda of the violent fringe that always shows up at protests against the World Bank, the IMF, or the WTO got the lion's share of public attention. Nevertheless, the antiglobalization agenda in the 1990s—one that sought to advance and protect labor rights, environmental rights, indigenous rights, local farming rights—was not an anti-American agenda; it wasn't even an antimarket agenda. But the debate between the two forces grew irretrievably polarized: The liberalize-at-all-cost voices appeared to conflate U.S. interests with corporate interests without acknowledging as much, whereas the go-it-slow approach came to be seen as opposing modernity and the United States itself.

By the early years of the twenty-first century, even as developing countries improved their overall macroeconomic performance, poverty and inequality remained entrenched. The advocates of the Washington Consensus came to recognize that the formula was not working: They argued that economic globalization had failed because true capitalism had not taken root in the formerly statist economies of the global South. They concluded that Washington's recipe for economic success needed freer trade, capital controls, and a second and third generation of domestic reforms "in-country."[28] Indeed, as the cacophony of anger around the collapse of trade talks in Cancun in 2003 demonstrated, many voices in government and civil society in the developing world held the view that the U.S. economic agenda had remained infuriatingly consistent: driving hard for developing countries to open their markets to U.S. goods and capital on the one hand, but retaining U.S. protectionist barriers to truly free trade, especially in agriculture markets such as sugar, corn, and cotton. Combined with the steady news of gross corruption in America's corporate giants of Enron and World-Com, and Argentina's and Malaysia's rebounds in defiance of the IMF formulas, the U.S. prescription for prosperity no longer looked so authoritative. Finally, in the context of the global falling-out with the United States over the war in Iraq, the perception among skeptics that economic globalization was primarily a front for parochial U.S. corporate interests rather than genuinely inclusive prosperity fed the growing anti-American wave.[29]

By 2005 the forces of economic globalization and the forces of democracy had collided not to reinforce each other, as was hoped at the end of the Cold War, but often to undermine each other. By any measure the world's population enjoys more democratic freedoms today than in 1989.[30] The United States is correctly seen as one of the key international players in that development.

This is true in Europe, Asia, Africa, and Latin America. But economic globalization, also sold as a U.S. project, has not fared so well. Instead, and despite evidence to the contrary from China, India, or the "Asian tigers" (Hong Kong, Singapore, South Korea, and Taiwan), where strong state institutions and subsidies for industry mediate the encounter with global capital, globalization is widely perceived to have worsened inequality and poverty, or at least not to have substantially improved the lot of the three billion people who live on less than two dollars a day. In Latin America, where the benefits of economic globalization have not trickled down to the impoverished majority, the left has taken power democratically in election campaigns that directly or indirectly blame the United States and its allies in the region for serving up economic recipes that don't put food on the table. Against the stark inequality and poverty of much of the developing world, America's association with globalization and the hypocrisy with which the United States rhetorically clings to the glory of the private space—despite continued government largesse directed toward agriculture, infrastructure, and the technology and defense industries—provide the mortar for the bricks of Anti-America's foundations of history, power, and powerlessness.

|

CHAPTER FIVE

|

What We Do

On top of those structural, even latent forces of history, power, and economic globalization sustaining Anti-America's pulse, U.S. foreign policies have exposed long-suppressed resentments among countries and populations the United States had assumed would indefinitely give it the benefit of the doubt on matters of international security. What the United States does and often does not do outside its own borders has long provoked international criticism, anger, or ridicule. Following a brief hiatus after convulsions caused by U.S. policies in Vietnam—when détente, the opening with China, and Middle East peace dominated the international agenda of the United States—the periphery again became the focal point of domestic and internationally divisive American foreign ventures, not surprisingly in the traditional U.S. sphere of the Western Hemisphere, over Central America. Tough-talking anticommunists carried the day in the 1980s, as the conservative U.S. political agenda made itself felt in a foreign policy that was then called "roll-back." Later, the same tactics would acquire a new name: "regime change." But in Central America, the stakes were hardly apocalyptic, and Secretary of State Alexander Haig's admonitions to the contrary, scantly geopolitical.

By the 1990s the sources of international instability had become genocide, terrorism, and failing states. But the United States was slow to recognize them. In Washington's national security culture at the time, individuals at the Rand Corporation or the National Security Council or CIA, for example, who predicted imminent doom at the hands of terrorists, were grudgingly tolerated but not seriously countenanced in a town trained to focus on conventional threats from nation-states. Especially when early guesses that Islamic terrorists were responsible for the 1995 bombing of the Murrah Federal building in Oklahoma City proved wildly off the mark, the threat of terrorism remained marginal to the big-ticket foreign policy debates, at least until the 1998 U.S. embassy bombings in Africa.[31] The United States was divided about the scope of its post–Cold War responsibilities and how best to fulfill them. Conservative isolationists in Congress attacked UN peacekeeping and gutted UN funding, while the Democrat-controlled executive-branch agencies struggled to conjure a U.S. response to genocide in Bosnia and Kosovo. The fractious disputes over Central America, peacekeeping, the Balkans, and the United Nations betrayed a brewing internal clash over U.S. power and the constraints of international institutions. September 11 briefly papered over the divide. Iraq reopened the breach.

During the 2000 presidential campaign, Latin America returned to U.S. foreign policy discourse when George W. Bush promised to make the region, especially Mexico, America's most important global partner. A bit of inter-American summitry and some flirtation with the new Mexican president Vicente Fox over a more sensible migration policy peppered the early months of

President Bush's first term. The enthusiasm for a deal with Mexico or making Latin America a greater priority than in the past faded well before 9/11. But even after the attacks, even as the neighborhood receded from the U.S. agenda, a whiff of the traditional U.S. style in Latin America hung in the air as the White House came to extend to the rest of the world the kind of big-stick-gunboat-proconsular treatment American presidents have traditionally reserved for their own backyard. It had been one thing for the great powers that once held a stake in the region to yield grudgingly to U.S. hegemony within the Western Hemisphere in the nineteenth and twentieth centuries. But it was quite another for the United States to subject the entire world community—including former and aspiring world powers—to the fast-and-loose approach to diplomacy, military intervention, sovereignty, and international law that had long been the U.S. currency in America's regional sphere of influence. Echoing the presumptions of the 1904 Roosevelt Corollary to the Monroe Doctrine, that "flagrant cases of wrongdoing or impotence" in the Western Hemisphere "may force" the United States, "some civilized nation," to "the exercise of an international police power," the White House's National Security Strategy Statement of 2002 continued this tradition beyond Latin America:

> [T]he United States has long maintained the option of pre-emptive actions to counter a sufficient threat to our national security. The greater the threat, the greater is the risk of in-action—and the more compelling the case for taking antici-patory action to defend ourselves, even if uncertainty remains as to the time and place of the enemy's attack. To forestall or prevent such hostile acts by our adversaries, the United States will, if necessary, act preemptively.[32]

Likewise, the country's foreign policy debates, though customarily heated affairs, adopted the airs of McCarthy-type suppression reminiscent of U.S. Cold War debates over Latin America. Within the government, dissenting views were squelched, distorted, parsed, or ignored. Individuals (and in some cases their families) who dared to challenge the new conventional wisdom on Iraq, Syria, Cuba, weapons of mass destruction, and how to fight a war on terror were harassed, sidelined, or driven to resign. For example, as the hearings over the nomination of John Bolton to become the president's representative at the United Nations revealed, individuals such as the CIA National Intelligence Council's chief officer for Latin America, Fulton Armstrong, the intelligence community's most senior Latin America official, and a more junior analyst at the State Department's Bureau of Intelligence and Research, Christian Westermann, had their employment threatened and were otherwise ostracized and harassed because their analyses did not conform with some political appointees' policy objectives of identifying Cuba, already on the State Department's terrorist list, as a bioweapons proliferator. The public exposure of the identity of once-covert CIA operative Valerie Wilson, the wife of career diplomat Joe Wilson, who challenged the Bush administration's contention that Iraq was seeking to purchase ingredients for a nuclear weapon from Niger, was another high-profile example.[33]

The White House seemed to give an airing to views offered by experts in and out of government only if they comported with those held by an extraordinarily narrow circle of trust around the president. Those who warned that the United States might have underestimated the nationalism of Iraqis or overestimated the persuasive power of U.S. military force were dismissed as negative and pessimistic—code for unpatriotic dissent. By evoking the prospect of a mushroom cloud as a distinct alternative to U.S. military intervention in Iraq, National Security Adviser Condoleezza Rice, subsequently to become secretary of state, conjured the Orwellian prospect that the bomb, generally de-fended in U.S. Cold War mythology as America's catastrophi-cally successful step to end a noble war, might be employed now by a madman to start a new one. Aside from some vigorous, healthy antiwar and House Democrat protests, the apparent unity of the country and support for President Bush that fol-lowed the September 11 attacks had the effect of erasing public criticism of the rationale for war in Iraq.

Enough Democrats in Congress complied with their votes in support of the October 2002 Joint Iraq Resolution to give the White House the legal and political cover it needed to send troops to war.[34] It helped that a midterm congressional election was around the corner. While effectively representing an alter-native to the Bush universe of socially conservative virtues at home, and despite ample evidence that the U.S. public outside of Washington was profoundly divided on the merits of the war in Iraq, the Democratic Party steered clear of a foreign policy vi-sion—not for the war on terror and not for Iraq—that substan-tially differed from that of the Republican Party. In the final stretch of his 2004 campaign, John Kerry recited the wrong time, wrong place, wrong war mantra and attacked the president for his bad judgments and miscalculations and for making our friends mad and emboldening our enemies. But the premium during the campaign was on toughness and the war-fighting ca-pacity of the presidential contenders: The Democrats did not fundamentally challenge the Republicans over issues of why, when, and how best to deploy U.S. power and force or on the overall strategy of the war on terror. Instead of debating what we were really doing in Iraq, or the real meaning of engaging in a war on terror or terrorists, U.S. officials focused instead on tacti-cal questions of troop levels, rotations, body armor, and Humvees. Not until Cindy Sheehan, the grieving mother of a twenty-four-year-old killed in Sadr City, camped out in Crawford, Texas, to highlight the folly of the war did figures of both political parties—from former Senator Gary Hart and Senator Russ Feingold to Senator Chuck Hagel and Henry Kissinger—begin to question the White House contention that "staying the course" in Iraq was a strategy for making the United States safer at home or respected in the world.

The effervescence of the new anti-Americanism is rooted in structural dynamics that have bubbled beneath the surface of international relations for decades. But individual presidential policies, personality, and style make a difference. The Bush II presidency's policies, specifically Iraq and the eruption of the detainee and "black" prison scandals, brought to the surface collective and cumulative resentments over U.S. power and its use; dashed expectations of the promise of economic globalization; and served to release a visceral anti-Americanism that for decades had remained latent or contained. Together with the president's cultivated plain-speaking bring-it-on braggadocio, the unilateralism of the first term's diplomacy especially, Washington's careless infatuation with power, the polarization it provoked in its with-us-or-against-us style, and the administration's outsider stance on a number of other international issues, from poverty to proliferation to global warming, provoked widespread international rejection of the United States and increasingly of its people. Structural dynamics of history, power, and economic globalization might have collided with specific U.S. foreign policies to provoke this new anti-American consensus under a White House populated by either party. But the style of the Bush presidency as well as the particularly provocative and poorly managed diplomacy over Iraq and subsequent occupation, and the lack of high-level accountability for the worst trespasses of it and the war on terror, explain why the global dissipation of trust in America and Americans occurred in the early years of the twenty-first century.[35]

Indeed, if popular protests, public opinion, or foreign press coverage offer any guide, there is an increasingly palpable perception beyond our shores that the United States no longer believes in the value of the international community.[36] Arguably, Washington has never been a "permission slip" town, and the only difference between the Bush II White House and its internationalist predecessors is one of form and process, not substance. Democrats and Republicans concur on the importance of reforming the United Nations, for example. But the Bush II White House was more than just impatient with the traditional mechanisms for international consensus-building, more than just interested in clarifying how the United States does and does not work within the strictures of international institutions. It appeared to see institutions of the state and suprainstitutions of states as a suffocating constraint on America's room to maneuver. Although couched as a celebration of the individual and the market, the Republican Party's ideological drive to overturn the twentieth-century social contract at home through privatizing public goods such as social security and health care, weakening labor rights, and transferring more wealth to the wealthy through tax reform, for example, finds its parallel in the unilateralist vision that sees international institutions as the global version of big government. The White House and its congressional allies' steady assault on the United Nations and the international legal regime it embodies reflects not just an American critique of a stodgy bureaucracy in need of reform but an organic disposition to scorn the international community's institutions unless and until they can be altered to directly serve America's unfettered freedom abroad.

The Bush administration revealed its unilateralist impulse soon after the 2000 elections when it signaled a departure from international norms and disdain for collective approaches to global (and once decidedly U.S.) concerns like the environment, human rights, and arms control. Kyoto, the International Criminal Court (ICC), the Nuclear Test Ban Treaty: The signal achievements perceived by opinion outside and many within the United States to collectively address environmental degradation, human rights, and weapons proliferation met with chilling derision from the Bush II White House. Even as the administration championed its support for women's education and franchise in Afghanistan, for example, the repeal of U.S. support for reproductive health and HIV/AIDS initiatives that include family planning and abortion risked adding women to the growing coalition of those offended by the United States. Well before the September 11 attacks, the Bush administration signaled a belief that U.S. power alone was adequate to the task of addressing what many at home and in the international community regarded as the critical global challenges of the twenty-first century.

After 9/11, the United States declared war on a tactic, terrorism, without a strategy to undermine those who employ terrorist tactics. As if straight out of some *Manchurian Candidate* spin-off, the White House conducted itself as though it somehow intended to hand one psychological victory after another to the truly dangerous (as opposed to just politically hostile) anti-Americans. After correcting his initial ill-advised description of the nation's post-9/11 mission as a "crusade," the president and the secretary of defense left Lt. General William G. (Jerry) Boyken, a self-described anti-Islamic Christian crusader, as the Pentagon's top policy official in charge of leading the hunt for Osama bin Laden. The arrests and jailing of thousands of Islamic men at home reinforced the message, intended or not, that Christian America was waging an anti-Muslim crusade.[37]

By summer 2002, with the formation of the internal White House Iraq Group meant to control and craft the war message, Iraq had become for the Bush administration the central front in its war on terror and remained so even as the line to Osama bin Laden had gone cold, even as the Taliban were resurgent in Afghanistan, even as U.S. ally Pervez Musharraf could barely contain radical Islam in Pakistan. Iraq continued to occupy this position from the perspective of the White House even as Bali, Madrid, Casablanca, and Riyadh were hit hard by al-Qaeda franchise organizations and their sympathizers.[38] By spring 2003, the conflation of the war on terror with regime change in Iraq had crystallized. This lazy linkage showed that for the White House and the Pentagon, it was easier and more consistent with Cold War thinking to focus the U.S. response on a state rather than to craft policies that wrestled with the new stateless enemy.

Save in the eyes of Tony Blair, José María Aznar, John Howard, Ariel Sharon, and a handful of lesser powers, the United States appeared to the world to have picked a fight in Baghdad—not, as the White House argued, to bring democracy to the Middle East, including peace to Israel and Palestine, but to bring closure to a Bush-family oedipal matter and feed the far more mundane resource needs of empire. Military bases, control of the oil fields, the largest U.S. embassy operation in the world—all these added up to far less than the quasi-Trotskyist global democratic revolution savored by some officials, such as then–Under Secretary of Defense Paul Wolfowitz, or the "forward strategy of freedom in the Middle East" that Bush called for in 2003.[39] By the 2004 election campaign, the president could invoke a flies-to-flypaper metaphor: By fighting terrorists in Iraq, whether Baathists or foreign jihadists, he had effectively prevented them from attacking the United States on its own territory. The conflation became part of the standard repertoire of U.S. officials talking about Iraq, and the strength of the insurgency seemed perversely to reinforce their contention, as Iraq became a training ground for a new generation of anti-American foreign terrorists. Yet it was the United States, not the insurgents, that had been weakened financially, militarily, and diplomatically by its venture in Iraq, not only on the ground but in the eyes of the world.

Not long after his reelection, President Bush awarded the

Presidential Medal of Freedom to Tommy Franks, George Tenet, and L. Paul "Jerry" Bremer for their contribution to the war in Iraq—three architects of what may well come to be known as the biggest failure in American foreign policy since Vietnam. Fallujah had been quieted in a devastating Marine assault earlier that month, but the Iraqi insurgency against the Americans and Iraq's civil war against itself had not slowed the growing body count of Americans and Iraqis killed and maimed as a result. The White House ceremony reflected more than just a yawning gap in perception over Iraq between official Washington and the rest of the world. It was a decision calculated to display affirmatively the president's belief in his choices and to honor them publicly, despite mounting evidence of catastrophic errors. The awards ceremony told the world that even after his reelection campaign, political theater when a certain amount of bluster was expected, President Bush held tight to the belief that his war in Iraq was truly the front line in an epochal civilizational battle. It was that conflation of the war on terror with the war in Iraq and the exaggerated and unproved assertion that Saddam Hussein possessed an arsenal of weapons of mass destruction— even more than the president's 24/7 all-terror, all-the-time approach to diplomacy—that stood out as a powerful source of America's abysmal credibility gap. The unwillingness to admit to error in Iraq reinforced the world's view of the United States as both arrogant and ignorant, a perception with negative consequences for American legitimacy and capacity to lead.

America's strategic thinkers and foreign policy practitioners— as well as the nation's friends, adversaries, and enemies—have by now incorporated the new anti-American instinct into the calculus that shapes U.S. foreign policy and the world's interactions with the United States. Recent anger at the United States may well have been in part a visceral reaction to President Bush's style. But he did not tip global opinion against the United States single-handedly. Indeed, because it was America's Iraq policy that played such an instrumental role in giving momentum to the new global animus, and that policy apparently was embraced by a fairly broad array of Washington's political class, including the media and punditry associated with both parties, the responsibility for blunders in Iraq falls well beyond the White House.

Even a partial list of gaffs is lengthy: the bullying diplomacy that led to the war in Iraq, including the derision meted out to the UN in general and specifically to recalcitrant Security Council members; attacks on the IAEA, the UN's nuclear watchdog; the erroneously substantiated rationale of weapons of mass destruction; the utter failure to anticipate the nationalist backlash and the related neglect to provide sufficient troops on the ground; allowing, even celebrating, massive looting; the exclusion of war opponents from bidding on reconstruction contracts; the smug declaration of "mission accomplished"; de-Baathification; the de facto nullification of the Geneva Conventions; handing over and then retracting from former Baathist generals the security of Fallujah; torture at Abu Ghraib; the "we don't do body count" dodge over civilian casualties; the relentless play of images of U.S. soldiers bombing and shooting at mosques and at dying Iraqis inside them; the failure to equip U.S. troops properly and the arrogance of Donald Rumsfeld's contentions that we "fight wars with the army we have, not the army we may want," and "freedom is messy."

In short, the war in Iraq brought an almost daily reminder to the world not of the kind of successful nation-building and reconstruction the United States undertook after World War II, but of naked American hubris in believing we could go it virtually alone in Iraq, and of ineptitude in meeting the immense challenges of the occupation and insurgency. Maybe the United States wasn't really any different from the empires that had come before it. Maybe American exceptionalism—the get-out-of-jail-

free card during the Cold War that helped explain and often ex-
cuse our contradictions and diffuse the potential impact of anti-
Americanism—had finally become more legend than truth.
Maybe America wasn't so special after all.

Still, as much as congressional Democrats made it easy for the
White House to go to war in Iraq, and the U.S. public's fearfulness and media's timidity after 9/11 limited dissent, the power of
the American presidency to shape the foreign policy of the
United States and how that policy is presented to the world remains paramount. Despite the cumulative evidence of failure,
the president's tenacious advocacy of the war in Iraq created a
global disillusion with the United States on a scale of that experienced by Frank Baum's great cultural icons Dorothy, the Cow-
ardly Lion, the Tin Man, and the Scarecrow. Hopes fall away
when they learn that the Wizard of Oz has no special powers but
is instead a normal human, faking his virtues to entice his
acolytes with the promise of universally appealing aspirations,
asking for pain and sacrifice as the price. The Iraq war and the
detainee scandals have tipped the world's gut reaction to the
United States from belief to skepticism, not only because of the
myriad problems intrinsic to Iraq but because of what the war
says about us. The yellow brick road of U.S. foreign policy leads
not to a nirvana where aspirations become manifest: Instead, the
reality-based world finds a dead end in the U.S. promise that its
military power alone could bring democracy, that votes could
bring peace or food on the table. Like the bumbling Wizard
found concealed behind a curtain yanking feverishly but fruit-
lessly at his ineffectual levers, the United States too has lost control of how it is viewed by its international constituents on whose
credence its power ultimately depends.

What, America's defenders asked, about the other side of the
story? What about the U.S. Army teams rebuilding hospitals and
schools? What about U.S. support for economic reform, women's

rights, and education in the Arab world? What about the elections in Afghanistan and Iraq, in Lebanon, Egypt, and the Palestinian Authority? Or the thousands of individual constructive acts carried out by servicemen and women doing their honorable best? Where was the outrage over the four contractors whose bodies were burned and hung in effigy or the Abu Musab al-Zarqawi network's gruesome slaying of foreign aid workers, diplomats, contractors, U.S. businessmen, and Iraqis brave enough to risk U.S. training to provide security for their country? Or over the death of hundreds of Muslims at the hands of other Muslims in the Iraqi insurgency? Hundreds of thousands of Spanish, French, British, German, Dutch, American, Mexican, and South Korean citizens have staged massive antiwar, anti-Bush protests, but precious few protested to call attention to Saddam Hussein's breathtakingly horrific violation of his people's human rights.

If one casualty of the war in Iraq has been America's standing in countries long thought of as reliably pro-American, a related casualty is our ability to tell our story in a way that is believable abroad. The strategy of embedding the media with U.S. forces during the invasion of Iraq was only fleetingly successful. The collapse of Baghdad was quickly followed by looting that showed the United States to be succumbing to, if not perpetuating, the forces of chaos on the ground. As the insurgency grew, and the casualties mounted, most of the wrongs the Bush White House had sought to right in Iraq—halting a weapons of mass destruction program, however incipient and containable, and removing a brutal dictator from power—have been almost totally overshadowed by the relentless and international public exposure of U.S. failures, whether political, diplomatic, or strategic in nature.

The bright spots in the Iraq story line—the drafting of a transitional constitution, the handing over of sovereignty to Iraqis, empowering long-suppressed Kurd and Shia communities, the national elections, efforts to integrate women or the Sunni minority into the political process, the constituent assembly's approval of a constitution (however deeply flawed), a national referendum approving it, and parliamentary elections for a new, constitutional government—have not had the effect of appreciably recovering U.S. standing for two reasons. First, none of these political milestones seems to have brought Iraq stability, prosperity, or the benefits of democracy: Deprivation, disintegration, and civil war are closer at hand than the ideals the Bush administration promised the world it could deliver with or without help. Second, although the demonstration that the Saddamist status quo in Iraq was not forever immutable did reverberate politically within and beyond the Middle East, the palpable disillusion with the United States that the Iraq ordeal brought to the surface was related not only to current U.S. foreign policy but also to the more deeply stored resentments over history and power. Iraq may further disintegrate into civil war. Or it may, a decade from now, bear a closer resemblance to the ideal the White House promised. But with the long-suppressed ill will toward the United States now freely expressed, it is difficult to imagine even that optimistic outcome alone directly recovering America's international standing. Iraq and its attendant blunders have inflamed Anti-America. The exercise of restoring a more predictable and manageable love-hate balance in the war's wake will have to go beyond Iraq in order to address the deeper dynamics behind current world pique at U.S. policy.

Compared with the war in Iraq, the photos from Abu Ghraib, or stories from Guantánamo or of "extraordinary rendition," the exercise of searching for the deeper dynamics underlying the rise of Anti-America takes on a distinctly academic air. Yes, America's love of power, money, sex, guns, and crass culture has always riled somebody somewhere. Yes, the Cold War in the periphery left a bitter aftertaste, and yes, the United States will always reserve for itself the pride of nationalism while dismissing or just missing it in others. Yes, the demographic explosion of young people in Islamic countries who have little space for expression and little hope for a future would have happened with or without a George Bush to inflame them with taunts of a U.S. "crusade." But none of these dynamics, not individually or collectively, was enough to have produced the cross-class, cross-ideology, elite and popular falling-out with the United States that polls have recorded since 2002.

As off-putting as the White House's zealous focus on terror may have been after 9/11, it was what we voluntarily, preemptively, and largely solely decided to do in Iraq that moved the global balance against the United States. Iraq came to embody many of the disparate dynamics underlying the new twenty-first-century anti-American consensus. Just as the United States first supported but ultimately turned against Third World allies during the Cold War—whether Manuel Noriega, Augusto Pinochet, or Ferdinand Marcos—unseating Saddam, to whom the United States had once sold chemical weapons to cultivate him as a balance to Iran, seemed motivated in part by a desire to cleanse this unsavory association from America's "permanent record." Losing contact with Iraqis on the ground, and facing a nearly complete absence of human intelligence to convey the subtleties of Baathist nationalism, the United States became stuck in a closed informational loop, relying on the very exiled intelligence assets we and the British intelligence services had created and empowered to drive a wedge against the Baathist regime.

In short, the 80/20 dynamic had us talking to ourselves rather than listening to others about what was really happening in the country. Once on the ground, with our free-market faith in hand and heart, we looked on and even helped as looters smashed the symbols of the state, and then we proceeded with a whole-cloth dismantling of the existing state apparatus. Under Paul Bremer's proconsulship, the market was to be the sole motor of economic development. Within months of the end of "major combat operations," the United States found itself confronting anti-American terrorist attacks, a nationalist insurgency, and an emerging civil war, all with a thick overlay of religious fundamentalism. The inescapable statistic arrived on August 26, 2003, when, with the death of 139 U.S. service members, more U.S. soldiers had been killed after the war was supposedly over than during the combat phase. By January 2006, nearly three years after the invasion of Iraq, more than two thousand more Americans had been killed, a total of 15,000 wounded, many severely, and 30,000 Iraqi civilians had been killed as well.[40]

The war in Iraq became an exercise in self-sabotage, a huge gamble, a diversion from what could have been an aggressive fight to eliminate or neutralize terrorists, a diversion from the critical and still unfulfilled task of domestic preparedness, a diversion from developing a strategy to drain the swamp of future generations of terrorists, and a diversion of what remained of global goodwill after September 2001. Americans have since become concerned with the decline in global respect for the country, and they are divided over the use of force, the war on terror, the United Nations, and the mix of soft and hard power America should use to promote its interests.[41] Although there is some overall consensus that the United States should preserve the right to preemptive defense and should protect itself from terrorists, there is a deep split over how these goals should be accomplished.[42] Indeed, by the end of 2005, some 60 percent of the country believed the United States should not have sent troops to Iraq at all.[43]

The overwhelming balance of America's twenty-first-century global projection—U.S. programs and U.S. rhetoric—increasingly favors guns over butter, God over the state, and the market (one not nearly so free as we pretend) over all. As a result, and despite the divisions within the United States, we are increasingly sending the message abroad that Christian America often sets the agenda for the country's foreign policy—and not only in Islamic countries. An unfortunate example came when Pat Robertson, founder of the politically influential Christian Coalition, broadcast his suggestion on public airwaves that the United States assassinate Venezuelan President Hugo Chavez, whereupon Chavez responded that Robertson was speaking for "the United States elite." This perception of U.S. foreign policy being guided by the Christian right was reinforced by a modest State Department rebuke of Robertson's comment as "inappropriate"; the secretary of defense's flat-footed reply that his department doesn't take such actions because they are illegal; and the White House's failure to say anything at all. Grassroots Christian America, though lobbying for more programs to end poverty and slavery and engaging in worldwide humanitarian action, seems also to promote the perception that it relishes in the proselytizing element of its messianic mission: Spreading America's word will bring the country's citizens closer to God.[44] Of course, evangelical Christianity is not the only force in U.S. politics that shapes and constrains what the United States does and does not do abroad: The private sector, labor, human rights and other nongovernmental groups, Jewish, Catholic, Muslim groups, women, gays, African Americans, and Latinos shape America's voice too. But evangelical Christianity may be the only formidable political force today whose socially conservative values are pulling the country precisely in the opposite direction from those progressive traits of the New Deal, the Great Society, and the civil rights agenda of the twentieth century that gave the United States its special standing abroad, its capacity to lead on the international stage. If at home social conservatives and their orthodox free-market allies succeed in cleansing the United States of its twentieth-century legal and social rights, abroad the United States will risk losing some of the very resources that once made it a credible purveyor of the American dream.[45]

CHAPTER SIX

Who We Are: Anti-America at Home

Americans can no longer take superior comfort from assurances that even our closest historic allies hate us only because of our power or wealth. In addition to the historical, structural, and economic dynamics feeding Anti-America, recent U.S. foreign policy—what we do—has provided a seemingly endless array of inflammatory gaffs that were born not in some madrassa six thousand miles away, nor in a plot hatched by a few neoconservative intellectuals, but of our own society, politics, culture, and actions.

America's global ethos today holds that the United States will be safer if the world emulates its model of democracy and capitalism. After the 2004 elections, polls showed that global publics were increasingly inclined to hold the United States to account for its international trespasses; responses in fifteen of sixteen countries surveyed rated the United States behind Australia, Canada, Great Britain, or Germany as a country they would recommend a young person go to "lead a good life."[46] Much of the recent outpouring of disenchantment with the United States has been related to specific policies. And yet there is also a danger that in addition to what we do, who we are becoming as a body politic may well reinforce the momentum toward a search by historic U.S. allies for alternatives not only in international leadership but also in domestic political and economic ways of being.

In the globalized, boundary-free, new twenty-first century, America's social and political identity at home increasingly bears on what we do abroad, how others see us, and the message we send. In the twentieth century, the American dream we advertised and others aspired to was our middle-class meritocracy, technical ingenuity, and optimism—not our warts, whether Jim Crow laws or gender inequality, urban blight, or rural illiteracy. During much of the twentieth century, the "wise men" model of U.S. foreign policy essentially held that a handful of worldly men could together assess and maximize the national interest. This model assumed there was a barrier separating domestic politics and national identity from what the United States did abroad.

The notion that U.S. foreign policy was independent of and functioned autonomously from domestic politics also applied to how American power thinkers and practitioners thought of other societies, whatever their ideology. The predominant realist thinking of the time saw states as power balancers or power maximizers: The domestic conditions that made the United States or other countries tick were the stuff of sociology, not international relations. The national interest transcended the peculiarities and contradictions within U.S. borders. It was enough to say that the United States represented freedom, equality, and opportunity. And for anyone taking the trouble to look, the twentieth-century's progressive trajectory at home largely bore out this contention, one that gave moral weight to U.S. claims to specialness and leadership in the world.

But domestic politics no longer stops at the water's edge; the foreign policy of the United States is increasingly and explicitly intertwined with its national identity. Today, precisely because the globalization we have championed has made the world smaller and vastly increased our role in it, media and technology make our domestic project also an international symbol: What we do and who we are at home are increasingly on display for the world to see and judge, to emulate or reject. This is precisely the phenomenon that George W. Bush alludes to when he contends that values and interests are now one and the same. Stated another way, national interests and domestic politics can no longer be disentangled. The same holds true for other countries. Democracy means that governments are increasingly accountable to their domestic electorate first. Regardless of the personality or political party occupying the White House, Americans can no longer expect that their power or interests will prevail over the preferences and demands of a global public that is increasingly democratic. America's constituents are now not only those who vote and pay taxes at home but also the billions of citizens abroad who watch and analyze every move we make.

Indeed, beneath the fights over inspectors, resolutions, yellow cake, and aluminum tubes, the core of America and the world's debate over Iraq came to be about whether what the United States proposed doing in Iraq reflected American values. Especially once U.S. claims over weapons of mass destruction in Iraq could not be substantiated, the White House transformed the conflict into a values war. At a World War II memorial service in August 2005, President Bush said of a U.S. Marine officer serving in Iraq that "he knows that he and his generation are doing the same vital work in this war on terror that his grandparents did in World War II," a war Americans collectively think of as a righteous war to defend universal values.[47] With Iraq as the vehicle, the United States asked the world to be like us, to adopt our core values, to embrace our universal truths.

Whereas the war on terror began as essentially a reactive U.S.

policy, transforming the Middle East via wholesale regime change in Iraq held out the promise of showing the world that the United States could offer something positive and proactive: The use of force was no longer a last resort but an engine that could accelerate history, and help people seize their own futures and escape their fates. Freedom from servitude for others meant security for America. President Bush went to war and spilled blood and billions to globalize that message. But exactly which American values do we hope the world will embrace from such a recklessly pursued exercise? Which American dream, if reproduced abroad, will make America more secure in the twenty-first century?

In the twentieth century, the New Deal, the Great Society, and civil rights became the signal domestic achievements for the United States, embraced eventually by Democrats and Republicans and that came to embody the American dream at home and represent it abroad. The core social goal of those programs was to bring federal protections of the state to a whole range of previously unprotected classes: African Americans, women, workers, immigrants—and later to the disabled and gays and lesbians. Liberals, progressives, small-d democrats, men and women of both political parties fought for and were empowered by these new federal rights. They believed in Martin Luther King's vision that the "arc of history" bends toward justice. They expected the New Deal and Great Society values of all America, including social security and a progressive tax system, to continue. Civil war, labor conflict, the depression, and racial violence had brought to the U.S. political mainstream the assumption that the union of democracy and capitalism could only be sustained with a state to invest in a safety net and enforce laws and regulations that level the economic and political playing fields. For a time, both parties shared this view.

But these core beliefs generated their own backlash, one not fully appreciated in its scope and political power until the turn of the twenty-first century. First the Dixiecrats in 1948, then the Goldwater campaign of 1964, the 1981 Reagan Revolution, the 1994 Contract with America, contemporary conservative Republican control of the Congress, the White House, and the Supreme Court—all with their underpinnings in an effective and well-funded idea industry—are developments that may well complete the consolidation of what some hope will become a permanent Republican majority. But it is not the Republican Party of Teddy Roosevelt or Richard Nixon. Though not without internal cleavages, the new Republican Party is bent on stripping away the very domestic legal and economic protections at home that gave the United States the moral credibility to lead abroad in the twentieth century. Hundreds of billions of dollars for military, intelligence, homeland security, or for politically earmarked pet projects folded into public works bills—often held up as proof that today's Republican Party has departed from its fiscally conservative traditions—cannot compensate for the structural inequalities increasingly manifest in the twenty-first century. Hurricane Katrina's hundreds of thousands of displaced victims in New Orleans, most of them poor and black, showed the world and Americans themselves that the United States can no longer sustain at home the ideals of equality and justice it purports to offer abroad.

After World War II, the international expression of America's domestic recipe for social peace and economic prosperity made itself manifest in the financial institutions of the Bretton Woods system and in the international laws, charters, conventions, and agencies that came to be understood as the United Nations system. These two networks were to provide collective economic insurance and an international legal framework to preserve the peace and promote prosperity following a half century of death and destruction. Americans viscerally understood the expedience of underwriting the creation of capitalist welfare states in Europe and Japan, as they had witnessed how their own social contract had also soothed the social tensions of rapid industrialization of the late nineteenth and early twentieth centuries. FDR's success in pulling the country from the brink after the Great Depression brought home the realpolitik of noblesse oblige within and outside of America's borders.

Underlying the domestic and international project of twentieth-century America was the assumption that to guarantee the values of freedom, equality, opportunity, and justice, government and international institutions had to play a role to mediate affairs between individuals and the market and between states. Neither God, nor an invisible hand, nor sheer power would suffice. Whatever the internal foibles and contradictions of the U.S. experiment, whatever the country's ignoble trespasses in the Third World and Latin America, the "wise men" model held up during the Cold War because America's domestic and social peace of the second half of the twentieth century helped generate global trust that the United States largely practiced the values abroad that it preached at home.

But just as the expansion of rights protected by the state at home produced a domestic political backlash, so too did the idea that the United States might subject its sovereignty to the dictates of international law or institutions. For example, by the 1990s, critics in Congress succeeded in weakening political and economic support for the United Nations. Democrats, too, had been itching to break free from the domestic and international constraints that bound individuals and states together during the Cold War. Reflecting an essential simpatico for corporate America, reinforcing the national move away from large federal programs, and trying desperately not to lose more political ground, the Democratic Party validated conservative antipathy toward state institutions with its reform of the welfare state at home and its embrace of free-market orthodoxy on the global stage. With a nudge from the center and a yank from the right, smashing twentieth-century state institutions at home and internationally became the ideological core powering the White House. The result is a rollback of the very protections and freedoms that gave the United States its moral authority during the American Century, at home and abroad. The boundaries that once balanced individual liberties with the common good are shifting: A new conventional wisdom on God, guns, money and taxes, science, and civil liberties is moving the center of social gravity in the United States backward in time, just as the White House has undertaken a global mission to propel what it views as arrested societies forward into the future. It is a bald contradiction for the U.S. government domestically to rein in the influence of the state in favor of individual agency while simultaneously asserting abroad the right of the state to remake societies from top to bottom.

Religion is a fine example of the shift. The lines separating church and state, regarded in the United States as a fundamental protection of religious freedom, are blurring. God has become good politics. The White House's faith-based initiatives, which direct government finances to religious institutions such as schools and churches, helped President Bush extend his base; without whose votes, he acknowledged, he could not have won the 2004 election. Poor, rural voters in southern Ohio's piece of Appalachia, for example, were among the new beneficiaries of God-driven state largesse and voted to stay on the God dole. The public education systems of forty of America's fifty states face legal challenges to the teaching of evolution brought by backers of the "intelligent design" proposal.

The religiosity of the American people is not in itself bad for the country's image abroad. But the merging of the private space of faith with the secular realm of politics undermines America's claim to represent a universal future colored by the values of the

Enlightenment, or a reason- and fact-based reality. The new U.S. experiment in blending state and faith initiatives to advance mutually reinforcing social projects on the domestic front and internationally evokes the blurring of mosque and state in the very societies whose whole-cloth reform the United States has demanded. This dissonance, and the failure so far of faith and market forces to replace the basic services of government, cannot help but undermine America's international credibility, not only within secular societies beyond our borders but with the moderates in Islamic countries whom we hope to help in their reform efforts.

Guns afford another example of this profound shift. It isn't only Michael Moore who has noted the uniquely revered role of guns in U.S. society. President Bush did as much when he allowed Congress to let the ban on assault weapons lapse. The United States spends billions in tax dollars to disarm and neutralize the warlords and terrorists who thrive in some of the world's most insecure places—Afghanistan, Pakistan, Iraq, Colombia—while permitting its own weapons firms to lead the global market in supplying all parties to these and many other conflicts in the developing world. Ten years after the wars in Central America ended, U.S. assault weapons once favored by guerrillas and death squads alike have flooded the market that now supports the drug and gang violence wracking the Andes and Central America.

Although without a civilian gun-ownership culture remotely comparable to that of the United States, the Russian, Jordanian, French, and Israeli arms industries similarly profit from conflict. But at the end of the day, because the United States represents itself as occupying higher moral ground than the rest, only its capacity for moral suasion suffers from its inebriation with guns and refusal to sign onto international conventions seeking to contain the illicit manufacture and trafficking of weapons and ammunition.[48] The second amendment of the U.S. Constitution referred to the right of a militia to hold arms when the militia was the new country's early form of self-defense. The United States is not the Wild West anymore; yet by insisting on the gun as a symbol of individual rights, we confirm the world's caricature of America as the violent cowboy state. Glorifying the gun at home plainly undermines America's credibility with the populations of countries whose help we seek in fighting the very fundamentalist terrorists who endow gun violence with spiritual content in their crusade against the West.[49]

Money and taxes create domestic tension as well. Should they succeed, domestic projects to privatize social security, or to render permanent a tax code that increasingly taxes work rather than wealth, will become the signal domestic achievements of the Bush II presidency. The consequences at home of these projects, dismissed as unthinkable or just plain quackery only twenty years ago when the American Century's social contract held fast even during the first Republican revolution of Ronald Reagan, will at minimum deepen the income divide between the poorest and wealthiest Americans, while further weakening the middle class. As white-collar American jobs are increasingly outsourced, with the depressing effect on wages at home, even America's trade enthusiasts are now asking themselves whether free trade will always maximize America's comparative advantage. As free-trade champion Jagdish Bhagwati warned in 1968, Americans might experience "immiseration" if trade in America's comparative advantage, skilled jobs, has the effect of lowering wages. Trade enthusiasts such as economist Paul Samuelson now fear that the United States could face a kind of growth where the narrow benefits of economic globalization "would flow mostly to companies and shareholders who profit from the cheaper labor, with little pass-through to workers and consumers"—precisely the contention of globalization's critics for nearly two decades.[50]

Indeed, rising income inequality seems to show that the middle-class meritocracy so cherished and advertised by the United States is indeed in a state of atrophy. In 1979 the average income of the top 1 percent in the United States was 133 times that of the bottom 20 percent. Today the top 1 percent earns 189 times that of the bottom quintile. And the top 1 percent of households now earn 20 percent of all income and hold over one-third of the country's wealth—a divide the United States has not experienced since the depression and one that still does not reflect the possible effects of the Third World–style tax programs the president has proposed.[51] As the race to the bottom becomes a cross-class phenomenon at home, touching on the poor, working poor, and middle class, economic globalization's foes will no longer find common cause only at gatherings in Porto Alegre or Genoa but will discover it within America's borders as well.

What of the consequences of the economic divide for U.S. influence abroad? The United States has prided itself on its meritocracy, for providing more equal opportunity to its citizens than any country anywhere in history. The prosperity of the country, the sheer size of its economy, and the pervasiveness and accessibility of its consumer culture seemed to bleach out the dark side of U.S. capitalism even to America's critics, save the left and, of course, the French. America's message to the world for much of the twentieth century was that a combination of government programs and market power guaranteed entry into the middle class and a piece of the American dream to anyone who worked hard. But now, with America's middle class working longer hours while earning less money, with blue- and white-collar workers vulnerable to what advocates call the greater "dynamism" of an unregulated market, the United States may be losing its claim to offer an economic model that truly promotes mobility, particularly as the other capitalist economies, the European Union, for example, have persuaded many of their own citizens that high productivity is indeed possible without a backbreaking work-week or substantially increasing inequality.[52]

How can the United States offer itself as a model to Third World elites, for example, those who have historically spurned the kind of social contract that gave America its strength in the twentieth century, to pay taxes and invest in their people, if in the twenty-first century the United States itself tosses aside that social contract for one that looks downright un-American in its insolvency, inequality, and plain unfairness? Hurricane Katrina definitively exposed the breach, confirming for one British observer "a basic understanding of American economics and history ... that, despite all the rhetoric, wealth—not hard work or personal sacrifice—is the most decisive factor in who succeeds." For *The Hindu* of America's new strategic partner India, Katrina told "a tale of systematic neglect, administrative incompetence, market-driven environmental destruction and desperate poverty" while "exposing squalor that would shame a Third World country, as well as racial and political divisions reminiscent of apartheid South Africa."[53] Similarly disillusioned observations poured from news outlets and commentary around the world, converging with the response to Katrina of Americans who seemed to have had the collective veil of denial about their country's racial and social divide peeled back for the first time since Bill Clinton told them the era of big government, and presumably poverty and racism, had officially ended.[54]

The rule of law may be another casualty. Is the White House's looseness with American laws (spying without warrants on its own citizens) or with international law and the Geneva Conventions so surprising from a country where over half the population finds the use of torture acceptable in some cases?[55] Are the sexual humiliations and extreme acts of cruelty at Abu Ghraib and Guantánamo very distant from the prisoner abuse that is a regular feature of prisons housing America's own criminals?

When Donald Rumsfeld was first asked about the abuses at Iraq's Abu Ghraib prison, he described the handful of guardsmen and soldiers as "un-American." It subsequently came to light that the military's own judge advocates had been overruled in interagency debates by civilian political appointees in the Pentagon, White House, and Justice Department—including Attorney General Alberto Gonzalez—who argued that the president's execution of the war on terror superseded prohibitions on torture set out by the Geneva Conventions. In its own tortured logic, the White House argued that "enemy combatants" fighting in irregular wars who bore no markings of national origin could not expect the same treatment as "prisoners of war," those bearing the insignia of nation-states fighting conventional wars. Should the United States suspect its own citizens of terrorism, the White House likewise concluded it could sidestep the Constitution by asking allies, say Saudi Arabia, to pick up and interrogate—and presumably torture—U.S. citizens along with nationals of other countries it now includes in the policy of "rendition"—a policy that allows intelligence services of countries such as Egypt to conduct interrogations with techniques such as torture that might violate U.S. laws.[56]

The United States signed and ratified the Convention Against Torture, and U.S. law prohibits transferring detainees to a country where they may be mistreated. After September 11, Americans began to face the consequences of having opted for stability over democracy and human rights in U.S. relations with its Persian Gulf–state allies. After the Iraq invasion, President Bush relished having liberated the Iraqi people from decades of unthinkable torture by Saddam Hussein's regime. But one executive order he signed overturned a half century of international legal practice in applying the rules of war. Abu Ghraib and Guantánamo scuttled America's claim as the standard-bearer of the rule of law. Contrary to the caricature at the time, it wasn't just a few burger-flipping-red-state-high-school-educated bad apples who committed the un-American acts of abuse or torture but the learned consigliere to the highest elected officer of the land whose rationales for such practices paved the way.

Bush may have won his reelection battle on the heels of the torture scandal, but U.S. credibility in the world had lost, not only because such practices shattered an ideal of the United States holding a higher moral ground but also because as a practical matter the detentions, incarcerations, and "renditions"— whether at Guantánamo, in other countries, or under direct U.S. jurisdiction—involved citizens of some forty-two different countries, whose treatment came to embody America's fall from grace.[57] Further corrosion of America's international reputation as a country committed to the rule of law, whether with the failure to hold accountable senior officials responsible for torture and other aggressive interrogation tactics in U.S. detention centers, or with elected officials and their supporters attacking the independence of the judiciary at Christian religious gatherings, has the potential to reinforce the global perception of an increasingly contradictory gap between the direction of America's domestic social contract and the values the United States purports to stand for abroad.

II

CHAPTER SEVEN

American Ubiquity—Chinmi, Sungmi, Banmi, Hyommi

In the language of South Korea, there are eight separate words to describe that U.S. ally's relationship to the United States. *Banmi* is anti-America, *sungmi* is worship America, *hyommi* is loathe America, *chinmi* is pro-America, *yonmi* is associate with America, *yongmi* is use America, *hangmi* is resist America, and *pimi* means criticize America. Just as the Inuits of Alaska have twenty-three words for ice, a part of nature that surrounds them and indeed defines their worldview, South Korea's relationship with the United States is sufficiently complex and defining that its language offers an entire vocabulary to capture the ambivalence (and worse) that is now shared across continents and cultures.[1]

Unlike citizens of countries the world over, Americans don't know what it is like to wake up every day to reruns of 1970s foreign sitcoms, or to news coverage about the vicissitudes of the president of some other country (unless the U.S. military is pulling him out of a spider hole). But for much of the world, the

United States today is ubiquitous, and not as some all-purpose element like water but as a power and presence that in the beginning of the twenty-first century has sparked considerable anger and contempt from the very partners and allies it once sought to inspire and lead. It doesn't take A–Z entries from the World Encyclopedia of anti-Americanism to prove the point.

Opinion polls, emerging attitudes toward U.S. corporate brands, and the membership of the Iraq coalition offer a window into the scope of Anti-America today. Since 2000, polls by over a half dozen organizations—from Pew to Zogby, German Marshall Fund to the *Guardian*, Eurobarometer to *Latinobarómetro*—have tracked the declining views about America, Americans, and U.S. foreign policy in every region of the world. The American private sector has begun to worry—with some evidence to support its concerns—that foreign tourists or consumers of American brands will vent their anti-American animus by vacationing elsewhere or steering away from products that in happier times sold well not only for their quality but because of their association with Americanness. Media coverage of the United States from the capitals of Europe to 24/7 Arab television offers a relentless flow of images and news coverage that even the most liberal of Americans might find offensive.[2] In France, anti-Americanism has become something of a niche industry, with a monthly paper, *L'Anti-Americain*, a somewhat tongue-in-cheek tabloid, selling 7,500 copies in its first week on the kiosks. In Great Britain, high and popular culture alike—*Jerry Springer the Opera*, *Guantánamo Baywatch*, *The Lardburgers* (a segment on the show *Big Breakfast* about fat "red-state" Americans), George Michael's Blair-as-Bush's-poodle video—captured a new anti-American zeitgeist expressing a palpable rejection of Tony Blair's embrace of George Bush and his war on Iraq, and of the vulgarity and tolerance for lawlessness Bush seems to represent. Street art and antiglobalization protests in Porto Alegre, Genoa, and Miami, political cartoons, and election campaigns have since 2001 thawed all manner of anti-Americanists out of their former freeze.

The insurgency against the symbols and representatives of the U.S. occupation in Iraq are a daily, vivid, and bloody reminder of the extremism of some anti-American hostility, as is the slow de-population by non-U.S. and non-British forces from the mile-wide, inch-deep "coalition" of military forces in Iraq. Less violent but no less important, regional intergovernmental entities where the United States once dominated, such as Asia-Pacific Economic Cooperation (APEC), are being challenged by competing entities from which the United States is excluded, including the Association of Southeast Asian Nations plus China, Japan, and South Korea (ASEAN+3), which are pursuing trade and economic ties quite independently of the United States. Latin America has recently formed the South American Community of Nations with the express purpose of countering U.S. power in the hemisphere. Led by Brazil, the region's largest economies in the Southern Cone plus Venezuela are also trying to revitalize MER-COSUR (Mercado Común del Sur) as a political mechanism to strengthen their hand with the United States in hemispheric trade talks. In 1971, when the world switched from the gold standard to the dollar as the dominant currency, it was a global statement of international confidence not only in the stability of the U.S. currency but also in the credibility and good faith of the United States as a responsible steward of the world economy. In 2004, in contrast, forty-five central banks attested to having increased their euro holdings in the prior year, mainly at the dollar's expense.[3] There may be solely economic factors in their decisions: The fiscal and trade deficits of the United States have weakened the dollar, and the world's central bankers are sensibly hedging their bets. But how much of the world's confidence in the dollar also has been diminished by the decline in overall American credibility and leadership?

The best, though admittedly eye-glazing, measure of the steep decline in America's world standing is, of course, polling data. Although the polls tend not to give much insight into the deep historical underpinnings of today's antipathy, nor into the intensity with which those polled hold their views, they clearly reveal a sea change. As a benchmark, the venerable Pew polls show that favorable views of the United States among three allies, Germany, Great Britain, and Indonesia, for example, reached 78 percent, 83 percent, and 75 percent, respectively, in 2000.[4] Among traditional and traditionally close U.S. allies, these numbers by and large show the reputation of the United States still in good standing. But between 2000 and 2003, favorable ratings of the U.S. government began to fall precipitously. The immediate cause of the world's falling-out with the United States was the war in Iraq. By 2003 the troika of France, Germany, and Russia that led the European opposition to the war, as well as populations of countries topping the A-list of the "coalition of the willing," such as Great Britain, Poland, and Spain, recorded dramatic declines in positive attitudes toward the United States. By 2005, the younger the individuals polled, the more consistently negative were their attitudes.[5]

Beyond Europe, public opinion in strategic U.S. allies—whether Jordan, South Korea, Saudi Arabia, or Egypt—also plummeted. By summer 2003, for example, Pew found that only 1 percent of Jordanians held a favorable view of the United States, with hostility toward the American people rising as positive views dropped from the mid-50s to the teens. One year after the war in Iraq began, Egypt and Saudi Arabia posted unfavorable attitudes of an almost statistically unimaginable 98 and 94 percent, respectively.[6] The measures of world opinion toward the United States were not limited to the general level of a popularity contest—the "do-they-like/dislike-Americans" type of question. Strong majorities in almost every country polled—in Europe,

Latin America, Asia, and the Middle East—consistently posted declining approval of U.S. foreign policy and declining trust in the ability and disposition of the United States to promote world peace and to play a positive role in fighting terrorism.[7]

Between 2000 and 2004, favorable opinion in Germany, Great Britain, and Indonesia declined by 40 percent, 25 percent, and 60 percent, respectively.[8] Once Americans affirmatively chose to return George W. Bush to the presidency, polls in France, Germany, Brazil, Turkey, Canada, South Korea, Argentina, Mexico, Great Britain, and South Africa indicated that the American people, largely given a pass during Bush's first term because of the controversy over the 2000 election, no longer escaped blame for their president's actions: The world's negative opinion of the Bush administration extended to Americans as a people.[9] The front cover of the British *Daily Mirror* the morning after the 2004 U.S. election captured the new unforgiving mood: "How Could 59,054,087 People Be So Dumb?"[10]

In the aftermath of the 9/11 attacks, the Bush administration was not entirely impervious to the global anti-American drift. Its answer? The United States needed some good PR. The State Department hired a star public relations veteran, Charlotte Beers, to overhaul U.S. public diplomacy. Beers's tenure was brief and much derided. Her Madison Avenue instincts told her that the trouble with America's world standing related to the decline of the American "brand." A little "rebranding" might give America's image a jump start. Marketing America as a brand fell flat, as did her tenure in the State Department, because the United States is much more than a product and because the forces breathing life into Anti-America were too multiple and too complex to be remedied by public relations alone. Although the idea of marketing America as a brand failed, the effort anticipated a shift in global attitudes toward American brands that would soon emerge as another measure of the crisis in U.S. credibility.[11]

In the past half century, American companies marketed their products abroad taking advantage of their Americanness as an asset to boost sales. Buying a Ford, a pair of Levis, or Nikes; drinking a Coke; devouring a Big Mac; or smoking a Marlboro offered a chance to possess a small piece of the American dream. These and dozens of other American brands capitalized on the appeal of their home country to sell their wares to international consumers. An American product in the American Century faced none of the psychological hurdles of a German or a Japanese product, which had to overcome decades of genocide- and fascism-related baggage to sell a car or a radio.[12]

Of course, some sectors of the U.S. economy operate in environments that are by definition somewhat or even substantially hostile. The defense, private security, energy, and insurance industries deal with political and physical risk every day; they factor it in as the price of doing business, and profit because of it. No downturn in global opinion was needed for women in Nigeria, indigenous Quichua, Achuar, and Shuar activists in Ecuador, or Tamil rebels in Indonesia to target U.S. (and, for that matter, Dutch or British) oil companies as rapacious profiteers. Antiglobalization protesters routinely launched boycotts against American icons such as Burger King, McDonald's, and Citibank long before global opinion of the United States declined in 2002.

Unlike the defense, security, and energy industries, the service and retail industries need a welcoming climate in the countries where they sell their products because they need consumers to pay voluntarily for them over and over. That choice depends on trust—not only in the product's quality but also in the emotional and psychological benefits associated with the transaction. But America's service and retail industries and the consumer-survey firms they employ have begun to detect a shift in preferences that, when placed alongside negative trends in opinion polls, suggests a deterioration of foreign attitudes toward Americans and American goods.¹³ Even if the quality of American products remains consistent, and consistently high, the experience of buying American may be souring because of the overall loss of trust in the United States.

By the end of 2003, consumer surveys in Europe, Canada, Latin America, Asia, and the Middle East began to show that public opinion toward the United States had started to creep into consumer choices. Still, in 2005 the United States ranked eleventh behind Australia, Canada, Switzerland, the United Kingdom, Sweden, Italy, Germany, the Netherlands, France, and New Zealand in a study of consumer attitudes and perceptions with 10,000 people in ten countries.¹⁴ Any sociologist will concede a basic mantra of marketing: There is a direct link between attitudes and behavior. This link may not be immediate, but it is causing ripples of concern in the U.S. private sector. In Europe, consumer-survey firms began to pick up on downward sales trends for Coca Cola, McDonald's, Marlboro, Gap, Disney, and Starbucks. Most of these companies explain any downtick in their market share contextually: The German economy is sluggish; older French coffee-drinkers want their coffee experience one way and not the other; taxes and health campaigns have put a dent in smoking habits. But in a survey of 8,000 consumers in eight countries, fully 20 percent of Europeans and Canadians said their objections to U.S. foreign policy would prevent them from buying American brands. The brands associated most closely with America, Marlboro and Coca Cola, have lost market share in Germany and France.

This survey by one of the world's largest consumer-survey organizations listed other brands explicitly identified with the United States as potentially vulnerable to anti-American buying practices: American Express, United Airlines, Microsoft, General Motors, Visa, AOL, Exxon Mobil, and Starbucks. Consumers polled assigned to many of these companies the same attributes they did to the U.S. government and President Bush: arrogant, intrusive, and self-centered.[15] In Latin America, a distinct generational attitude had emerged by 2004, with younger people in Chile, Argentina, Brazil, and Mexico, by far the largest markets for American products in the hemisphere outside of Canada, reacting to American brands negatively and searching for alternatives.[16] More neutral American brands, those not easily identified as American and that have "localized" their identities, have fared better: SPAM, Estée Lauder, Kleenex, Sara Lee, and a range of Proctor and Gamble products, for example, have so far avoided association with the decline in U.S. credibility and doubts about the consistency of American values. The downward trends in consumer attitudes or choices do seem to be related in part to the availability of high-quality alternatives to American products, and in part to factors affecting preference such as greater public health awareness, but also in part to the tarnished U.S. image that is so amply demonstrated by polling, protests, and the polarization over the Bush administration's particular style of unilateralism.

With some exceptions, the U.S. private sector remains loath to openly attribute any decline in market share to a specific U.S. government policy, preferring to point to local economic conditions or misunderstandings. These businesses assert that quality above all drives consumer choice, and they resist efforts to engage the private sector in global public diplomacy as a cover for a partisan anti-Bush agenda of which they want no part. After all, anti-American and antiglobalization protesters in capitals around the world can be seen on television running from the cops in their Nikes. American companies may alter their marketing strategies to put a higher premium on "localization," a shift forced in the last decade by the backlash against globalization, and explore opportunities for "corporate social responsibility" to enhance consumers' perceptions of their commitment to the common good.[17] Some American corporations have begun to acknowledge the softening of their overseas markets and even gingerly concede the slackening may have some connection to America's standing in the world. The U.S. tourism industry worries that both the obstacles to getting visas to visit the United States and the country's overall decline in appeal reinforce each other and are together making a significant dent in business. McDonald's, American Airlines, and ExxonMobil, for example, are quietly supporting private diplomacy initiatives aimed at softening America's image abroad and launching modest efforts to educate Americans to behave as better world citizens. But in general, and perhaps because the weak dollar has boosted U.S. exports and helped short-term profits, the American private sector outwardly remains in denial about the potential relationship between the downturn in global attitudes toward the United States and the shift now under way in global market choices.

Still, symbols matter, and the performance of large American companies has become closely associated with that of their home country. Even before the war in Iraq, America's private sector had come under considerable scrutiny abroad. Corruption scandals at Enron, WorldCom, and other business titans tarnished the image of the great American corporate citizen. Even if, for example, the face-off over the General Electric–Honeywell merger pitting Mario Monti, the mild-mannered Italian economist running the European Commission's antitrust office, against Jack Welch, the high-flying, hard-bargaining CEO of GE, was only a matter of safeguarding competitiveness for the European defense industry, the Brussels ruling against the merger, and against monopolistic design and marketing practices of Microsoft and Coca-Cola, became a metaphor for Americans and especially Europeans of the latter's capacity to take the empire down a few notches. Whatever the real numbers—and U.S. companies generally will not divulge them—there is undoubtedly a new and palpably stronger perception, particularly in Europe, that punishing U.S. companies through technical European Union rulings in Brussels or by buying a non-American product offers a chance to chastise the United States for its hubris and unilateralism. Anti-Americanism is, after all, very much about perception. And when it comes to America the brand and American brands, there is very definitely a perception—as the general opinion polls bear out—that both are becoming increasingly unworthy of that critical dimension of brand loyalty: trust.[18]

A very public measure of the world's falling-out with the United States is the much-derided composition of the coalition it assembled to participate in the invasion and occupation of Iraq. On March 18, 2003, Secretary of State Colin Powell announced that the United States had assembled a thirty-country coalition prepared to give concrete military and other support to the invasion of Iraq. The list was soon expanded to forty-eight countries. The braggadocio that accompanied the White House depiction of the alleged international support was captured by then–press secretary Ari Fleischer, who had the chutzpah to tell reporters that "all told, the population of the coalition of the willing is approximately 1.18 billion people around the world."[19]

The initial coalition included Afghanistan, Albania, Australia, Azerbaijan, Bulgaria, Colombia, the Czech Republic, Denmark, El Salvador, Eritrea, Estonia, Ethiopia, Georgia, Hungary, Italy, Japan, South Korea, Latvia, Lithuania, Macedonia, the Netherlands, Nicaragua, the Philippines, Poland, Portugal, Romania, Slovakia, Spain, Turkey, the United Kingdom, and Uzbekistan. It was painful to listen to the president and his cabinet members assert the global nature of the new coalition. The hollowness of the suggestion that the United States would be accompanied in Iraq by a great global coalition was reinforced by the State Department's rating of eighteen coalition countries as having poor

or very poor human rights records, and Freedom House's rank-
ing of seventeen coalition countries as "not free" or "partially
free."[20] Like the case for Iraqi possession of weapons of mass destruction presented to the United Nations just weeks earlier, this
U.S. diplomatic assemblage, widely mocked as the "coalition of
the coerced," reeked of slap-dash illegitimacy. Only the United
Kingdom, Australia, Poland, Spain, Italy, and South Korea contributed substantial troops to the effort, and only the first three
contributed any during the "major combat" phase, at great political and human cost. Especially by comparison with the 1991
Gulf War coalition in which dozens of countries joined the
United States and truly did commit troops, bases, and financing
to the effort, the 2003 coalition came to demonstrate America's
isolation rather than its global leadership and convening power.[21]

By 2005 only the United States and the United Kingdom kept
more than a symbolic number of troops in the country: roughly
150,000 for the United States and only 8,000 for Great Britain,
down from 45,000 at the beginning of the war. As for Poland,
some 75 percent of the population opposed participating in the
"coalition," but the country was lauded by the United States as a
sign of "new Europe's" democratic promise and deep commitment to fighting terrorism. Still, Poland began a phased withdrawal of its 2,500 troops after Prime Minister Marek Belka
barely survived a vote of confidence that hinged on his commitment to remove troops. South Korea struggled to keep its 3,000-
troop contingent in Iraq. Spain withdrew its troops after the
March 2004 Antocha train bombings brought down the government of conservative Bush ally José María Aznar. Most Latin
Americans followed Spain's lead, with the exceptions of U.S.-fa-
vored El Salvador, which kept some troops in Iraq, and of that
country's former guerrillas and paramilitary fighters hired by
private contractors. Gloria Macapagal-Arroyo, president of the
Philippines, pulled out her country's 51 troops to gain the release

of a Filipino contract worker taken hostage by the al-Zarqawi network. Even Ukraine, America's new "new Europe" ally, decided to withdraw its 1,650 troop presence in a vote before Vladimir Yushchenko took office. Bulgaria, another "new European" ally facing equally strong domestic opposition, also began withdrawing the few hundred troops it had in Iraq in 2005 after a Bulgarian soldier was accidentally killed by U.S. troops.

In Australia, although Bush ally Prime Minister John Howard may have wished to send more than 400 Australian troops to Iraq, enormous antiwar demonstrations and popular opinion against the war restrained him from doing so until he had succeeded in winning reelection. He then reneged on a campaign promise not to send more troops and doubled the Australian troop presence in 2005: In the aftermath, the Australian public's support for Howard dropped from 62 percent to 54 percent. Opinion toward the United States, which had remained respectable in the early years of the Iraq war, dropped in 2005: Only 58 percent of Australians had positive feelings toward the United States, and 57 percent were worried about the potential threat posed by U.S. foreign policies (the exact percentage that were worried about the threat of Islamic fundamentalism).[22]

Public opinion in Italy turned definitively against the United States and led to Prime Minister Silvio Berlusconi's decision to begin withdrawing Italian troops after an incident of friendly fire by U.S. forces killed an Italian hostage negotiator just after he secured the freedom of a compatriot journalist. Despite the happy gloss on visits to Europe by Bush, Rice, and Rumsfeld early in the president's second term, the United States has been able to secure very little from the war's opponents within "old Europe": NATO members committed a paltry $5 million for equipment and training of Iraqi security forces, and the European Union Community budget pledged $400 million for humanitarian assistance and reconstruction aid; by comparison, the

United States has spent more than $300 billion since the war began. Even if European governments might wish to extend a hand to the United States, their populations—both elites and the broad public—are united in exercising a significant check on their governments' room for maneuver. Not insignificantly, it was James Baker, the old-school architect of the first Gulf War coalition, who secured agreement of the most symbolically significant European contribution to Iraq: forgiveness of 80 percent of some $39 billion in Iraqi debt owed to members of the Paris Club, a far more palatable agenda item—few expected a future Iraqi government ever to pay it off—for publics that regard Third World debt as the symbol and substance of an ever-tightening noose of globalization and Americanization.[23]

As the war in Iraq, coupled with repeated U.S. assertions of global support for the war effort, damaged American credibility, few if any of the governments in the coalition could demonstrate to their publics that their sacrifice had delivered tangible benefits either to the common good or to their own body politic. Many participants in the coalition paid heavy political costs at home, with little to show from the United States by way of material or even spiritual quid pro quo. After the first Gulf War, Bush père's diplomatic team directed White House power directly toward Arab-Israeli peace. It was only Yasser Arafat's death, not a sense of obligation to Bush's closest coalition ally Tony Blair, that revived U.S. reengagement in Middle East peace—from the start among the central stated objectives of the regime-change strategy.

CHAPTER EIGHT

Who They Are

The capacity of the United States to unleash a flood of resentment is particularly striking in countries where it has maintained close strategic relationships over the years. By the end of the American Century, the United States had itself become a domestic political actor to greater or lesser degree, by design or default, in nearly every part of the world now in open rebellion. Historians will debate how instrumental U.S. power has been in shaping the domestic politics and foreign policies of its allies and dependents. But whatever the particular national identity, domestic pathology, or historically or culturally driven problems of a given country, elite, or public now at odds with America, these homegrown traits have become intimately intertwined with how the United States is regarded, rationally or irrationally, whether in Europe, Asia, Latin America, or the greater Middle East.

This book is not about the fundamentalist clash with the West. It is not about jihadist terrorists, nor about the states that sponsor them. But in order to face the threats to U.S. and global

security posed by truly dangerous anti-American cells, movements, or states, the United States needs to count on the political
will of populations, governments, and elites long regarded as
friends, cultivated as allies, or otherwise depended upon. That is
why the progress of Anti-America in countries that have a long
and strong history of close relations with the United States is
more revealing, and potentially more serious, than in states or
among groups that define themselves by ideological opposition
to the United States.

Since 2002, when publics and governments around the world
began to openly express their anger at the United States or its
role in the world, a lengthy list of long-standing U.S. allies or
partners from around the world have registered strongly negative views. In Europe, this has included Spain, Italy, Portugal,
the United Kingdom, Germany, Turkey, France, Belgium, the
Netherlands, and Greece. In Asia, public opinion in South Korea, Indonesia, the Philippines, and Malaysia has grown sharply
negative. In Africa, opinion in Kenya, Nigeria, and South Africa
also has soured. In the Americas, including Canada, there has
been a virtually uniform slide in attitudes toward the United
States. And in the Middle East and South Asia, populations
whose governments have sustained deep ties with the U.S. government, such as Egypt, Jordan, Pakistan, and Saudi Arabia, now
register profoundly negative attitudes toward the United States.
In a visceral sense, this catalogue of nations now fundamentally
ill at ease with the U.S. gravitational pull is significant—and not
only because of the sheer numbers of countries: During the Cold
War it also was easy to tick off a long list of countries in the Soviet bloc that were geopolitically and propagandistically anti-
American, on the Eurasian continent as well as in the Third
World.

What is shattering about the new list is not just its length or
scope but rather, outside of the Middle East, the politically

"Western" and essentially pro-American character of the new anti-American countries, as well as the tendency for younger generations to be more likely than their elders to see the United States as a negative influence in the world. For example, a 2005 survey found that the younger generations (ages 18 to 29) in twenty of twenty-three countries, including Italy, Canada, and Australia, preferred European over American influence and rated the United States below the European Union, France, and even China. From the perspective of tomorrow's leaders, the United States is neither the admired beacon of freedom nor an avatar of beneficent global power. As these individuals age, their tendency to prefer Europe or China to the United States as a world power and their broad-based skepticism will have a corrosive effect on U.S. influence.[24]

Notably, many of the most glaring exceptions to the international community's anti-American impulse are those countries that during the Cold War were part of the Soviet bloc, such as Poland, Bulgaria, and many other eastern and central European countries where even though the Iraq war was unpopular, America's anticommunism, commitment to freedom, support for democratic and market reforms, and advocacy of NATO enlargement are widely appreciated, and where anti-Americanism is regarded as an opportunistic political redoubt of former communists.[25] Another exception is India, a leader during the Cold War of the Non-Aligned Movement and longtime economic beneficiary of the Soviet Union, where a positive sense of U.S. economic prosperity, scientific accomplishments, and intentions is now palpable and where, as in "new Europe," the United States is cultivating a fresh strategic alliance as a way to balance a rising China, moderate tensions with Pakistan, and gain access to the enormous consumer and labor market India represents.[26]

There is one other important exception to the global anti-American trend: Japan. Unlike India or the former Soviet bloc countries of "new Europe," all of whose ties with the United States are comparatively fresh, Japan at first blush would seem to be a leading candidate for an anti-American outbreak. A country that the United States burned, bombed, and then stripped of any remnant of military wherewithal before reconstructing, Japan during the Cold War accepted a relationship of tutelage with the United States almost as intimate as U.S. ties with Germany became. By the early 1990s, Japan's economic growth was widely touted as having the potential to overshadow that of the United States. Its rise helped prompt debate over the end of American primacy, and a new generation of Japanese technocrats and public at the time bristled over U.S. attempts to pry open protected markets in technology and agriculture. Yet in the twenty-first century, the United States has, for strategic reasons, such as balancing China's rise, grown more comfortable with and even promoted a more activist Japan and, as with India, has sought to deepen ties, especially in the realm of security, a step the Japanese appear to welcome and to have cultivated.[27] Although some 70 percent of Japanese public opinion opposed the war in Iraq and later favored withdrawing the five hundred soldiers Prime Minister Koizumi contributed to reconstruction, the war did not catalyze a broader Japanese rejection of America or Americans, unlike in "old Europe" and other parts of Asia. With a political culture that remains deferential of authority, and with business, government, and the media organized to limit dissent, Japan's democracy is not as robust as that of other Cold War U.S. allies rebelling against America. This has had the effect of limiting exposure of both the government and the United States to the kind of anti-American groundswell seen elsewhere in Asia, Latin America, or Europe.[28] Finally, the absence of a strong anti-American backlash in Japan and India is the result of an affirmative U.S. policy decision to actively forge strong bilateral ties with both countries.

What is new about Anti-America today is not what is old or intractable about it: Just as jihadist fundamentalism is not the focus of this book, neither are expressions of Mexican and French anti-Americanism. Both are old news. The United States has long grown accustomed to bemoaning French defiance of U.S. strategic interests, taking in stride the cultural and political airs of superiority of both the French left and right. French opposition to U.S. aspirations in Iraq should have been among the most anticipated of any of the members of the antiwar coalition. Precisely because the United States and France have a long history of challenging each other's aspirations to universalism, and because France especially has a far more obsessive interest in the United States than is the reverse case, as Philippe Roger has amply demonstrated, French anti-Americanism will indefinitely remain a feature of international life.[29]

Likewise Mexico. The United States seemed to usurp France's universal pretensions, but Mexico suffered the indignity of losing a third of its actual territory to American manifest destiny a full century before the young nation had reached the status of world power. Because of that history, anti-Americanism is part of Mexico's national identity, a sentiment that stretches across class and race and along the length of the three-thousand-mile border the two countries now share. Even during the Cold War, when the United States had virtually all of Latin America in its diplomatic corner, Mexico managed to carve out a foreign policy independent from the United States; multilateralism became a defense of Mexican national sovereignty.

Paradoxically, it was the end of the Cold War and Mexico's transition from authoritarian rule toward democracy that prompted a drive to build a closer alliance with the United States. This impetus came from a coalition of Mexico's traditionally anti-American elite, business class, intellectuals, aspiring democrats, and nascent civil society. But the seeds planted in the

1990s had little time to flower. Other than a free-trade agreement that brought more U.S. investment to the country, neither the United States nor the transitional government of Vicente Fox provided sufficient nurturing to counter the deeply held anti-American instincts of Mexico's traditional political, diplomatic, and security institutions. There are upward of ten million Mexican citizens living and working in the United States, paying taxes and sending money home to family, and doing so mostly without legal status. Their presence in the United States is both an irritant and a salve: a reminder of America's bounty and its quasi–open door, and of Mexico's seemingly intractable poverty and the sense of injustice and exploitation Mexican citizens experience when they cross the border.

Well before the September 2001 attacks, it had become clear to Americans and increasingly to Mexicans that the United States was either unprepared or politically unable to deliver to Mexico the one thing that Mexico's new democrats believed might fundamentally alter their country's indelible distrust of the United States: a comprehensive immigration agreement. The new generation had taken a giant political risk in attempting to anchor Mexico's democratic transformation to a hypothetical agreement that was never as much a priority for the United States as for Mexico. And, with Mexico in a two-year rotation on the United Nations Security Council just as the Iraq debate reached fever pitch, the United States, by giving Mexico's new government nothing to take home to its citizens, squandered an enormous opportunity to help Mexico deepen its democratic transformation and move closer to the United States, diplomatically and politically. As in France, the decibels of Mexican anti-Americanism might increase or decrease, but it remains a permanent feature of the country's domestic politics that may never fully subside, even as the country grows more democratic.

A look at only a smattering of countries that have experienced a strong anti-American backlash in recent years is a reminder that comprehensiveness may be the enemy of synthesis. No two countries are alike. Each has its own character and its own particular encounter with the United States that helps explain today's pique or outright fury. Yet, as diverse as many Cold War U.S. allies were and remain, patterns in their story lines do emerge, making it possible for a handful of countries to illustrate the broader phenomenon. It is among America's historic friends, partners, allies, or dependents that Anti-America is becoming entrenched, precisely because of the intimacy of the bilateral relationships solidified during the Cold War era. The list is unsettling: Great Britain, the Anglo-Saxon cousin and beneficiary of America's most special relationship; Germany, the junior partner and pillar of postwar European containment in Western Europe; Turkey, early NATO member, Cold War buffer separating West and East, and now an Islamic democracy; South Korea, the former Japanese colony and strategic U.S. anchor against China and the Soviet Union in Asia; and finally, back in the Western Hemisphere, much of Latin America, not just one country but a subcontinent that of all the cases listed here has been the most deeply entwined with the United States.

|

CHAPTER NINE

|

Great Britain

"Tony and Gordon have to ring up George and say, 'Do this, George, do this one thing for me, it's going to cost you fuck all, do it for me.'"—Singer/songwriter/activist Bob Geldof at launch of the British-led Commission for Africa Report, March 11, 2005

"Because I'm a politician in a suit I wince at the occasional word—but actually what he said is really what I think."—Prime Minister Tony Blair, in response to Geldof, March 11, 2005

In an indication of the breadth of the new anti-American consensus, three years after the Iraqi intervention, the British public and its policy elites, including the Bush administration's ally Prime Minister Tony Blair, were finding it increasingly difficult to define the benefits to Great Britain of the special relationship with the United States. Other than the divisiveness over Iraq, and unlike Germany, the United Kingdom apparently had nothing to rebel against, no postwar molds to break. Whereas the Bush presidency roughly coincided with the arrival of a new generation in power in Germany, the transformation of British domestic politics under Margaret Thatcher in the 1980s and Tony Blair in the

1990s was already complete by the turn of the century. At first blush, then, Great Britain has no place in the pantheon of Anti-America. Tony Blair survived his firm embrace by George Bush, day-to-day cooperation within the Anglo-American alliance ticks on, and British forces, although in vastly reduced numbers, have stood by their U.S. comrades in Iraq. But this cheery picture of an enduring special relationship belies the brew of strong anti-Americanism bubbling in British society, culture, and electoral politics. As an indicator of the British fixation on what's gone wrong with America, Michael Moore's *Dude, Where's My Country* and *Stupid White Men,* also best-sellers in Germany, ranked second in British book sales only to J. K. Rowling's Harry Potter series as the George W. Bush presidency began. Well before his reelection, British anti-Americanism had become, one observer wrote, "the dirty little secret of the war on terror."[30]

Whereas traditional twentieth-century British anti-Americanism was confined mainly to the British elite, left, and intellectuals, or to tensions of declining empire, in the new century the phenomenon is both personal and political: Blair's zealous support for George Bush and his Iraq venture divided the Labour Party and damaged British institutions, while the perceived U.S. intransigence on Israel-Palestine, climate change, the International Criminal Court, and Third World debt relief reinforced the sense among the British public that they, and Blair, had been betrayed by a once knowable and trusted partner.

In the twentieth century, for Britain, the "special relationship" in part had meant using its familiarity with the quirks of the young American empire to serve its own interests. As the fate of their empire became clear toward the end of World War II, and without financial or military power after the war, the British sought to defend their interests with their version of soft, special power—to tame the United States on the sly. In 1943 future Conservative Party Prime Minister Harold Macmillan tapped into the recipe for controlling the Americans through proximity, writing of British operations at allied headquarters in Algiers: "We ... are Greeks in this American empire. You will find Americans much as the Greeks found the Romans—great big, vulgar, bustling people, more vigorous than we are and also more idle, with more unspoiled virtues but also more corrupt. We must run [Allied operations in Algiers] as the Greek slaves ran the operations of the Emperor Claudius." Macmillan speculated later in the war that the British would have to "guide" the Americans "both for their own advantage and ours for the future peace of the world."[31]

After World War II, the British came to believe that their proximity and subordination to U.S. power had been instrumental in pushing the United States to recognize the severity of the Soviet threat and to develop a strategy to contain it. Later, with British forces fighting alongside U.S. troops in Korea, Prime Minister Clement Attlee came to believe he had persuaded the Truman administration against the use of nuclear weapons. But the hardening of anticommunist ideology within the United States and Senator Joseph McCarthy's denunciations of the British Labour Party kindled a more fundamental disdain toward the United States and presaged a chastening by the "great big, vulgar, bustling people" on the international front. Distinguishing between communism and Labour's socialist "idealistic, anti-imperialist, anti-privilege and social reform principles" in the pages of *Foreign Affairs*, Attlee wrote in 1954:

> I think that here we should recognize that there is a certain difference of outlook between the British and American people. I think that Americans tend to see things in black and white where we see shades of grey. . . . The Labour Party is not anti-American ... but it is right that I should express some feelings of disquiet which have arisen in our ranks re-

cently. The Labour Party has had nearly 40 years of fighting Communism in Britain and despite war and economic depression, the Communists have utterly failed. We are pardonably annoyed at being instructed by a beginner like Senator McCarthy.[32]

Within two years, Attlee's frustration with a hardening American posture at home would find its international counterpart: By the middle of the 1950s, the Americans were guiding the British. The 1956 Suez crisis ended any British pretensions at empire by proxy. When President Eisenhower caught wind of the Anglo-French-Israeli assault on Egypt aimed at overthrowing General Gamal Abdel Nasser to punish him for nationalizing the Suez Canal, Eisenhower condemned the attack. A sterling crisis ensued; Prime Minister Anthony Eden was forced to call off the venture in humiliation. In part as a result, Eden's government collapsed. Great Britain's diplomatic dependence on the United States was sealed, as was the atrophy of its place on the global stage.

In the 1960s through the 1980s, the Anglo-American alliance nevertheless prospered. Successive British governments—Labour and Tory—backed the United States on the international stage despite popular protests against the Vietnam War or U.S. failures to consult over controversial proxy wars in Africa and Central America. Although the United States infuriated Margaret Thatcher when it did not consult her prior to invading Britain's former colony, Grenada, she ultimately supported the intervention. Ronald Reagan's deployment of Pershing missiles in Europe to counter the Soviet build-up in the 1980s deepened the British public's antipathy toward the "cowboy nation" and awakened a sizable antinuclear political movement that, after the Cold War, took up various causes of the day—against bombing Belgrade, against globalization, and against the Cuba embargo, for example.

The Euromissile crisis shared the decade with the collapse of the Labour Party and, later, the end of Thatcher's tenure. There was a fair amount of overlap between those who regarded the Iron Lady's free-market economics and hawkish foreign policies as an assault on proper English restraint and those who found "Ronny" equally offensive. The pair, many on the British left feared, would bring the world to war if not tamed by the forces of civil society in both countries. But short of the agitation over Thatcher's romance with Ronald Reagan and Milton Friedman, and in the absence of a crisis in bilateral relations that might mobilize broad public opinion in the United Kingdom, anti-Americanism during the Cold War was largely confined to British intellectuals and cultural figures associated with the old Labour Party and others on the left.

During the 1990s, Anti-America remained a peripheral phenomenon in Britain. Whether worrying about the influence of a violent and drug-infested American society or lamenting Hollywood's pervasiveness, the British were cautious of the United States but rarely viewed it as a destructive force in the world. Instead, as the United States moved toward rapid economic growth and social dynamism, a model greatly admired by finance minister Gordon Brown, for example, most Brits dismissed the anti-Americanism of the Cold War left. Some even suggested that a bit of U.S.-style vitality, diversity, and democracy might reinvigorate Britain's ossified and elitist political culture.[33] The intervention in Kosovo aroused some antiwar anger, but as was the case after previous spikes in anti-Americanism in Britain, it eventually receded.

When the Oxford-educated Bill Clinton left the White House in 2001, Tony Blair lost an American president with whom he had a substantial political and personal affinity. Who could forget the two—rock stars both—waxing eloquent on the Third Way, their vision for a world economy and domestic policy safeguarded from the unseemly ravages of globalization but catapulted to new heights by its dynamism. Or the phone calls placed from 10 Downing Street in the middle of the Monica Lewinsky imbroglio to reassure a friend under withering domestic pressure. Both Blair and Clinton believed they had reinvented and led their po-litical parties to victory after dark days of conservative govern-ment, renewing the sense of high but modernized moral and social purpose to which both men aspired.

But what would be special in the relationship for Blair and Bush? On the eve of Blair's first visit to Camp David to get to know the new president, speculation swirled over whether the refined, cosmopolitan leader of New Labour would find any common ground at all with the recently crowned Texan heading a Republican Party significantly to the right of Ronald Reagan's. The early news was not encouraging. Their one discovered shared taste was for the same brand of American toothpaste. But in matters of social policy, politics, and foreign policy, the two at first had little else in common.

The September 2001 attacks rapidly revealed the substance of the special relationship, in large measure because of Tony Blair's immediate and uncompromising commitment to support the United States in pursuing its attackers. There seemed to be no light whatsoever between the United States and Great Britain, and no ally more sincerely ready to stand in solidarity. To be sure, NATO for the first time in history invoked article five of the alliance's treaty, declaring the attacks to have been an assault on all NATO members. But of all the European leaders, it was Blair who flew to Washington, to stand with the president and speak to the American people. The outpouring of emotion on British streets was equally effusive. Queen Elizabeth ordered the "Star-Spangled Banner" played at the changing of the guard at Buckingham Palace. There were some exceptions, of course: The playwright Harold Pinter blamed the United States for having provoked the 9/11 attacks, describing them as "predictable and inevitable . . . an act of retaliation against constant and systematic manifestations of state terrorism on the part of the United States over many years, in all parts of the world."[34] But the view that the United States had provoked the attacks and deserved to be humbled by its newfound vulnerability had yet to seep into the mainstream.

Blair and Bush remained outwardly in sync on their analysis of the attacks and of the appropriate response. Well before the allied Afghanistan operation had conclusively knocked the Taliban from power, the Bush administration focused its sights on Iraq. Blair followed and mobilized the British intelligence services to do so as well. As world skepticism intensified on the merits of a case for invading Iraq, Blair's speeches since well before 9/11 revealed an individual who believed in his core that the Westphalian notions of national sovereignty no longer held in the age of stateless terror.[35] He seemed more passionate, and certainly more articulate, than President Bush when he argued the centrality of defeating terrorism to accomplishing virtually every other global objective of the world community. In his noted speech on terrorism in March 2004, Blair did not hesitate: "[T]he nature of the global threat we face in Britain and round the world is real and existential and it is the task of leadership to expose it and fight it, whatever the political cost."[36] His powers of persuasion probably helped American blue-state doubters give their president the benefit of the doubt early in the war. The two leaders no longer shared only toothpaste but a sincere and messianic faith in their mutual conviction that taking the war on terror to Iraq was critical to their calling to reorder the world in their decidedly Western democratic image.

Blair had always been a high-stakes risk-taker. He gambled that by keeping Britain as closely aligned as possible with the Bush White House on Iraq, he would secure British leadership and leverage U.S. support on a number of other issues he held dear. First among these was the Israel-Palestine peace process, or the "road map." Bringing the United States back into the Kyoto Protocol on global warming was another, as was African debt relief. If he succeeded, Blair and the Labour Party would emerge politically victorious at home. He might go on to assume the mantle of European leadership in lieu of the French or Germans and prevent the breakup of the transatlantic alliance, which after all had provided the United Kingdom with its counterbalance to continental Europe for a half century. Iraq was Blair's opportunity to become a towering statesman on the world stage. But if he was wrong about Iraq and unable to parlay his allegiance to the United States into action on Israel-Palestine and other issues, he would pay a heavy political price.

The Iraq venture quickly split British society. In September 2002, as the UN weapons-inspection agency was still asking for time to complete its inspections in Iraq, the Blair government released a dossier alleging that Saddam could launch a chemical or biological weapons attack against British soldiers stationed in Cyprus—the media misrepresented the target as the United Kingdom itself—with forty-five minutes' notice. A top weapons inspector, David Kelly, allegedly told a BBC journalist in spring 2003 that the document had been "sexed up" by British intelligence. During the ensuing investigation and just one day after his testimony to the Foreign Affairs Committee in summer 2003, Kelly killed himself. Subsequent investigations led to resignations by top figures at the BBC. The BBC, MI-5, Whitehall, and 10 Downing Street all emerged damaged from the scandal that had erupted in the rush to rationalize the war.

After the September 11 attacks, a number of British citizens picked up in Afghanistan and elsewhere were held by the United States without charge at Guantánamo. It seemed a small matter, requiring little political capital, for the Americans to help an ally on his home front by allowing the prisoners to return to Britain to face charges. But Blair could not secure their release until nearly three years after their capture. The courts-martial of several British soldiers for abuses in Iraq in 2005 further turned British opinion against Blair and against the United States for its corrupting influence. By March 2003 favorable opinion of the United States had dropped to 48 percent from 75 percent in 2002.[37] Blair's approval rating had plummeted as well, to 33 percent in October 2003 (from 49 percent the previous April).[38] If Harold Pinter's schadenfreude was outside the British mainstream in 2002, by 2003 the novelist Margaret Drabble's bitter words reflected a new, more widely shared popular view:

> My anti-Americanism has become almost uncontrollable. It has possessed me, like a disease. It rises up in my throat like acid reflux, that fashionable American sickness. I now loathe the United States and what it has done to Iraq and the rest of the helpless world. . . . I have tried to control my anti-Americanism, remembering the many Americans that I know and respect, but I can't keep it down any longer. I detest Disneyfication, I detest Coca-Cola, I detest burgers, I detest sentimental and violent Hollywood movies that tell lies about history.[39]

Revelations of torture and aggressive interrogation techniques at Abu Ghraib and Guantánamo accelerated the downward slide in Blair's, Bush's, and America's standing.

Within Iraq, British forces, 45,000 of them (compared with the U.S. average of 130,000 to 150,000), had been largely confined to the south, in and around the city of Basra. During the initial invasion, the British ability to quickly pacify the south was widely attributed to the country's long-honed colonial skill at quieting the natives. U.S. forces, which were confronting a growing insurgency in the Sunni triangle, might have something to learn from the British, it seemed, when major combat operations ended and British forces in Iraq dropped to 16,000. They remained, for the most part, in the south of the country until the United States prepared for the second, presumably definitive attack on the insurgents who had taken over the city of Fallujah to the west of Baghdad. Then, in October 2004, a simple U.S. request to transfer 650 British soldiers and 200 support personnel to Fallujah angered Labour backbenchers, enraged military families, and created a perception, however inaccurate, that Bush was using British military resources to ensure stability in Iraq immediately prior to the American presidential election. The perception held that U.S. recklessness and electoral opportunism in the war would place British troops in harm's way. (Seventy had already been killed and 800 wounded.)

Further, the insurgency in Iraq seemed to have no end. The regime had fallen, Saddam had been captured, but Blair's main rationale for backing the Iraq invasion had proved false. By the beginning of 2005, 50 percent of British public opinion regarded U.S. influence in the world as negative, while Blair's approval had climbed slightly to a still-low 35 percent.[40] By midyear favorable opinion of the United States hovered at 55 percent, still the lowest rating from Great Britain documented by Pew since 1999. After reaching 39 percent approval following the London terror bombings in July 2005, Blair's approval rating dropped again by September to 31 percent.[41]

The United States did resume a more active role in Middle East diplomacy after Yasser Arafat's death. It also, if grudgingly, joined in Blair's and finance minister Gordon Brown's campaign to reduce Third World debt. But other than the removal of Saddam from power, it was not immediately apparent what the British political, moral, and human sacrifice in Iraq had delivered. The venture had produced enormous strain on the Anglo-

American relationship, grief for the prime minister, divisiveness within his cabinet and his party, and an increasingly widespread anti-Americanism that now spilled well beyond the historic territory of the British left and elite.

Outside of the "Prime Minister's Question Time" in the House of Commons, or at Labour Party annual conferences, and beyond the frequent *Guardian* editorial, there was evidence in the cultural realm of a fundamental distancing between the two countries, caused by Iraq and its numerous attendant assaults to the British (and, for that matter, continental European and American) conscience but palpable well before the war. Philip Lader, the Clinton administration's ambassador to the Court of Saint James from 1997 to March 2001, had appeared on a live, popular BBC television program also called "Question Time" just two days after the attacks of September 2001. Lader had long traveled in the circles of Britain's "20," studying at Oxford as a young man, managing the U.S. investment portfolio of the late Sir James Goldsmith, an international business tycoon and political figure, and otherwise deepening his knowledge of British society before and during his ambassadorship. He believed he knew the country top to bottom, having literally walked its length while ambassador. But apparently neither the walk nor his years of study, private business, or public service had put him in touch with the full range of British public opinion, the "80." When confronted by an angry preselected television audience with suggestions that U.S. Middle East policies had provoked the attacks, Lader found what British journalist William Shawcross described days later as "a darker side" of British attitudes toward the United States, one that revealed the "awful truth that these days there is just one racism that is tolerated—anti-Americanism. Not just tolerated, but often applauded." So aggressive and hostile was the audience that some 2,000 viewer calls and e-mails to the BBC forced the network's director general to issue an apology, but not before millions of viewers witnessed the former U.S. ambassador moved nearly to tears by the assault. His pain came to foreshadow what the U.S. political class as a whole would soon experience.[42]

To be sure, British satirists had long taken aim at their and our political leaders. But this time, the new decidedly anti-American zeitgeist in British society was reflected in wickedly pointed satire: the West End hit "The Madness of George Dubya," which compared President Bush to Dr. Strangelove; "A Weapons Inspector Calls," which took its shot at Blair over the weapons-of-mass-destruction fiasco; and "Guantánamo Baywatch," which excoriated the United States for its treatment of prisoners. There were tragedies as well: "Guantánamo: Honor Bound to Defend Freedom," which drew directly from testimonials of imprisoned inmates and their families to paint a graphic and damning portrait of prisoner abuse under the U.S. watch; or "Stuff Happens," David Hare's deadly serious look at the lead-up to the war in Iraq and the cast of American and British architects behind it; or massive protests against the purchase of Manchester United by the American owner of the Tampa Bay Buccaneers.

The parodies and the tragedies came to occupy a space in the Anglo-American dialogue about the war that only Michael Moore seemed ready to explore in the popular realm on the U.S. side of the Atlantic in his film *Fahrenheit 9/11* and, compared with David Hare at least, with far less nuance. If Tony Blair had hoped to exercise any restraining influence on Bush by accompanying him so closely on the road to Iraq, British dramatists did a far better job at speaking truth to power in Blair's stead. To digest one's flaws in a theatrical recipe concocted by a close intimate was surely a healthy experience, in a cooked-spinach-and-cod-liver-oil sort of way. It is hard to imagine French or German or Mexican playwrights getting so close to the nut of the American post-9/11 psyche.

But the Blair-Bush alliance and the havoc it wreaked in Iraq

for the moral authority of both countries has not remained confined to the realm of culture or foreign policy. In the Anti-American Century, the new anti-Americanism in Great Britain had
become part of British domestic politics to a degree not previously on display. Michael Howard, the once staunchly pro-U.S.
Tory Party candidate, accused the White House of being "very
protective of Mr. Blair" and hesitated during the 2004 U.S. presidential campaign to overtly support President Bush. Later, during the Labour Party's campaign for reelection in 2005, public
pressure forced the Blair government to publish two highly controversial and confidential memos. The first memo, dated July 23,
2002, and released just days before the May 2005 election, substantiates the inevitability of U.S. action and British acquiescence to U.S. invasion plans months before the public debate
had occurred and despite British concerns that "the intelligence
and facts were being fixed around the policy." The second shows
Attorney General Lord Goldsmith's reluctant approval of the legality of the Iraq war in March 2003.[43] In large measure because
of Tony Blair's willingness to join the Americans in Iraq despite
questionable factual and legal grounds, Labour's majority in Parliament shrank from 161 to 67 in May 2005. Howard's refusal to
congratulate Bush after the latter's 2004 reelection and particularly the marked decline in Labour's reelection majority suggest
the special relationship may have become a political liability to a
degree Winston Churchill, Harold Macmillan, and Margaret
Thatcher might never have imagined.

CHAPTER TEN

Germany

When the sheriff goes riding, everyone goes riding with him,
Wants the sheriff to go riding, everyone goes riding with him.
When the sheriff celebrates, everyone celebrates with him.
Everyone has to respect,
Everyone has to accept,
Everyone has to grasp, who the sheriff is.
Three criminals stole an egg from the kitchen once.
They already hung on the gallows on the next beautiful morning.
And everything was over.
Because the sheriff had said: "Never steal an egg!"
Everyone has to respect, what the sheriff says.
Everyone has to accept, what the sheriff does.
Everyone had to grasp, who the sheriff is here.
    —"Der Sheriff," song released in 2002 by the German punk-
    techno group DAF, Deutsch Amerikanische Freundshaft
    (German American Friendship)

In the fall of 2004, General Motors announced plans to cut
12,000 jobs in its European operations, mostly from its Opel factory in Bochum, Germany. The German magazine *Stern* published a front-cover image of a giant cowboy boot, embossed on
the side with an American flag. Under the cocked and descending
toe appeared the letters "GM." The boot was poised to crush tiny,

helpless German workers arranged in the formation of what looked like a peace sign but was actually the insignia of the Opel car. "Wild West Way" read the headline splashed adjacent to the big boot.[44] The visual analogy was clear enough: Corporate America—Nazi-esque, Texan, jackbooted—was stomping all over the helpless workers of Germany. Factory workers at protests outside the plant said as much. General Motors had dared violate a taboo of postwar German labor-management relations by announcing layoffs, a costly proposition under Germany's half-century-old *Kundigungsschutz* labor law, without first consulting with the local union. That many other German firms, including Siemens and IG Metall, almost simultaneously instituted mass layoffs and extended the workweek to forty hours was irrelevant in the new zeitgeist; corporate America, the illustration suggested, was responsible for broader structural changes within Germany.

Prior to, during, and following Prime Minister Gerhard Schroeder's 2002 presidential campaign, Germans themselves had broken a number of postwar taboos. Some began talking openly about themselves and their country as victims of World War II: stories of women and children and refugees bombed by allied forces; the "crematorium" of the Dresden firebombing. Taboos against anti-Semitic slurs were broken no longer only by marginal neo-Nazis and skinheads but even by politicians and high-culture critics: One derided the Holocaust museum under construction in Berlin as a monument to the "banality of the good." Another attacked a prominent German-Jewish television personality and defended Palestinian terrorism as the appropriate response to Israeli occupation. Some on the left argued, as Günter Grass illustrated in his novel *Crabwalk*, that the postwar culture that suppressed discussion of how Germans themselves suffered from Germany's dark side was breeding a new generation of neo-Nazi youth and strengthening right-wing political parties. These were not isolated incidents—they reflected broader sentiment. Germans, as one psychiatrist put it, "will never forgive the Jews for Auschwitz," because the price Germany paid was impotence.[45]

Gerhard Schroeder broke some critical German taboos as well. During his campaign he tapped into popular desires and resurrected the importance of the *deutscher Weg*, the German Way, a phrase that within Germany evoked the prospect that Germany might become again a "normal" country, capable of the sovereign and independent pursuit of its national economic and security interests. Schroeder's choice of words also evoked the fearsome prospect of a strong, united Germany unimpeded and undeterred by its neighbors or by the transatlantic alliance with the United States. Schroeder openly opposed the war in Iraq, a policy that Germany's longtime benefactor regarded as in its vital interest. For many Americans for whom a peaceful, democratic West and, later, a unified Germany represented the signal accomplishments of the Cold War in Europe, the spectacle of Gerhard Schroeder running an election campaign on an anti-American ticket was akin to watching a child buy drugs by pawning the family silver. In breaking the taboo of all taboos, Schroeder defied not only the United States but potentially the international community as a whole: In his commitment to oppose the war even if it were sanctioned by the United Nations, he made it fair game for Americans and Europeans to ask themselves whether they should again be worried about a return of the "German question."

Schroeder's 2002 reelection campaign took place against the backdrop of a sluggish German economy: nearly 12 percent unemployment, a growth rate of less than 2 percent, huge budget deficits, a demographic slump, and an economy that would be paying the high costs of reunification with the East for at least another ten years. Voters were beginning to put Christian Democrats and other center-right parties back in local office to punish the governing coalition for this malaise. Schroeder's 2002 electoral comeback—though politically unsustainable in the face of profound economic malaise by 2005—hinged in no small measure on his pointed attacks on the United States. During his 2005 electoral campaign against Christian Democrat Angela Merkel, he revived such blatantly politicized anti-American attacks—this time in reference to a potential U.S. strike against Iran.

But Schroeder and his party, the Social Democratic Party of Germany (SPD), with Foreign Minister Joschka Fischer's Greens, hardly represented an aberration in the desire to break with the United States. German public opinion strongly opposed the U.S. proposal to invade Iraq and, like the French and many others around the globe, increasingly viewed the American "hyper-power" as a global threat, in need of chastening. As far back as the German romanticism movement of the early nineteenth century, Germans have held Americans to task, seeing their capitalism and democracy as violations of the purity of the soul, an ideology later evoked in Hitler's mythologizing about the superiority of the German essence. But it would be grossly unfair to argue that the German rupture with the United States over Iraq was a sign of a resurgent Nazi fascism. By the late 1990s, Germany had undergone a significant shift in generations. Well before Bush II's first term had gotten its sea legs, it became clear that the generations of 1968 and of 1989, and even a younger generation that cut its political teeth on the first Gulf War, had substantially replaced the generations of Konrad Adenauer, Helmut Schmidt, and Helmut Kohl, the earlier German partners in U.S. reconstruction of the country.

The 1968 generation that Schroeder and Fischer represent was shaped by protests against the war in Vietnam, against U.S. imperialism, and against U.S. nuclear missiles and military bases. Students, Greens, and civil rights and antiwar activists who once protested the United States in the streets could now do so from the Reichstag and the Chancellery. Democracy and power in Germany for this generation meant a break with the father in every sense: their own as well as the paternal tutelage of the United States. Much of the tension in U.S.-German relations during the Iraq war, while genuinely about the wisdom of going to war, with or without a Security Council resolution, without letting the inspectors complete their jobs, and without clear evidence of WMD in Iraq, was the product of a new generation of leadership that, although grateful to the United States for the Cold War's economic and security blanket, regards itself as having been cleansed by the country's 1968 political awakening and now fully equipped to establish its own security agenda. Like South Korea, Germany has hosted several hundred thousand U.S. troops on military bases for decades and as a consequence is plainly ambivalent about American military power. The bases brought economic good times to Germany, on the one hand, but also became a symbol of Germany's impotence after the war and shame about its Nazi past. Germany's economic and political success in the postwar era was in large measure an American success. But that very feeling of having been "made *by* America" caused its own resentments. The younger generations now in or aspiring to power feel that Germany has paid for and continues to repent for the Shoah (the Holocaust) and is now ready, without burying that past, to become a normal country. They are resentful of the grinding and unreciprocated U.S. expectation of deference and gratitude. They feel far from an irrelevant player in international security whose protests were better off ignored, as Condoleezza Rice once suggested.[46] Germany under its Red-Green alliance has earned its place at the grown-ups' table: leading the country away from pacifism with troops in Kosovo and later in Afghanistan in a combat role for the first time since 1945, training Iraqi troops, cooperating against terrorists, and championing both European integration and a strong transatlantic alliance.[47]

Signaling its newly discovered determination, Germany is actively campaigning for a permanent seat on the United Nations

Security Council. The new Germany, in Fischer's, Schroeder's, and now Merkel's vision, could be an equal partner in fighting jihadist totalitarian terrorism without first having to pass Germany's proposals for global security through the U.S. filter that earlier German generations reflexively—even gratefully—accepted. Within Germany, the physical manifestation of that filter is also vanishing: Under new U.S. plans, many military bases and installations in Germany will be closed and transferred to central and eastern Europe. With fewer U.S. troops on German soil, the country is more likely to act independently on the world stage, no longer requiring U.S. cover to signal that it is a trustworthy member of the international community.

When Americans think of their contribution to Germany, they think of the fight against fascism, of the Marshall Plan, of the Berlin airlift, of Kennedy's and Reagan's visits to Berlin, and of their sustained contribution to the country's international rehabilitation, rearmament, security, postwar economic boom, and support for reunification with East Germany. But these memories no longer occupy center stage for the new generations in Germany's streets, suites, board rooms, and ministries. The war in Iraq, George Bush's particular style, and his cabinet's dismissive and derisive attitude toward Germany accelerated the force of generational changes already under way and reinforced the new German argument that the time had come for "a more assertive and sovereign Germany." The war in Iraq also gave the German public a taste of the moral high ground. Perceiving the United States as an imperial aggressor that launched a "war of choice," primarily as a resource grab, evoked for some Germans, including Schroeder's repudiated minister of justice, preposterous comparisons to Hitler's international aggression. It was one thing to issue a declaration of independence from the American father but quite another to compare him to the architect of the twentieth century's greatest evil.[48]

But having single-handedly accelerated Germany's declaration of independence and unified much of the Continent, against America, with scornful gibes about "old Europe," the United States may now be ill-prepared to adapt to a Germany that wants to be a strong Atlantic partner while also a major player in the European Union, and a member of an expanded United Nations Security Council. To many Germans, it appears that the country that once championed a united Europe and succeeded in bringing France and Germany together for Europe's defense can now live with the fruits of its success only if "atlanticist" priorities—code for U.S. hegemony—prevail.[49]

In some ways the United States has fulfilled Germany's wish to be treated like a normal country: No country, not even Great Britain, the closest U.S. cousin and ally, can honestly claim to be accorded the same reciprocity in the recognition of its interests by the United States that the United States requires of others. In that sense, Germany is quite normal. From the German perspective, domestic politics and generational changes make it hard to imagine that lockstep deference will return to the bilateral relationship, even under a Christian Democratic–led government. Though some Americans reactively assume otherwise, an independent foreign policy does not necessarily correlate with anti-Americanism. But in Germany, now that the old domestic taboos about victimhood, Jews, and Israel have been broken, and with the country facing no clear path toward strong economic recovery in the short term, it remains to be seen whether the crude, but for now mostly benign, style of anti-Americanism depicted by the media and invoked at times by German politicians might be replaced by something far more problematic. Germany needed U.S. protection to reinvent itself after the Nazi era. Many Germans believe their work is done in this respect, and yet the blessings of normality have yet to come.

|

|

CHAPTER ELEVEN

Turkey

"As tomorrow's novelists prepare to narrate the private lives of the new elites, they are no doubt expecting the West to criticize the limits that their states place on freedom of expression. But these days the lies about the war in Iraq and the reports of secret C.I.A. prisons have so damaged the West's credibility in Turkey and in other nations that it is more and more difficult for people like me to make the case for true Western democracy in my part of the world."—Orhan Pamuk, Turkish novelist, the *New Yorker,* December 19, 2005

Although an undertow of anti-Americanism in Turkey was palpable during much of the Cold War, today there is almost no sector of Turkish public opinion that has not in some way adopted an anti-American default and an increasingly anti-Semitic tilt. What has changed? Turkish Anti-America is bound up in many of the themes that emerge elsewhere. Turkey's historic suspicion of outside powers, ambivalence about its dependence on the United States during the Cold War, the impact for Turkey of the Cold War's end, globalization, democratization, religious and ethnic politics, regional politics, transatlantic realignments, and the pull of European Union membership—all these combine with specific U.S. policies to produce the starkest anti-American sentiment in Turkey on record. By 2005 a BBC poll found that 82 percent of Turks believed that U.S. influence on the world was "very negative."[50] Indeed, anti-American views in Turkey are no longer confined to intellectuals, the left, or the nationalist right but extend across class, profession, religion, and political ideology and include the Turkish military, once the closest U.S. ally in the country.

As the "sick man of Europe" and center of a dying Ottoman Empire by the early twentieth century, Turkey has a national identity that is deeply intertwined with the experience of fighting to establish national independence from occupying powers. The twentieth-century narrative from which Mustafa Kemal Atatürk drew during Turkey's nationalist war of resistance derives from the humiliation over the terms of the 1920 Treaty of Sèvres abolishing the Ottoman Empire. Signed by the victorious allied powers after World War I, the treaty obliged the Ottoman Turkish government to renounce rights over Syria, Iraq, Palestine, Armenia, and Italy and conceded to Greece control over parts of Anatolia and over several of the Aegean islands close to the Dardanelles. Within two years, and driven in part by their dishonor over the Sèvres agreement, Atatürk's nationalist forces drove Greece, Britain, and France out of Anatolia, the eastern portion of contemporary Turkey, founded the modern republic of Turkey, and in 1924 abolished the Ottoman Sultinate, which during four hundred years had been the Caliphate, or seat for the worldwide community of Islam. Inspired by Atatürk, the core of "Kemalist" nationalism held that for Turkey to take its rightful place on the world stage, the new nation required a secular, modern state firmly anchored in the West. The practice of Islam was to remain a private affair and the expression of cultural ethnicity suppressed; the state and its principal arm, the nationalist military, would lead the Turkish people toward greatness through modernizing legal and economic reform.

Although neutral until nearly the end of World War II, Turkey declared war on Germany in early 1945, in time to become a founding member of the United Nations. By 1947, Stalin's interest in access through the Dardanelles to the Aegean Sea was among the flashing lights that provoked the announcement of the Truman Doctrine, the first large-scale postwar declaration of American containment strategy in Europe. With the Soviets literally at its northeastern border, Turkey could not sustain its heralded independence from great powers and joined NATO in 1952. Throughout the 1950s, Turkey was governed by one party, Atatürk's Republican People's Party. The Turkish military and security establishment formed what came to be known as the "deep state," a web of closely related networks that saw to all aspects of Turkish public life, including the economy.

During the Cold War, Turkish-U.S. security cooperation grew extremely close. In the 1950s, Turkey sent forces to Korea under the U.S.-led United Nations command. In the 1960s, the military allowed the United States to use its air base at Incirlik, some 250 miles southeast of the Turkish capital of Ankara, to stage ground and air reconnaissance missions into and over Soviet territory and to house nuclear missiles on Turkish territory. In the 1970s and early 1980s, Turkey's military and intelligence services cooperated with the United States to end the Turkish heroin trade. The military establishment sought but failed to leverage its compliance with U.S. strategic interests into support by the United States of the Turkish invasion of Cyprus in 1974. From the Turkish nationalist and military perspective, U.S. compartmentalization of the Cyprus conflict separate from its responsibilities to Turkey within NATO became cause for deep and long-lasting resentment of the United States. Likewise on the left, Turkey's identity with and ties to the West and Europe meant it was as much exposed to the ideological crosscurrents of the era as Germany or France. Opposition to the Vietnam War on the streets and anti-imperialist, Third World–oriented politics became part of Turkey's political and intellectual currency. Throughout the 1960s and 1970s, the perception that the country's Cold War alliance with the United States violated Kemalist sovereignty became part of the internal narrative driving Turkey's deepening and often deathly violent domestic politics.

Until the early 1970s, the separation of mosque and state remained an article of faith for Turkish nationalists in the military and throughout the country's state institutions. But political violence by left- and right-wing nationalist forces had begun to fray the Kemalist consensus, strained further by rising inflation and unemployment. An idea first floated by a group at Ankara University, known as the Intellectuals' Hearth, that a new Turkish-Islamist synthesis might best pacify society and diffuse the pull of the left gained currency among the nationalist elite, including the military. The Turkish state began to fund the construction of mosques and schools for Islamic clerics, control messages pronounced by clerics, and allow the teaching of Islam in private lycées, with the expectation that the Islamic tenets of community and consensus might dampen social conflict. Islam gradually became a part of modern Turkey's late-twentieth-century political identity: from the top down through state-funded mosques, private schools, and universities; from the bottom up, through grassroots mobilization by Islamist political parties; and eventually in the Millet Meclisi (National Assembly) and at Çankaya, the Presidential Palace.

By the end of the 1970s, a depressed economy, the stirrings of political Islam, violence on the left and right, demands for Kurdish expression and representation, and the internationally isolating Cyprus venture had produced, from the Turkish military's perspective, the conditions for a return to first "Kemalist" principles. In the wake of the 1979 Iranian Revolution, a 1980 coup put in place a new military regime that took a more ecumenical view of political violence: It enlisted a crackdown against the left, right, Kurds, and dissidents of all stripes, including against the shadow right-wing militia it had once deployed against all of them. Turkish jails became the scene of torture and brutality against American drug traffickers—the images of a destroyed Brad Davis in the film *Midnight Express* was an offense in Turkey and to Turkish-Americans and a cultural coup for U.S. antidrug warriors of the time—and Turkish jails served as incubators of political Islam and ethnic Kurdish nationalism. In 1984 the Kurdish Workers Party (PKK), which since the 1970s had been agitating against long-standing laws prohibiting Kurdish language, newspapers, schools, and organizations, began its guerrilla campaign targeting Turkish military, security, and civilians. The military responded with a counterinsurgency campaign that lasted well into the 1990s, complete with the creation of armed "village guards" that obliged local civilians to cooperate with the military or see their villages burned.

The end of the Cold War heightened Turkish sensitivity to the threat of encroachment by its historic enemies. Greece and Syria continued to sponsor Kurdish separatists, creating pressure on the Turkish military to increase defense spending even as other European NATO members decreased theirs.[51] Turkish nationalists in and out of the military believed that their NATO allies, including the United States, had little appreciation for Turkey's sovereign security interests. Politically, the late 1980s and early 1990s represented a time of transition as well. Turkey began to liberalize its highly closed economy in the 1980s. By the end of that decade, with the resumption of civilian rule under Prime Minister Turgut Ozal, Turkey had laid the groundwork for the democratic opening that would follow. Yet in the same period, the military cracked down on dissidents—left, right, Islamic, and Kurdish. The Kurdish campaign alone resulted in the deaths of some 35,000 Kurds, the assassination of 17,500 others, and the imprisonment of several thousand more.

Between 1952 and 1997, the United States provided Turkey with nearly $15 billion, or an average of $316 million annually, in military assistance, mainly grants and credits for the purchase of American-made equipment. During that period, the Turkish military carried out four coups d'état, went to war with Greece over Cyprus, waged a campaign to quash its own ethnic and political dissidents, and conducted a largely successful and vicious dirty war against the Kurds. The early 1990s, the most intensive years of the counterinsurgency campaign against the Kurds, coincided with the years of greatest U.S. military assistance: $903 million in 1993 and $811 million in 1994. Indeed, in 1995 the State Department concluded that since the United States was Turkey's principal arms supplier in the early 1990s, it was "highly likely" that U.S.-origin military equipment had been used in the "evacuation and/or destruction of villages."[52] Despite the military's contentions that the United States lacked an appreciation for Turkey's security needs, it remained an active if indirect partner in the efforts of the Turkish "deep state" to restore uniformity to the country's political canvas.

Still, it was only the first Gulf War, with its arousal of Kurdish autonomy, and a related economic crisis later in the decade that marked the beginning of today's hardened anti-Americanism in Turkey. In addition to the troops, airspace, and basing rights Turkey provided, its most strategic contribution to the war was to cut off the oil pipeline that runs from Kirkuk in northern Iraq to the Mediterranean port of Yumurtalik in southeast Turkey. That concession cost Turkey upward of $30 billion in lost revenue.[53] Later in the decade, when Turkey's economy crashed following a crisis in its banking sector, Turkey's elite and public blamed the country's high inflation and collapsing currency directly on that loss of revenue and indirectly on the United States. Also in the 1990s, the substantial electoral gains at the national level of political parties that openly identified themselves as Islamic, and the public displays by their supporters of the Islamic faith, shook the nationalist orthodoxy of the Turkish military and secular elite. By 1997 the Welfare Party, the conservative Islamic political party that was the precursor of today's more progressive ruling Justice and Development Party, took 25 percent of the nationwide vote running on a starkly anti-American ticket that also played off long-accumulated frustration with the economic mismanagement and corruption of Turkey's traditional ruling parties.

After the first Gulf War, and while still receiving substantial U.S. military assistance, Turkey continued to stage raids into Kurdish zones of Iraq in pursuit of its own Kurdish separatists, keeping as many as 12,000 troops in northern Iraq until 1997. The last thing the Turkish military wanted to see from its contribution to the Gulf War was an autonomous Kurdish success story in Iraq. From its perspective, the U.S.-British enforcement of the "no-fly" zone over the Kurdish north of Iraq effectively undermined Turkey's Kurdish campaign and inflamed autonomous urges within. By the end of the decade, the Turkish military had concluded that the American incitement of Kurdish nationalism constituted a direct threat to Turkey's national security: The United States had become a fickle ally ungrateful for decades of Turkish service in the name of the NATO alliance and Soviet containment.

With anti-American hackles raised by the arousal of the Kurds and the economic crisis, Turkey at the end of the 1990s formally embarked on the process of preparing to apply for membership in the European Union. The prospect of EU membership did not immediately translate into antagonism toward the United States. In fact, the United States antagonized Europe by openly lobbying Brussels on Turkey's behalf. But the chance to gain the right to apply for consideration to join the European Union—approved unanimously by EU members in December 2004—prompted a series of reforms regarding women's rights, human rights, press freedom, prison conditions, public administration, and regulatory alignment with other EU laws that substantially exceeded any for which the United States had pressed in the heyday of its alliance with Turkey.

For Islamists in the mainstream of Turkish politics, EU membership had become a way to safeguard their inclusion in Turkey's political process. Indeed, by the turn of the century, the steady opening within Turkish politics could best be measured by the rise to power of the Justice and Development Party in 2002, under the leadership of Abdullah Gul and Recip Erdogan, who later became prime minister. A former mayor of Istanbul, Erdogan is a practicing Muslim who grew up in Kasimpasa, a working-class neighborhood known for its hard edge. While preparing to run for national office, Erdogan was banned from politics and jailed for four months in 1999 for inciting religious strife by publicly reciting a poem, which, though written by a prominent Turkish nationalist, compared mosques to helmets and minarets to bayonets. Although his children attend American universities, they and Erdogan's wife appear publicly in Turkey wearing tight head scarves, a statement of faith that instills fear among nationalists that despite Erdogan's professed European outlook and reformist zeal, his presidency may be an early step in Turkey's conversion into an Islamic state.

By the time Erdogan stepped into the prime minister's seat on the eve of the Iraq invasion in March 2003, no sector of the country—secularists, Islamists, the military, or the public at large—was in a mood to accommodate the United States in another foreign venture. The United States woke up to Turkey's ambivalence toward it only on the eve of the second Bush administration's invasion of Iraq. The U.S. military had left Saudi Arabia after the 9/11 attacks and needed Turkey because of its contiguous borders with Iraq. The Pentagon's architects crafted their plans for the Turkish northern rearguard based on 1990 assumptions about Turkish politics and an offer of $28 billion. But Turkey had changed since the first Gulf War. Its democracy had grown stronger if more complex. Domestic support for a second and decidedly American war in Iraq was no foregone conclusion. Over the previous two decades, Turkish society had done something of a flip-flop with respect to the role of Islam in the country. By the beginning of the twenty-first century, political Islam had come decidedly out of the closet, and, although not without great discomfort to traditional nationalists, had gradually inched its way toward coexistence within Turkey's secular institutions. Prime Minister Erdogan, who calls himself a Muslim democrat, played an instrumental role in forging the contours of a new, but by no means consolidated, consensus within Turkey that combined elements of Kemalist nationalism and affinity for the West, particularly Europe, with greater tolerance for Islam in politics and society.

Although Turkey had sent 2,000 troops to Afghanistan in late 2001 to help overthrow the Taliban, the Turkish public at the time regarded the U.S.-led effort as a Christian war against Islam. By 2002 neither the Turkish public nor the military would countenance allowing U.S. troops to use Turkish territory and airspace as a base for the Iraqi deployment. The Turkish military harbored suspicions that deposing Saddam in Iraq signaled that the United States was prepared to help establish a Kurdish state with the capital in Kirkuk, just as the Kurdish conflict within Turkey had begun to simmer down. With an eye on membership in a European Union dominated by countries that opposed the war, with the new Islamic oxygen in the air, and with an economy still barely out of the recovery room, there was little incentive for the Turkish public, whether the traditional Kemalist elite, its Islamic parties, its business class, its intellectuals, or its state-controlled media, to back a second U.S. venture in Iraq. In March 2003, when the Turkish parliament rejected the proposal to assist the United States in Iraq, albeit by a technicality, a nearly complete anti-American consensus had already emerged in the country. That month, only 12 percent of Turks polled expressed a favorable view of the United States, compared with 52 percent three years earlier.[54] The vote in parliament enhanced Erdogan's standing at home and in Europe and demonstrated definitively that the Turkish military had lost whatever leverage it once held over the United States, making the institution that was once the closest U.S. ally in the country now among the most anti-American.

By 2005 a reflexive suspicion of U.S. motives and of U.S. allies—particularly Israel—had become the new default in Turkey, from the malicious to the ridiculous. Some Turkish media reports alleged, for example, that the Americans were fighting with their Israeli or Jewish friends in Iraq and took to comparing George Bush to Adolf Hitler; others promoted conspiratorial notions that the United States was colonizing the Middle East to escape a meteor headed to destroy the North American continent; still others described al-Qaeda as a code name for a CIA operation or as a means to promote U.S. imperial interests.[55]

The widely reported reference by anonymous U.S. officials to Turkey as a nation of "carpet merchants" and the July 2003 arrest and hooding by U.S. forces of eleven Turkish soldiers in northern Iraq had further poisoned the well. Like much of Europe, Turkish media and intellectuals, with few exceptions, cannot forgive the United States for its imperial pretensions and have come to see multimillion-dollar military assistance packages and multibillion-dollar IMF loans as covers for a conspiracy to Americanize and, increasingly, to Christianize their country.

Anti-Semitism has not been traditionally part of Turkey's political culture. The Turkish intelligence service and military had developed close relations with their Israeli counterparts in the 1990s. But Prime Minister Erdogan and Foreign Minister Abdullah Gul have long held less than fully enthusiastic views toward Israel. As the U.S. relationship came under strain, Turkish-Israeli relations also frayed over Turkey's suspicions of Israeli flirtation with Kurds in northern Iraq. Simultaneously, Israeli incursions in the West Bank and Gaza inflamed Turkish public opinion. The hostility toward Israel, Jews, and the United States that has crept into Turkish state institutions is increasingly palpable in the Turkish media and in the broader public: Sales of Hitler's *Mein Kampf* reached disturbingly high numbers among university students, and a best-selling novel, *Metal Storm*, contained a fictional account of a Turkish defeat of invading American forces.

The United States has not adjusted easily to the idea of a more independent Turkey willing to flout the historic alliance in pursuit of its evolving national interests. Americans are dismayed by the venom readily accessible in Turkish media. As an editor of one conservative U.S. daily lamented, the United States has a debt to call in for a long list of friendly gestures undertaken on Turkey's behalf. These include decades of military assistance, protection from the Soviet Union, efforts to secure for Turkey a pipeline route for Caspian oil, successfully beating back congressional resolutions condemning Turkey for the 1915 Armenian genocide, the return of PKK leader Abdullah Ocalan to Turkey, support for Turkey's membership in the EU, and rapid recognition of the political victory of an Islamic president. These gestures, from the U.S. perspective, demonstrate a commitment to Turkey born not merely of selfish strategic interests but of common interests, jointly pursued.[56]

America's Cold War alliance with Turkey largely reinforced the historic Kemalist subordination and suppression by secular institutions of the country's ethnic and religious identity. But that orthodox secular Turkish identity is now a feature of the past. It was only the war in Iraq that forced American assumptions to catch up with Turkey's new political and religious landscape. Despite America's praise for Turkey's successful integration of Islam with democracy or its support for economic reforms, the second war in Iraq unhinged much of the remaining value or affection for the alliance and its benefits perceived or felt by a broad cross-section of Turkish society. Public criticism of the controversial Ottoman Turkish massacre of anywhere from hundreds of thousands to well over one million Armenians in 1915 and of thousands of Kurds remains virtually taboo and can still mean jail time or threats to offending critics. Still, as Turkey diversifies its foreign policy and struggles to establish its newest synthesis of religious, ethnic, and democratic identity, and as the prospects for joining the European Union rise and fall, Turkish Anti-America is likely to diminish, provided that the United States can accept a more autonomous Turkey within a more autonomous if not fully unified Europe and can dispel the widely held impression that the United States is at war with Islam.[57]

|

CHAPTER TWELVE

|

South Korea

Did you see the short-track speed skating race?

What a vulgar country, fucking U.S.A.!

You'd go that far just to win the Gold?

What a nasty country, fucking U.S.A.!

Is the U.S.A. still a nation of justice?

Why the hell can't we even say what we want to say?

Are we slaves in some colony?

From now on we will shout: "No! to the U.S.A."

Such a wretched thief that stole our Olympic gold medal,

Fucking U.S.A.!

Such a wicked robber that tries to rob everything by force,

Fucking U.S.A.!

Did you hear Bush's abusive words?

Such a shameless country, Fucking U.S.A.!

Threatening the North with war;

Politically intervening in the South

Such a country of gangsters, Fucking U.S.A.!

Is the U.S.A. still a beautiful country?

Is the North still an "enemy" to be killed?

When are you gonna get a clue?

From now on we shout: "Yankee, go home!"

You Americans are really gonna pay when we reunify.

A magnificent reunification,

Through the strength of our race!

A magnificent reunification!

Don't forget the blood and tears we've shed!

You, the cause of our division, Fucking U.S.A.!

Don't forget the No Gun Ri massacre of civilians!

You, country of murderers, Fucking U.S.A.!

—Yun Minsoku, "Fucking U.S.A.", February 2003*

After over a half century under the American security umbrella, and nearly four decades of substantial military and economic aid, South Korea has emerged as a thriving economy and democracy. Yet, anti-Americanism there is one of the most striking results of this apparent U.S. success. South Korea's full political independence, largely thwarted for much of its history, and the rise to power of a new, post–Cold War generation of leaders have opened the door to a wave of anti-American sentiment strong enough to swing elections and to alter the long-standing security arrangements at the core of U.S. interests in the peninsula and beyond.

In a country where every citizen can recite the history of occupation by foreign powers, struggles for predominance in Asia by great powers in the early twentieth century mark the first time that Koreans came to view Americans with a distrust historically reserved for China, Japan, and Russia. With the exception of a brief Japanese invasion in the late sixteenth century, China had dominated the Hermit Kingdom until the end of the nineteenth century. In 1905, imperial Japan defeated Russia in the Russo-Japanese War, leading to Japanese occupation of Korea. Despite direct appeals by Koreans to reject the Japanese occupation,

*This song was released as an MP3 file in February 2003, shortly after Kim Dong Sung lost the short-track speed-skating gold medal to U.S. athlete Apolo Anton Ohno at the Salt Lake City Olympics. It reportedly received over 30,000 hits during the first day. It was produced in South Korea and then aired by a North Korean news program.

Teddy Roosevelt instead recognized the occupation in exchange for Japanese acceptance of the U.S. occupation of the Philippines. While under Japanese control in the first half of the twentieth century, Koreans formed an independence movement influenced by cultural nationalists, anti-imperialist nationalists, and communist nationalists. Like their peers around the globe, these activists took their inspiration from the anticolonialism of Woodrow Wilson and the anti-imperialism of Vladimir Lenin. Following the first Roosevelt's slight, and after a half century agitating for independence, Korean nationalists viewed the absence at Yalta of any mention of their fate as a second U.S. betrayal.

Indeed, for the United States, Korea remained an abstraction—a colonial dependent of a defeated fascist power, not a country in its own right. When the Japanese surrendered in August 1945, Korean nationalists formed an interim government in Seoul. But rather than transfer sovereignty to the interim government, the United States and Russia instead established an international trusteeship over the peninsula. Back in Washington, two young U.S. colonels then inadvertently stoked anticolonial, nationalist suspicions by proposing to divide the country at the thirty-eighth parallel: Russian forces would occupy the North and Americans the South. Massive anti-American and anti-Russian demonstrations erupted to protest this insult to Korean sensitivities. The Americans were unaware that earlier in the century Korea's Japanese and Russian occupiers had once proposed dividing the peninsula along the same line.[58]

The great-powers' World War II promise of a "free and independent" Korea proved elusive. There was no internal consensus within Korea for permanent division—quite the contrary. The first elected president, the Princeton- and Harvard-trained Sygman Rhee, resisted the increasing permanence of the division, as did Korean nationalists from left to right. The longer the division lasted, the more fractious it became, and the more the division and the U.S. and Soviet occupations came to incite Korean nationalism. By 1948 the Truman administration terminated its military occupation and created a separate Republic of Korea in the South, leaving the North to the Soviet Union. The Korean War of 1950 to 1953 had the effect of weakening the political forces in the South that opposed the country's division and of renewing the presence of American forces on the peninsula. The U.S. defense of South Korea and U.S. willingness to sacrifice during the three-year war cost many lives; 33,000 Americans and 500,000 South Koreans died, as did an estimated nearly 2 million from the North and China. The Korean War solidified an intensely anticommunist ideological climate in South Korea and changed the psychology of the U.S. presence there. America's defense of the South and its resolve even at the cost of American lives had a profound effect on Korea's national consciousness and identity. The generation of Koreans who had lived under Japanese occupation and later fought the Korean War emerged with a sense of duty, obligation, and gratitude—described by Koreans as bonds of blood—for the United States.

But the war also made the U.S. occupation permanent and temporarily dashed the nationalist aspirations for a unified Korea. The 151-mile by two-mile boundary separating North and South Korea, known as the DMZ (for demilitarized zone), became a militarized border, not a temporary partition. Hostility toward the North and, gradually, toward the United States became a channel for South Koreans' frustration over their centuries-long thwarted independence. The regional containment strategy of the United States required a permanent U.S. presence to protect the South and restrain Soviet and Chinese communism. Domestically, America's association with the ensuing decades of authoritarian military rule would gradually convert the American wartime sacrifice for Korea—at least among many younger Koreans—into a symbol of suppressed nationalist aspirations.

By the end of the 1950s, Sygman Rhee's increasingly corrupt civilian rule met with a popular storm of criticism. In the wake of a massive student protest in spring 1960, Rhee fled the country on a U.S. military plane. In 1961, General Park Chung Hee overthrew the interim president in a military coup. Park, unlike Rhee, was no U.S.-trained aristocrat: He was a peasant who had been trained by the Japanese in Manchuria, with none of the politesse of the Koreans with whom the United States had grown accustomed to working. The U.S. ambassador, chargé d'affaires, and U.S. commander of United Nations forces conveyed their doubts to Park about the illegality of the coup. The Voice of America broadcast statements in support of the elected government, but Park ordered them suppressed. Park imposed martial law, purged many pro-American officers from the military, censored the press, abandoned a new constitution, and disbanded the National Assembly. But Washington took the view that it would be impractical to get in Park's way. U.S. officials in South Korea believed that any attempt to soften the edges of *yushin*, the system of repression Park introduced, would be interpreted by the Korean military and public as U.S. endorsement of the general thrust of the coup. What to U.S. officials must have felt like a sophisticated balancing act, to Koreans appeared as acquiescence and contributed to the mythology feeding a simmering anti-Americanism.

Between 1961 and 1979, the year Park was assassinated by the head of his own intelligence service, the *yushin* system of repression intensified, particularly in the 1970s. Political leaders and opposition figures, including journalists, Christians, labor organizers and workers, students, and intellectuals, were arrested, tortured, jailed, or exiled. The Korean Central Intelligence Agency (KCIA), perceived by Koreans to be tied closely to its U.S. counterpart, became notorious for its invention of the "Korean barbecue," a method of torture that involved stringing up victims by their hands and wrists and holding them over flames. In the decades of U.S. presence on the peninsula, the Korean political, economic, and security establishment learned to play off tensions between various Americans stationed in the country. State Department efforts, especially under the Carter administration, to temper the Park regime's human rights abuses were undercut by sympathetic allies from the CIA and the U.S. military, who had extensive ties to their Korean counterparts. Playing the "North Korea card"—an often deadly game in which the North was a willing partner—kept in check the increasing U.S. discomfort with the South's heavy tactics against its own population. "What," Park was known to mutter, "did the American bastards know?"[59]

But the regime that followed Park's 1979 assassination proved even more repressive. In May 1980 an army massacre of students, opposition activists, and protesters in Kwangju, hometown of a leading prodemocracy dissident, Kim Dae Jung, resulted in the deaths of several hundred, with thousands more wounded. The new military ruler, Chun Doo Hwan, and his deputy, Roh Tae Woo, had ordered Korean special riot forces and Korean marines to Kwangju without notifying the American officer in charge of the U.S.-Korean Combined Forces Command. At the time, all Korean forces were technically under the control of the U.S. commander. Chun made it known, falsely, that the United States had approved the troop deployment. Like Park, he suppressed U.S. statements against the crackdown to promote the popular perception that the great protector had blessed the repression. Muddled U.S. denials reinforced suspicion of complicity. As with the 1961 coup, the popular perception was that the United States had given a wink and a nod to the massacre. Chun Doo Hwan imposed martial law, brought the press entirely under government control, and shut down universities and the National Assembly. Despite open and muted U.S. attempts by the Carter and the

Reagan administrations to encourage a transition to civilian rule, by 1981 Chun became president. Kim Dae Jung and other opposition leaders were sentenced to death for inciting violent revolution. *Yushin* and still more national security laws allowed Chun to further repress labor, civil servants, journalists, and politicians well into the 1980s. Eventually U.S. pressure, including a last-minute phone call from the White House to the Blue House that literally prevented the execution of Kim, and domestic protests combined to oblige Chun to permit a political transition at the end of the decade.

Between 1948 and 1987, the United States provided South Korea with almost $9 billion in economic assistance and, excluding the cost of stationing troops at the DMZ, nearly $15 billion in military assistance—including grants, credits for weapons purchases, and training.[60] The bulk of those funds went to Korea during the harshest years of repression, between 1961 and 1987. In that same period, the Korean economy took off. A middle class developed. Democratization did follow. But the U.S. policy of containment was costly for Korean domestic politics and exacted a high toll on the younger Korean generation's views of the United States. In the 1980s, anti-American anger grew particularly fierce. In 1980, 1982, 1983, and 1985, U.S. cultural and information centers were burned. In 1987, students protesting the death of a student in Korean police custody set fire to U.S. government housing in Seoul; in 1989, Korean farmers and villagers stormed and looted barracks and destroyed virtually all the infrastructure at a U.S. military base near Seoul. The Korean War generation's reverence, *chinmi*, for the U.S. protector was yielding to *banmi*, open hostility and resentment, and it extended from the Korean elite and military best skilled at manipulating American power to a much broader and younger array of the population.

By 1987, Chun yielded to domestic and international pressure for a new constitution and democratic elections. Bill Clinton visited South Korea in 1993, when Kim Young Sam became the first civilian president in thirty-two years. Kim Young Sam and Kim Dae Jung continued the transition in the 1990s. With democracy, the intensity of Korea's anti-American animus dramatically subsided: The Cold War had ended, the United States had finally played an overtly and unambiguously active role in the democratic transition, and the Korean economy was prospering. Against that backdrop, Korea's new civilian governments launched a fresh approach to North Korea. Well aware of the economic and political shock to the Federal Republic of Germany of its rapid unification with the East, the South adopted an approach of gradual engagement, or "soft landing," in anticipation of a change of regime in North Korea and eventual reunification, which later in the decade came to be known as the Sunshine Policy. Humanitarian assistance, economic investment, family reunification, and a joint application for a seat at the United Nations, Kim Dae Jung hoped, would steer the North back toward its Southern brothers, toward the community of nations, and offset its nuclear temptation that had emerged in the 1980s. From the South's perspective, bilateral relations with the United States, including the mutual defense treaty, with 37,000 U.S. troops on the border and at U.S. bases throughout the country, would strengthen rather than supplant Korea's initiative toward the North.

Over the course of the 1990s, however, South Korea and the United States began to fall out of sync with respect to Pyongyang's plutonium enrichment activities, beginning with the first North Korean nuclear crisis of 1993. The tensions began when North Korea threatened to withdraw from the Non-Proliferation Treaty. The United States excluded the new democratic government in South Korea from its bilateral security talks with the North that eventually led to the Agreed Framework in 1994. That snub touched the bone of South Korea's deeply rooted nationalism and exposed shame at its dependence on outside powers. By the Clinton administration's second term, the United States managed more successfully to include South Korea in its North Korea security talks, and it appeared South Korea had found a way to pursue its engagement policy, keep North Korean nuclear ambitions in check, and maintain a productive alliance with the United States. But U.S. pressure on Korea to open its highly symbolic and closed agricultural, steel, and auto markets, the 1997 financial crisis, and revelations in 1999 that U.S. soldiers at No Gun Ri had fired on and killed 400 civilians during the Korean War, including women and children refugees, battered the image of America as the immutable Cold War protector and fueled a revival of anti-American sentiment across Korea's ideological canvas. This trend gained footing particularly among the younger generations who felt less beholden than their elders to the United States.

In 2000, President Kim Dae Jung, who had risked harassment, exile, torture, prison, and near-execution at the hands of South Korea's ancien régime, won the Nobel Prize for his efforts to bring peace and democracy to the Korean peninsula. Kim had spent nearly three decades accusing leaders in both the North and South of using tension—real and often inflated—to keep themselves in power. Unlike the once dominant Grand National Party, which thrived on hostility toward the North and was suspicious of the Sunshine Policy as a ruse for less noble economic interests and as a magnet for corruption, Kim represented a current of thought in Korea that regarded keeping tensions low and contained as the best path to consolidating democracy in the South and eventually harmonizing, if not reunifying, with the North. On the eve of George W. Bush's election that fall, and before the full extent of North Korea's secret uranium enrichment program came to light, it became clear that the United States and South Korea held divergent priorities regarding North Korea.

Indeed, not long after taking office, the new Bush administration had caught the scent of that Cold War nemesis, neutrality, wafting out of the South. Pyongyang, as it happened, was farther along in its uranium enrichment goals than Kim Il Sung had let on to the United States, to the International Atomic Energy Agency, or to Kim Dae Jung at their historic summit earlier that year. In his first visit to Washington as president, Kim Dae Jung was greeted by President Bush with a frontal and public assault on the Sunshine Policy: Both the Korean president and population at large took great offense over the loss of face and lack of respect implied by such an overt rejection. After the September 11 attacks, the White House's elevation of North Korea's status to membership in the "axis of evil" was digested by the new generation in power in South Korea as a purposeful and unequivocal attempt by the Bush administration to insert the United States again in Korea's domestic politics, undermine its "soft-landing" and Sunshine Policy, and sabotage North-South relations. An ally of President Kim Dae Jung referred to Bush in the National Assembly debate as "evil incarnate," hardly imaginable from a Korean politician who shared Kim's historically pro-U.S. inclinations. South Korean public opinion toward the United States began to decline steadily after 2001.[61]

In 2002, in the latest reminder of South Korea's humiliating dependence on American security, a U.S. military court acquitted two U.S. soldiers who accidentally ran over and killed two South Korean schoolgirls. Massive anti-American protests called for U.S. troops to leave the country. In his presidential campaign then under way, Kim's successor, the current President Roh Moo Hyun, significantly galvanized his still-underdog candidacy by playing to the unleashed anti-American sentiment of Korean twenty-something cyber-surfers, and to the generation of labor, student, and other political activists who had been in the streets in the 1970s and 1980s protesting America's allies Park and

Chun. Roh's platform echoed the demands of the street, suggesting that U.S. troops withdraw from the country and that South Korea might sit out any conflict between the United States and the North.

Well before the White House had fully clarified its intentions to go to war in Iraq, domestic politics in South Korea had turned against the United States. After less than one year in office and with declining popular support, Roh withstood a flimsily based impeachment challenge staged in parliament by the traditionally pro-U.S. opposition Grand National Party, the party of the ancien régime. The Korean opposition actively cultivated Washington's sympathies, accusing Roh's generation and postimpeachment parliamentary coalition of endangering the peninsula's security with its softness toward North Korea's nuclear program. Roh's ruling Uri Party professed its desire for dialogue and consensus but relished using public debate and scrutiny of the role of the United States in Korea's authoritarian past not only to solidify the new Korea's independence but also to delegitimize its opposition.

Symbolically, after the impeachment defeat, the Grand National Party came under new leadership: Its president is Park Geun-hye, whose father was strongman Park Chung Hee and whose mother was kidnapped and killed by North Korean agents. After nearly ten years of democratic rule, the rough-and-tumble of Korean politics, one observer noted, still resembled "a bacon grill uncleaned for fifty years."[62] By 2003 the country had split along generational lines. Some 71 percent of young South Koreans held unfavorable views of the United States, compared with 47 percent of those age 30–49 and only 30 percent of those over age 50. All in all, half of South Koreans surveyed in May 2003 held an unfavorable view of the United States, up from 44 percent in July 2002.[63] The United States, which in the late 1980s and 1990s had gradually reformed its image in the country by unambiguously supporting a clear transition to democracy, was again at the center of the country's conflictive domestic politics.

Despite his campaign platform, after the impeachment episode Roh could not risk alienating his military and intelligence services with an abrupt breach with the United States. North Korea's nuclear pretenses were real, and the South, which had armed forces numbering nearly 700,000, needed U.S. troops at the DMZ as a symbol to the North, to the opposition, and to Japan and China of the South's aspirations for a heightened regional security profile. History, the bonds of blood, and the savvy of a politician keen to be treated by the United States with respect drove Roh's decision to commit what became a total of 3,700 troops to the Iraq effort, despite massive opposition from his political base. Yet as in most of the rest of the world, the war in Iraq proved extremely unpopular in South Korea—and not only because its citizens were kidnapped and beheaded there. The failure of U.S. diplomacy prior to the war, the cockiness with which the Bush administration approached the prospect of regime change, the gruesome nature of the insurgency, and the revelations of torture under the U.S. watch conjured memories of Korea's own past and, with North Korea on America's potential hit list, stirred fears that such violent conflict might come spectacularly close to South Korea. From the Korean perspective, the American talk of regime change for North Korea, and with it the specter of hundreds of thousands of refugees pouring across the border and of the economic shock that would surely follow, reinforced the appearance of a nearly total disconnect between South Korean and U.S. interests. And all this surfaced at a time in the country's history of thwarted nationalist aspirations when the prospect of democracy, independence, and even eventual reunification might finally give Korea the strength to assert itself as a respected, if relatively small, regional power.

Indeed, during the same period that U.S.–South Korean relations deteriorated, Korea pursued a strategic economic relationship with China, another former imperial power. South Korea and China normalized diplomatic relations in 1992. Even with occasional disputes over the patrimony of the ancient Koguryo kingdom, an uncomfortable reminder of China's power, bilateral trade with China is set to reach $100 billion by 2006, surpassing South Korea's trade with the United States.[64] More than half of Korean foreign direct investment is in China, often as an export platform to the United States. Korean students in China outnumber all other foreign students studying in Chinese universities. Korean restaurants, film, television, computer games, music, makeup, and hairstyles are trendy in China and much of Asia. The South Korean central bank holds only 4 percent of total foreign treasury holdings, but when it reported plans to diversify its holdings away from the weakening dollar, it seemed to be flexing more than just economic clout and sparked fears of a Chinese and Japanese sell-off that might do severe damage to the U.S. economy. Even as Korea competes with Japan to be the base for U.S. security operations in North Asia and engages in occasional nationalistic spats over disputed islands, a boom in Korean pop culture in Japan and Japanese pop culture in Korea is softening historically anti-Japanese suspicions and supplanting the lure of Americana. For America, it must feel like a surprise kick in the gut that nearly 40 percent of Koreans polled in 2004 found the United States to be a greater security threat than Pyongyang or China.[65] For Koreans, the nuclear threat and China's potential in resolving it had reinforced the importance of China as a counterweight to the United States.

During the Cold War, South Korea's domestic politics became intimately entangled with American power. The new generation of ideologically diverse reform-minded forces in office today has turned an old dynamic on its head. Instead of playing the North Korea card to jockey for U.S. financial, security, and diplomatic patronage and tolerance of authoritarian repression, the split with the United States over North Korea has become an opportunity for South Korea to break from the postwar status quo, to establish independence from the United States, and to assert itself as a regional player within Asia. The South Korean military, itself divided along generational lines over how to deal with the North, has become increasingly independent of the United States and under greater civilian control and scrutiny. Between 1950 and 2000, more than 3 million U.S. troops served tours in Korea. American troops are now leaving South Korea for Japan, which is fast becoming the new base in Asia for the U.S. strategy of rapid troop deployment. Roh Moo Hyun's anti-American presidency may prove shrewd enough to successfully diversify Korea's dependence without entirely severing its security cooperation with the United States. South Korea is now cutting the umbilical cord to the United States, a process that derives significant political support from younger Koreans who did not live through the Korean War. At the popular level, the era of *chinmi*, pro-America, has ended.[66]

CHAPTER THIRTEEN

Latin America: The One-Fingered Wave

We live in a time in which the satanization of the United States doesn't just belong to the extreme left or right. . . . What indignant screeching the world would hear if there was put in place, headed up by the United States, a mobilization of all democratic countries for the final fight . . . against the remaining dictatorships.

—Mario Vargas Llosa, September 20, 2001

It isn't an exaggeration to say that [the images of Abu Ghraib and Gaza] have done more damage to the United States and Israel than all the bombs and the suicide attacks of the Islamic extremists in the last few months. What credibility can the affirmation have of President Bush or Secretary of Defense Rumsfeld that the United States is in Iraq to bring liberty and law to the Iraqi people, compared with the photos of these naked prisoners, forced to masturbate and sodomize, submitted to electric shock or the fangs of fierce dogs before the smug imbecility of their guards?

—Mario Vargas Llosa, June 3, 2004

Latin American grievances were balanced by a perception that the U.S. never formally renounced the principles of international law and the hope that it would reaffirm them again. What is alarming about the Bush administration is its formal denunciation of the basic rules of international intercourse. With us or against us, President Bush declares starkly and simplistically. . . . Is it strange that many Latin Americans should see in these statements an aggressive denial of the only leverage we have in dealing with Washington: the rule of law, the balance obtained through diplomatic negotiation?

—Carlos Fuentes, September 26, 2004

Unlike Europe or Asia, in the years between the fall of the Berlin Wall and the September 2001 attacks, the United States had little Cold War capital on which to draw in Latin America, long a wellspring of anti-Americanism from the ambivalent to the visceral. During the Cold War, the United States generally aligned itself with and underwrote a repressive status quo, or was instrumental in rolling back popular, even democratic, challenges to the status quo in the region. America's Cuba obsession had poisoned the atmosphere and substance of U.S. policies in the region more than even Fidel Castro's support for revolution there. With the exception of the militaries, mercenaries, oligarchies, and now discredited political parties that benefited from their alliances with the United States, Latin Americans by and large regard the Cold War as having exacted a high political and human cost. Latin Americans thus greeted the end of the Cold War with relief, hopeful that the United States might no longer find cause to compress its regional policies into the politically deadening and socially destructive shackles of anticommunism and containment.

U.S. foreign policy during the Cold War had been relentlessly obsessed with Cuba for its own sake and as a symbol. Preventing a repeat of 1959—whether through force of arms or the ballot box—was paramount. By the end of the Cold War, the United States had largely accomplished this goal: Fidel was still in office, but by the 1990s the United States had put its weight behind peace processes in Central America and the end of authoritarian rule in the Southern Cone. Latin American governments, with some exceptions, were by and large occupied by U.S.-friendly center and center-right political parties.

Indeed, in the 1990s the United States set forth a positive agenda for the region, supporting civil society after decades of authoritarian rule and civil war, promoting economic prosperity and political democracy. U.S. security preoccupations did not subside: The ideological and geopolitical emphasis on fighting communists and guerrillas yielded to a new war—this time on drugs. Yet the new U.S. agenda was a far and refreshing cry from the tired saws of the previous four decades, and Latin America welcomed the new approach. The region was not a priority for the United States, but the message from the North was largely positive, inclusive, and respectful. An era of summitry—breathless meetings of heads of state committing to critical goals of democracy, development, and the rule of law—generated momentum, energy, and hope.

Over the course of the 1990s, the United States proved to be entirely sincere about its commitment to market liberalization, democracy, and the war on drugs—but to a fault. In time, the myopia characteristic of Cold War policies, albeit with a different set of priorities, set in. The Treasury Department and U.S. Southern Command became the principal drivers and public face of Washington's projection in the region. Authoritarian governments such as that of Peru's Alberto Fujimori stood out as palpable reminders that the American security agenda—fighting drugs and Maoist rebels in Peru's case—could often overtake refreshing democratic instincts from the United States for the hemisphere. Sober and patronizing admonitions from the Treasury Department about fiscal probity and currency stability came to supplant talk about creating vibrant civil and political cultures. Nor did the United States put any obvious pressure on governments in the region to tend to what economists often dismissed as the "distributional" aspects of economic policy; it was enough to adapt the macroeconomic measures that would keep Wall Street investors interested in the new emerging markets. Growth, the message seemed to be, was in itself the answer. By the end of the decade, it grew clear that neither the market orthodoxy of the Treasury Department nor the domestically driven zeal of the drug war was sufficient to help overcome the region's grinding poverty, inequality, insecurity, and illegality. If the 1980s were known in Latin America as the "lost decade" because of hyperinflation and stagnation in growth rates, the 1990s became the decade of lost hope when Washington's answer failed to bring the region any appreciable recovery.

Still, by the turn of the century, despite the perception that U.S. economic prescriptions of trade integration and market liberalization were to blame for widening inequality and poverty, Latin American public opinion toward the United States remained largely positive. The greatest symbol of Latin America's instincts to accept, even help reinvent, a new Pax Americana was Mexico's attempt under Vicente Fox to deepen significantly its ties with the United States, bucking the anti-American default of Mexican elite and popular opinion. But in only a handful of years following the 2001 attacks, the ambivalence of the Cold War and the hopefulness of the 1990s had yielded, in Mexico and the entire region, across class and ideology, to unequivocal distrust in U.S. global leadership and U.S. intentions for the region. In part because of the failure of U.S. economic recipes and of local elites to invest in their own countries, and in part because democracy really has taken hold, a significant realignment of power, ideology, and diplomacy is under way in Latin America. If the signal accomplishment of the United States in the American Century was keeping the left out of power, the Anti-American Century is witnessing a significant reversal of this investment. Left and center-left governments and movements, most of them democratic and most of them nonviolent and noncommunist, are stronger than the region's revolutionaries could have hoped even at the height of Soviet global aspirations.

The Anti-American Century began with a campaign promise by George W. Bush to put Latin America front and center on the U.S. foreign policy agenda. Vicente Fox, a former Coca Cola executive elected to office in Mexico in 2000, was America's new best friend, with prospects of a dignified immigration agreement tantalizingly dangled at the bilateral table. The Bush administration continued his predecessor's Colombia policy of training that country's military for drug-interdiction activities, a backdoor way of boosting U.S. support for counterinsurgency against the radical right- and left-wing armies there. Whatever Bush's sincerity of alleged commitment to Latin America, his administration sent mixed signals not long after his election. When Argentina's central bank could no longer sustain its currency peg to the dollar and the economy began to collapse, the administration left what had been the hemisphere's only "non-NATO ally" (a privilege now enjoyed by Pakistan) to fend for itself: no Mexico-style bailouts for the Argentines. The United States blamed Argentina for corruption, profligate spending, and a flawed tax system as five presidents came and went in ten days, unemployment soared to more than 25 percent, the bottom fell out of the middle class, and poverty consigned millions to line up at soup kitchens and pick at garbage dumps. The crash of the Argentine economy spelled the political death of the Washington Consensus for Latin America.[67]

Ideology, thought to be buried with the Cold War, soon made a comeback. During Brazil's presidential election season, a whisper campaign spread between Wall Street and "K" Street casting doubt over the capacity of longtime leftist Luiz Inacio "Lula" da Silva to keep "the markets" happy and sowing panic over his comparison of the U.S. Free Trade Area of the Americas (FTAA) project to an annexationist plot by the United States. Cold War ideologues and senior Republican legislators in Washington circulated memos warning of Lula's nuclear pretensions and of his potential to form an "axis of evil" with Venezuela and Cuba. The hysteria subsided only after Lula, before even winning the presidency, announced a deal with the IMF to maintain a healthy budget surplus.

Nor did the Bush administration's choice of appointees to manage Latin America policy inspire confidence in the millennium's promise for a new approach to the region. The staff of Senator Jesse Helms and other relics of the Cold War, who spent years explaining away the human rights abuses of Augusto Pinochet in Chile while promoting the contras in Nicaragua, counterinsurgency in El Salvador, the destabilization of Jean-Bertrande Aristide in Haiti, or, most consistently, an ever-tighter embargo against Cuba, were rewarded with top jobs in the Organization of American States (OAS), the State Department, the Pentagon, and the White House. For example, Roger Noriega, a Helms staffer, went first to the OAS as U.S. ambassador and later became assistant secretary for Western Hemisphere affairs after the White House's unconfirmable first choice served a brief recess appointment. That individual was Otto Reich, who during the 1980s had run the White House Office of Public Diplomacy, responsible for planting puff pieces about the Nicaraguan contras in U.S. newspapers and otherwise propagating the comparison of the contras to America's founding fathers. After his service in the first Reagan White House and then as ambassador to Venezuela, Reich became a lobbyist, counting among his clients Bacardi Rum, one of the major advocates behind the 1996 Helms-Burton law that tightened the embargo against Cuba and has the potential to allow companies and individuals that have had their property nationalized to sue the Cuban government in U.S. courts. Roger Pardo Maurer, who in the 1980s was a Washington spokesperson for the Nicaraguan contras and involved in their training, became deputy assistant secretary for the region over at the Pentagon. Dan Fisk, also a Helms staffer, veteran of the congressional battles over Central America in the 1980s, and one of the authors of the Helms-Burton law, became a deputy assistant secretary, with Cuba and Central America in his portfolio; he moved to head Latin American affairs at the National Security Council in Bush's second term. The appointments signaled to the region's policy and intellectual classes, and to those congressional Democrats and Republicans who had worked to bring bipartisan comity at the end of the Cold War, that because of domestic politics, the senior figures on the Bush foreign policy team were content to allow Latin America to remain in the tenacious hands of cold warriors, for whom the most important priority appeared to be the overthrow of Fidel Castro and keeping the left out of power.

The only policy area where the Bush administration initially appeared sincere in its embrace of a new day for the hemisphere was with respect to democracy. Under the Clinton administration in the 1990s and the leadership of former Colombian president and then-secretary general César Gaviria, OAS members had worked to craft what would come to be known as the Inter-American Democratic Charter, a covenant that would bind members to oppose and penalize military coups and other unconstitutional power grabs in Latin America. On September 10, 2001, Colin Powell arrived in Lima, Peru, for what was to be a three-day visit to attend the signing ceremony of the new charter. Powell's presence in Lima, which had just emerged from a decade of virulent insurgency and corrupt authoritarian rule, reinforced a sense of hope in Latin America that the U.S. commitment to democracy might be truly sincere, even bipartisan.

The terrorist attacks in Washington and New York the next day had the effect of scuttling these hopes. Democracy receded to the back burner of the U.S. agenda for the hemisphere. Fighting communists during the Cold War and coca cartels during the drug war had presaged what would become the new U.S. default: Counterterrorism overtook the U.S. priority list for the world, and the hemisphere was no exception. Instead of talk about consolidating democratic institutions, strengthening civil society, promoting the rule of law, and advancing economic opportunity, Washington started asking a different set of questions. Were Hezbollah and Hamas nurturing terrorist cells in the triborder area shared by Argentina, Brazil, and Paraguay? Did Fidel Castro have a secret plan to manufacture, export, and even use biological weapons against the United States? Could al-Qaeda take advantage of the Mexican border with the United States to infiltrate the country? Was Venezuela becoming a haven for Colombian narco-terrorists and terrorists of international reach? Might the Colombian government better defeat its enemies if these were thought of as ideology-free terrorists rather than as quaint guerrillas? The United States Southern Command, responsible for all U.S. military activities in Central and South America, issued statements and testimony about the nexus among drugs, terror, and insurgency, and the Pentagon declared that Latin America's vast ungoverned spaces offered a potential haven for terrorists. In the war-on-terror environment, security again became the overarching agenda for U.S. policy toward Latin America, and with that returned ideology and the politicization of what is called "democracy promotion."

After a post–Cold War short-lived attempt by the United

States to more diplomatically subordinate its overt dominance through a web of regional democratic and economic institutions, the focus of the war on terror, combined with the old-school staffing of Washington's Latin America bureaus, very quickly plunged the United States back into its earlier twentieth-century role as the elephant in the room of Latin America's domestic politics. In elections in Bolivia, Nicaragua, and El Salvador, U.S. officials threatened grave consequences should voters elect a *cocalero*, Sandinista, or former FMLN candidate who had taken the commitment to democracy to heart and run for elected office. As a result, a once obscure peasant organizer, Evo Morales, gained the national stature to help make Bolivia practically ungovernable in 2005 and captured the presidency by 2006. The Sandinistas under former president and revolutionary Daniel Ortega are winning municipal and provincial elections playing on the antigringo nationalism of the contra war and more recent warnings from Washington about the consequences of a Sandinista political comeback. In El Salvador, U.S. officials let the public know in the 2004 presidential elections that a vote for Shafik Handal, former head of the Communist Party, member of the FMLN, and critic of the war in Iraq and the Cuba embargo, might endanger the permanent-residency status of Salvadorans living in the United States on whose remittances home much of the country depends. Although the statements were by no means decisive—Handal stood no chance anyway—they sent the message that the United States was not prepared to accept the pillars of democratic politics: free speech and dissent. And in Haiti, the United States used its weight in multilateral development agencies to withhold millions of dollars in aid for policing and humanitarian initiatives from the increasingly autocratic but nevertheless elected leftist priest Jean-Bertrande Aristide. One effect of the squeeze was to deny Aristide the ability to control security in his country. By 2004, he was forced to flee the country in a U.S. military transport plane—a dream come true to Bush Latin America hands who could not forgive Aristide and his allies in the Democratic Party for persuading the Clinton administration to return him to power in 1994 after his earlier overthrow.

But the signal clearer than truth that the United States had fallen into its old ways was the manifest relief over the success of a coup in Venezuela that had briefly removed Hugo Chavez from power in April 2002. On the day of the coup, the White House and State Department issued statements giving this impression, as did the congressionally funded International Republican Institute.[68] A former assistant secretary of state saw a counterpart at a tony Washington breakfast spot and, referring to Chavez, remarked, "Ding dong, the witch is dead." The Latin American diplomatic corps came away from a meeting convened the same day by Otto Reich convinced that the United States would recognize the provisional government then in formation. Even as the civilian-military interim junta that took power dissolved the National Assembly, the constitution, the Supreme Court, and the National Elections Council, the U.S. ambassador and his Spanish colleague in Caracas were meeting with those involved in the power grab and issuing polite and positive statements acknowledging the work ahead for the interim government. Chavez's own military brought him back to Caracas in a matter of days, and many of the coup organizers eventually fled to exile—some to the United States—dooming relations between the United States and Venezuela. But Chavez's standing soared.

Before the coup, favorable opinion toward Chavez had dropped from the high 70s in 1998 and 1999 to the high 30s in 2001 and 2002. Massive capital flight and mismanagement of the economy had increased poverty and unemployment. But after the coup and bolstered by oil revenues, Chavez used America's ideological antipathy toward him to paint his opposition into a *golpista*, or coup-mongering corner, and to raise his own profile within the country and in Latin America as the twenty-first-century version of David slaying Goliath. Chavez and Lula have opened trade and investment deals, as have Chavez and Argentina's Nestor Kirchner. Venezuela has joined MERCOSUR as a full member. The oil-for-medical-care arrangement Chavez struck with Cuba has put doctors in poor neighborhoods where private Venezuelan physicians would not travel. Together with land and property titling, microfinance, and education programs, this has established Chavez as the best, though far from perfect, hope for Venezuelans long marginalized politically and economically. For all of his demagogic warts, Chavez has become a symbol of defiance against globalization and Americanization, whether at the World Social Forum, the Ibero-American Summit, or most recently, the Summit of the Americas, where, complemented by the more sophisticated foreign policy style of Lula's Brazil, he helped derail America's plans for hemispheric trade integration.

Venezuela has also used the tension with the United States as an opportunity to reorganize—though not nationalize—its energy industry and to diversify its supply and investment relations to include now Brazil, India, and, importantly, China. Traditional U.S. allies within Venezuela, whether in the energy industry, the old and now thoroughly discredited political parties, the private sector, the corporatist labor movement, the church, or the large and powerful private media conglomerates, have been unable to shed the stain of their involvement in agitating for the overthrow of Chavez. Although Venezuela remains highly polarized, the opposition and Chavista forces are united in the view that the United States has served neither well. The opposition believes the United States purposely overlooked signs of fraud in the 2004 referendum in which Chavez again prevailed and that, in thrall to big oil, the Bush administration talks tough but carries only a flimsy stick. By boycotting legislative elections at the end of 2005, the opposition again strengthened Chavez's political control and raised international eyebrows about its commitment to the democratic process. No democratically elected Latin American heads of state want to be seen by voters as doing anything but supporting constitutional rule in Venezuela, especially on America's behalf, lest they open the door to undemocratic power grabs in their own countries.

However put off some Latin Americans may be by Hugo Chavez's bravado and his often petty and needlessly provocative anti-American rhetoric, they also see him as a symbol of defiance of the United States, just as Fidel Castro was in the twentieth century. Only instead of Soviet backing, Chavez has oil revenue that he can leverage domestically, regionally, internationally, and, until the United States diversifies its energy consumption and determines a political strategy for the region, bilaterally, as the donations of cut-rate oil and gas to Boston, New York, and Chicago demonstrate. He can declare himself a socialist and decry capitalism and the United States, all in an economic and political environment where indigenous and social movements and leftist political parties are thriving in the face of relentless poverty and inequality and often violent threats to security over legal and illegal resources—whether water, oil, natural gas, coca, or cash at an ATM. However messy and even illiberal Chavez's domestic programs, Latin Americans see the American hostility toward Chavez as an indication that the United States is unwilling to accept the reorganization of power relations within societies and supports democracy only when "our son of a bitch" wins an election.

Unfortunately for the United States, its endorsement of the Venezuela coup tarnished its reputation with Latin America at a bad time internationally, beyond the hemisphere. By the second half of 2002, the United States had focused the world's attention on Iraq. Latin America at the time had two countries in rotating seats at the UN Security Council: Mexico held a seat in the 2002–2003 session, and Chile's term would overlap in 2003–2004. But by the end of 2002, the Bush administration had allowed the relationship with Mexico to fall into stasis by comparison with earlier promises. Vicente Fox had been slow to offer supportive remarks after the attacks of September 11—a pause in leadership that encouraged Mexican public opinion to revert to its historically anti-American bent. The outwardly pro-U.S. socialist president of Chile, Ricardo Lagos, had yet to see a long-promised free-trade deal materialize from the United States and led a citizenry that, after seventeen years of military dictatorship under U.S. ally Augusto Pinochet, had grown allergic to the use of force and was preternaturally suspicious of the U.S. rationale for a "war on terrorism," the very language used during the Pinochet era to justify kidnappings, assassinations, torture, and repression.[69]

Within Latin America, Venezuela had come to symbolize the ambush of a scarcely recovered U.S. credibility in the hemisphere. Internationally, the Chilean and Mexican refusal to support the United States at the UN Security Council represented a diplomatic blow: The United States could no longer count on even its neighbors in the hemisphere for backing of its Iraq war plan. In stunning contrast, during the first Gulf War, Secretary of State James Baker had secured support for two Security Council resolutions—the first approving the use of force against Iraq and the second establishing the terms for a cease-fire—from a government with which the United States lacked diplomatic relations and which it had repeatedly tried to overthrow: Fidel Castro's Cuba, then representing Latin America on the Security Council.

As the war in Iraq dragged on, without the international legal authority Latin America had insisted upon, whatever well of goodwill the United States might have drawn upon for its post–Cold War embrace of democracy in the hemisphere had run virtually dry. On the eve of a World Trade Organization ministerial meeting in Cancún in fall 2003, the governments of Brazil, Argentina, Mexico, and ten other Latin American countries joined with India, South Africa, China, and even U.S. war-on-terror allies Colombia and Pakistan to form the "Group of Twenty." Though the Cancún summit was aimed at achieving an agreement on agricultural issues, the draft proposals, heavily influenced by the United States, Europe, and Japan, kept the agricultural subsidies in place. The Group of Twenty's collective demand that developed countries first eliminate their agricultural subsidies effectively scuttled the U.S., European, and Japanese negotiating position, which held that they would cut subsidies only in return for guarantees that developing countries would grant improved market access. Although the developing countries' opposition was directed also at the European Union and Japan, coming on the heels of the failed diplomacy around the Iraq war, the show of defiance represented a significant diplomatic defeat for the United States.

In another sign of diminishing U.S. influence, and with the United States still fighting a ruthless insurgency in Iraq, China's President Hu Jintao swept through Brazil, Argentina, Chile, and Cuba on a twelve-day swing through Latin America the next year, in fall 2004. Other communist officials had visited Latin America during and since the end of the Cold War. But in the new Latin American and international context—one of resounding dissatisfaction with U.S. primacy along with greater scrutiny of China's rise—Hu's visit came to represent, for Washington's worriers, the first symbolic violation of the Monroe Doctrine since the Soviets inserted their nuclear missiles in Cuba. However mercantilist and focused on enough commodity extraction to make Lenin turn in his grave, China announced multibillion-dollar investment deals that came colored in the language of prosperity and cooperation.

Indeed, China's wooing of Latin America—and the enthusiastic response in the region—stood in sharp contrast to the tone of fear and insecurity that surrounded overlapping visits in the same period by Donald Rumsfeld and George W. Bush and to the entire tone set by the Bush administration since the September 2001 attacks. Rumsfeld lectured defense ministers about their countries' vulnerability to terrorism, while eye-rolling and hallway chatter reflected a sense that the United States had few answers for the causes behind Latin America's vulnerability—poverty, pervasive illegality, and common crime. By advocating a greater role for the military in the civilian domain of policing, the Pentagon gave the impression that the United States was willing to risk a return to the infringements on human rights and democracy of the region's authoritarian era to satisfy its counterterrorism objectives. Bush's arrival days later to attend with Hu the Asia-Pacific Economic Cooperation (APEC) head-of-state summit in Santiago, Chile, brought out the most virulent anti-American protests in decades. Effigies depicting Bush as Hitler, flag burning, and signs protesting everything from globalization, the U.S. human rights record in Chile, and the more recent revelations of torture at Abu Ghraib marked a stunning show of antipathy from a country that the United States routinely—and with no shortage of self-congratulatory relief—hailed as the greatest economic and political success of Latin America. By the end of Bush's first term, free trade—and then only with those countries on the U.S. "friends" list (Central America, the Dominican Republic, Colombia, Peru, and Ecuador) and even then only on U.S. terms, which did not include eliminating U.S. agricultural subsidies— remained one of the few tangible features of U.S. interests in the hemisphere that the United States did not frame in terms of fear and insecurity.

A fundamental realignment is under way in Latin America. The nonviolent left—some with a history of insurgency or involvement in military coups—is coming to power within government and gaining a voice outside of it. Chile, Argentina, Brazil, Uruguay, Venezuela, and Bolivia now have governments that range from European-style social democrat to left-populist. Ecuador and Peru are headed by presidents or interim leaders who barely cling to power, with single-digit popularity ratings and hostile oppositions in parliament or the streets capable of making their countries ungovernable. Only Colombia, which tops the list of America's best friends in the hemisphere, has a head of state as popular as Hugo Chavez, and like Chavez on the left, Alvaro Uribe governs as a populist of the right, doling out patronage directly while, most important to his success, taking on left- and right-wing illegal armies that thrive on the country's legal and illegal resources. But even Colombia's capital, Bogotá, has a left-wing mayor with presidential aspirations dashed by a controversial constitutional amendment that will allow President Uribe to run for a second term. Mexicans too may vote into Los Pinos Manuel López Obrador, the recent mayor of Mexico City, a populist-nationalist who left the once ruling party to join the left's Revolutionary Democratic Party (PRD).

Save Chavez and Morales, none of the new left-leaning elected Latin leaders are talking revolution: They are pragmatic, understand firsthand the risks of unmanageable domestic conflict and the U.S. temptation to step in to fill the breach, and are searching for a middle way somewhere between the heavily state-dominated economic model of their authoritarian pasts and the politically unsustainable market orthodoxy of the Washington Consensus. They recognize that Latin America has experienced zero net growth since 1980, and that despite stable and low inflation and more trade and foreign investment, poverty and inequality are worse than when their economies began to open toward the end of the Cold War. Even without the highly unpopular war in Iraq, anti-Americanism in Latin America has returned with a vengeance as a cross-class phenomenon, not only because the U.S. economic model has failed to deliver but, most important, because of strong evidence—in Bolivia, Venezuela, Haiti, and Central America—that for Washington, despite the solemnity of rhetoric, the promise of summits, and earnest intentions of charters, ideology still trumps democracy, and social exclusion remains the rule.

Regionally and internationally, under Brazil's and Chile's leadership, Latin America is reorienting its historic trade and diplomatic habit of looking first to the United States to set the hemisphere's agenda. With the exception of Colombia, Peru, and Central America—the small island-states of the Caribbean essentially broke with the United States over Haiti—U.S. influence is diminishing. The Free Trade Area of the Americas, planned for 2005, was dead on arrival. New regional organizations have been created and old ones strengthened with an eye toward deepening market integration in order to better leverage an eventual trade deal with the United States, particularly once U.S. agricultural subsidies are eliminated. With Venezuelan money and Cuban know-how, the two countries have launched Operation Miracle, aimed to cure cataracts for Caribbean residents, and are reaping the political benefits of PetroCaribe, a venture to provide Venezuelan oil at discounted prices to Caribbean nations, the twelve of which vote as a bloc at the OAS, often against the United States. In the meantime, individually and collectively, the major countries of South America and Mexico have diversified their trade substantially, reaching agreements with the European Union, Japan, China, and India. Argentina has defied the IMF, and implicitly the United States, by successfully refinancing its own debt. No one knows for sure whether Chavez is distributing money to indigenous social movements in Bolivia, Ecuador, and Peru (and if so, how much), nor can anyone know the precise political value to Fidel Castro of subsidized Venezuelan oil and more generally of the hemisphere's move to the left. Brazil's historically inward-looking diplomatic corps, colloquially known for the name of its foreign ministry, Itamaraty, is elevating the country's diplomacy internationally—building ties with other middle powers of Brazil's stature such as India and South Africa while waiting for the United States to come around on a mutually agreeable trade deal. Emerging as the political and diplomatic heavyweight of South America, Brazil is building its international capital to press its case for a permanent seat on an expanded Security Council by leading the UN peacekeeping forces in Haiti. In an arrangement that is surely practical but nevertheless would have been unthinkable before the loss of U.S. credibility in Latin America and the stretching of U.S. military resources because of Iraq, Chinese police forces now make up part of that UN contingent.

These realignments have pulled the rug out from under America's historic sway in the region. Neither the Alliance for Progress of the 1960s, the North American Free Trade Agreement (NAFTA), the summitry of the 1990s, the Free Trade Area of the Americas at the end of the American Century, the billions of dollars in military assistance and training, nor even the largely sincere but at times half-hearted embrace of democracy at the end of the Cold War could bring the United States lasting goodwill. But even by a colder calculus, these U.S. investments have not yielded their expected returns. Just as the United States seeks to extend the power and influence it once exercised over Latin America to much of the rest of the globe, save China, Latin America can no longer be relied on to support the U.S. global trade, market, and security agenda.

Nor can the United States be counted on to support the agenda for Latin America now under development by those countries with the greatest political heft. Rather than throw its weight behind either Chile's or Mexico's candidacy to lead the OAS, the United States backed a right-wing former president of tiny El Salvador as a reward for being the only Latin American country with troops in Iraq and as an OAS candidate under whose leadership the United States might use the organization to impose sanctions against Chavez's Venezuela. The strategy failed, however: With the rejection by most of the hemisphere of the war in Iraq, the controversy over the collapse of the Aristide government in Haiti, and the disillusionment over the U.S. confrontation with Hugo Chavez, the United States could not muster the votes for its candidate. As a result, in a retreat that surely symbolizes the end of its uncontested political dominance of the region, the United States ultimately was forced to defer to warnings from most of South America and stand aside while for the first time in nearly sixty years a candidate not of its backing, a Chilean, assumed the chairmanship of an organization which for almost its entire history had been a reliable tool of U.S. diplomacy in the Western Hemisphere.

In the lead-up to the war in Iraq, a U.S. diplomat at the United Nations, asked whether Mexico would follow the French in opposing the United States at the Security Council, roared with laughter. "Follow the French?" he replied. "Hell, Mexico *is* France." Politically, he may as well have been talking about nearly the entire region.

.   .   .

Shortly after his reelection in 2004, President George W. Bush took a quick trip north in the hemisphere to Ottawa, Canada. Canadians had grown decidedly more hostile toward the United States and President Bush, partly over its citizens' experience in U.S. detention and rendition programs and generally over the war in Iraq. To greet the president's arrival, Canadian protesters erected and then ceremoniously pulled down a statue of Bush designed to resemble the statue of Saddam Hussein toppled by U.S. soldiers in April 2003 in Baghdad. Bush took the jab in stride, remarking to reporters at a press conference in Ottawa with Prime Minister Paul Martin that he appreciated how crowds had come to greet him on his way in from the airport, especially those polite enough to bestow upon him what he called "the five-fingered wave."

With this reference, Bush put his own finger on a phenomenon that by the end of his first term and well into his second had become the new international default. Anti-America is almost everywhere, and his administration, the policy community around it, and the punditry that dissects it have adjusted to the new global environment. U.S. power has walked into the buzz saw of domestic politics and history around the globe at a particularly propitious time, lining up the stars for the emergence of Anti-America across continents, in varying degrees of robustness and intensity. Even in "new Europe," where generally pro-U.S. heads of state participated in the Iraq coalition against the will of their constituents and where anti-Americanism is seen as a cynical way back into power for former communists, public and government opinion lines up consistently with "old Europe" against the United States on critical "core belief" issues such as the International Criminal Court and the Kyoto Protocol. Among U.S. allies in the Arab world, Egypt, Saudi Arabia, Pakistan, and Jordan, for example, the United States has spent billions of dollars for peace with Israel, oil, Soviet containment, and now the war on terror. In Nigeria, especially in the Muslim North where local imams spread the rumor that the United States had laced polio vaccines with HIV virus, parents won't vaccinate their children, and polio has now spread beyond sixteen countries. In South Africa, heads of state for years refused to finance the proper treatment of HIV/AIDS because they believe the diseases and their treatments are part of a malevolent U.S. conspiracy.

As diverse as U.S. allies from the Cold War are—ethnically,

culturally, historically, and geographically—the respective story lines of their falling-out with the United States are remarkably similar, even outside the traditional West. After World War II, the United States came to replace the former colonial powers in Asia, Africa, and the Middle East. To promote its national interests, whether security, energy, or ideology, the United States allied itself, its capital, and the international financial institutions it controlled with unsavory regimes that repressed and stole from their own populations. Often such regimes justified their frequently ruthless authoritarian rule and breach of basic human rights as the political cost of providing the United States with whatever specific tangible applied: oil and stability from Saudi Arabia and Nigeria; a truce with Israel from Egypt; balance against Iran from Iraq and vice versa; an anchor of security in Asia from South Korea and Indonesia; and so on. In the absence of open, democratic politics during the Cold War, religion often filled the breach. The United States came to be identified with the repressive and authoritarian status quo not only in Latin America but throughout much of the developing world: an enemy of the sacred, in an increasingly profane and hopeless world.

The sameness of this pattern is of course a testament to the strategically comprehensive nature of containment during the Cold War. It also suggests that the United States can again, in demeanor and policies, alter course to regain the trust not only of governments but of entire populations who, once trapped by their powerlessness, are now, because of democracy, media, and communications technology, unalterably alert to prospects—both peaceful and violent—to change their history and hold their governments, and the United States, accountable. The United States may well be powerful or stubborn enough to throw up its hands in the face of the structural foundations that make Anti-America feel inevitable. America may be arrogant or frustrated enough to expect that it will inevitably trip over domestic political, cultural, and historical qualities abroad that are simply beyond U.S. control. But the United States must avoid the tempting trappings of intellectual idolatry—the conviction that certain features of international life are immutable and thus immune to nuanced policy. To follow such a path would be paradoxically to concede that America lacks the very power that found expression in specific U.S. policies, those that so dramatically provoked world opinion in the Anti-American Century. Structure aside, policies matter, and the United States has the power, still, to change course.

III

|

CHAPTER FOURTEEN

|

Friendly Fire

> So if you're unilaterally declaring Kyoto dead, if you're
> declaring the Geneva Convention is not operative, if you're
> doing a host of things that the world doesn't agree with
> you on and you're doing them blatantly and in their face
> ... without grace ... then you've got to pay the
> consequences.—Col. Lawrence Wilkerson, Ret.*

The United States has lost the intangible resource it had cultivated in the twentieth century: the benefit of the doubt. But does that lack of trust really get in America's way? Isn't the world big enough and aren't America's prospects sufficiently robust to survive the scorn of the members of an increasingly antiquated and frayed Cold War coalition? And if the United States loses its preeminence internationally as a consequence of the emergence of new powers and viable alternatives to the American model, isn't that something to be applauded as the logical result of the very globalization and democracy the United States has championed and encouraged others to harness?

For much of the twentieth century, the United States grew to

*Col. Lawrence Wilkerson, Ret., Former Chief of Staff, Department of State, 2002–2005, "Weighing the Uniqueness of the Bush Administration's National Security Decision-making Process: Boon or Danger to American Democracy," New America Foundation Policy Forum, Washington, D.C., October 19, 2005.

expect a "damned-if-you-do-damned-if-you-don't" reaction to its power and policies, feeding a conclusion by power thinkers and practitioners that assessing and realizing the national interest was different from politics and should not have as its baseline the goal of pleasing or being liked. Tension over policies was a natural feature of a complex international environment, but it was a milieu the United States had largely mastered. Still, it isn't America's style to conduct itself merely as a heartless, interest-maximizing rational state actor. Americans think of themselves as kings and queens of the world's prom, presiding fairly over their less wise, less powerful, or less strapping subjects with policies that, though perhaps imperfect, have the effect of advancing U.S. interests while promoting the common good. But in the recent period of a decidedly more contentious international landscape, controversial policies and nonpolicies of the Bush II administration stripped bare the latent structural anti-American animus that had accumulated over time.

The consequences for the United States are far more momentous than losing likeability. The new anti-American default has accelerated the process of the diminution of U.S. power. It has exposed a fundamental rift in American society over how to use our power. It has left the United States isolated in Iraq, hobbling America's ability to focus attention on other international issues. It has further weakened the United Nations and efforts to reform it, and it has slowed the process of trade integration, among other items on the U.S. foreign policy agenda. It has severely damaged credibility of the United States as an advocate of democratic values. Anti-America, though, is not just the result of immutable organic conditions that necessarily inspire resentment of U.S. power by those with less of it. If the rebellion under way against America were only a result of fixed inequalities ossified by history, money, and power, Anti-America would now be an institutionalized and entrenched characteristic of twenty-first-century international life, impervious to any efforts to roll it back, full stop. That hasn't occurred—yet. Although the disillusion with America felt far and wide may permanently tarnish the country's once sparkling appeal, Anti-America need not spread or remain entrenched, despite its structural roots.

That is because Anti-America at home and abroad is also the outgrowth of policy choices, self-inflicted wounds deepened by the retreat of progressive values at home, and international disillusion with both. With its prestige, influence, and image diminished, the United States has been hit by the friendly fire of its longtime acolytes and dependents. In a sense, it is good news that specific U.S. policies of the early twenty-first century were so central to the unfurling of Anti-America's flag among longtime allies and friends. The structural foundations feeding Anti-America will remain deep-rooted, but American citizens still have a choice about whether they and their children will have to lie and say they are Canadians in order to travel the world unharassed. Americans still have a choice about whether their country can again be seen as a desirable leader internationally with a domestic social contract that sustains their country's global appeal.

There may well be no practical formula to eliminate the fundamental dilemma that no matter how the United States uses its power, a certain, even significant degree of resistance will remain a chronic feature of the world's reaction. The approach to this phenomenon, to which the American people and international community are already in the process of adjusting, should not be tactical, public diplomacy–type questions such as what the White House should do to persuade foreign and domestic publics of the virtues of its war in Iraq, of its intentions in the Middle East or at the United Nations. Instead, we need to ask and answer two far more basic questions. By the end of the twenty-first century, what kind of reception might Americans hope to encounter when they leave U.S. shores? And what kind of America do we want international visitors to find when they come to the United States?

Unfortunately, the answer du jour to the question of how to improve America's standing in the world has all too often been public diplomacy. Described by the State Department as "engaging, informing and influencing key international audiences," public diplomacy—transparently progovernment propaganda at its worst or smart, nuanced, multifaceted outreach at its best—has been offered up all too often as the logical answer to America's image problem.[1] Precisely because of the historical and structural nature of today's backlash; the misleading rationale, polarizing diplomacy, and conduct of the war in Iraq; and the abuses, torture, and secret detentions associated with it and the war on terror, public diplomacy cannot be honestly expected to tame the scope of Anti-America. Public diplomacy is not a panacea or a substitute for fairness, good policy, and substantive engagement with the international community.

At the start of his second term, President Bush indicated that he was committed to giving better explanations of America's decisions to the world. But public diplomacy has a bad name these days, and not because America is misunderstood. More explanations, however handsomely crafted the message is or how accessible or pleasant the messengers, won't help temper anti-American attitudes or interrupt hostile anti-American actions. Public diplomacy during the Cold War, especially in Europe—through radio programs, cultural exchanges, libraries, and a whole host of informational efforts—was an effective complement or force multiplier to the U.S. strategy of containment, because the United States was a credible messenger of desirable values and because the alternative to the United States revealed itself to be so much worse. Until the United States has a coherent and positive set of priorities it can make manifest in international policies, money spent on public diplomacy may generate lucrative contracts for the communications, polling, and public relations industries, but it is not likely to substantially improve America's image. It may even make it worse. We can expect public diplomacy to help recover the credibility and trust we have lost as a country only when we give thought to how we use our power and to the potential impact of our policies. In the interim, treating public diplomacy as a political campaign, in which the daily message crafted to create a particular perception may be light-years from the reality on the ground, will only reinforce international suspicion of the United States.

Karen Hughes, President Bush's longtime campaign and communications adviser and later undersecretary for public diplomacy, encountered firsthand on her inaugural trip to Turkey, Saudi Arabia, and Egypt exactly how our credibility with respect to women's rights, a fundamental component of personal freedom and democracy, has been grossly undermined. In Turkey, where Hughes introduced herself as a "working mom" who drives and represented Americans as "a people of faith," women audiences were unimpressed with appeals on gender or religious grounds. Instead, they challenged her to defend the war that in their view had made the lives of Iraqi women and their children patently miserable. Hughes's response, one that would never pass muster with an American audience, was to insist that "'my friend President Bush' did all he could to avoid a war in Iraq."[2] This incident illustrates the inadequacy of public diplomacy in such a strongly anti-American context. But more critically, Hughes's experience demonstrates the capacity of poorly and incautiously deployed American power to undercut thoroughly the country's ability to draw upon its own domestic strengths—women's rights and religious freedom in this case—as a source of its specialness.

Indeed, the blur between perception and reality is such that it is hard to imagine how, in an increasingly democratic and technologically connected 24/7 environment, government-sponsored public diplomacy can ever come to substitute for policies that are perceived as fair and lawful. The presidentially appointed Defense Science Board concluded in 2004 that when it comes to crafting a strategy to counter anti-Americanism in Islamic populations, perception plainly is reality from the perspective of those angered by U.S. policy in the Middle East or U.S. support for Israel or resentful of U.S. support for authoritarian regimes.[3] In the Muslim world and on more familiar territory alike, allegations and documented reports of psychological and physical torture, sexual humiliations, desecrations of the Koran, and publicized photographs of naked and near-naked prisoners—from the nameless to the notorious—have cast a cloud of suspicion over U.S. motives that makes each new allegation of mistreatment increasingly believable, whether true or not. How can public diplomacy overcome images of torture? It can't. The answer is not to assert that the United States is committed to human rights but to implement policies that ban the practice of torture and hold accountable those responsible, especially at the highest levels. To make headway in reducing the scope and intensity of Anti-America, public diplomacy will have to be part of a much more significant and long-term course correction.[4]

CHAPTER FIFTEEN

Shedding the Unreality

Since the United States is not seen by others in the same light as we Americans see ourselves, the overarching requisite now and for the future is to shed the unreality that has characterized our habitual approach to how we project our power and respond to international dissent. The purpose for such a top-to-bottom overhaul is not to ensure that we are likeable. The objective is to regain the benefit of the doubt we have lost and to soften the visceral anti-American instinct that is now all too pervasive in international political life. Anti-America poisons the atmosphere and reinforces the U.S. preference for bucking the international consensus on major global issues while signaling to other, especially emerging powers that they too can opt out. This cycle slows the pace of and dilutes the content of multilateral cooperation whether on climate change, poverty and debt, protectionism, the treatment and spread of infectious diseases, compliance with international human rights law, or the proliferation of weapons—light, biological, or nuclear. On the latter, for example, the anti-American international environment, enhanced by the legacy of exaggerating WMD claims in Iraq, has left the United States dependent upon (and thus beholden to) China to keep North Korea at the negotiating table, and unable, even with the enticement of civilian U.S. nuclear technology, to persuade the new strategic U.S. ally India to declare a position against Iran's nuclear activities. The fog of Anti-America makes it virtually impossible to sort out when a U.S. proliferation objective is really about preventing WMD and when it masks a desire for regime change. That fog now blankets much of the global dialogue with the United States.

The rise of Anti-America has converted the once nearly sacrosanct bonds of alliances into what increasingly resemble profane liaisons of convenience that can forward the interests of their participants first and the collective goals of the common good a more distant second at best. In part this is because fighting terrorism does not offer the kind of ideological umbrella the Cold War provided. Without a persuasive and effective organizing principle for its foreign policy, the United States is now seen to be behaving as other countries do: picking and choosing relationships exclusively to maximize its narrow interests, giving slim consideration to their broader impact. To deepen the difficulty of regaining a benefit-of-the-doubt reflex, democracy and technology have unleashed politics within and among nations to a degree well beyond the conditions that once enabled the Soviet Union and the United States to organize and lead blocs of nations.

Further, U.S. foreign policy has become domestic politics in societies that are both intimately familiar with the United States, such as Germany, or relatively isolated from and ignorant of America, such as Brazil. Some anti-Americanism will always be fake, contrived for domestic political consumption, such as Gerhard Schroeder's almost wishful evocation during his race against Angela Merkel of the prospect that the United States might in-

vade Iran. In these cases, the United States and others should de-
nounce such remarks for their bogus quality and call to account
those who make them. But whether fake or real, the fundamentals of structure and policy that in the twentieth century laid the
foundations for Anti-America can also help shape an overall approach for the future that will isolate the former and undercut, or
at least limit, the damage of the latter.

Much of the logic of this book is grounded in the assumption
that on balance the consequences of U.S. isolation and loss of
credibility are negative. Has anything positive come of this current bout of anti-Americanism? Returning to the fits and starts
of heavy anti-American resistance in the twentieth century
might help answer the question.

The U.S. loss in Vietnam and the international disgrace that
befell the nation over the war had the effect at home of ushering
in a series of laws and a new political culture that heightened
public accountability and scrutiny in the conduct of U.S. foreign policy. The issue of morality of nuclear weapons aside, a
plausible argument could be made that the nuclear build-up of
the 1980s was well worth the heated backlash in European capitals because it was among a number of factors—external and internal—that led to the collapse at the end of the decade of the
Soviet Union. Anti-American outbursts over the Vietnam War
and the Euromissile crisis were contained: Unlike in Iraq, there
was no spillover that tainted other critical issues, nor did these
episodes unfold in a broadly anti-American international climate. If, in a matter of decades, the United States can claim to
have undercut substantially the recruitment, financing, proliferation, and operational capacity of al-Qaeda and other terrorist
networks, and if Iraq becomes a stable, relatively peaceful,
somewhat democratic country, and if Iran's and North Korea's
nuclear ambitions are successfully contained, this current
episode of anti-Americanism may well be regarded in the future

as a manageable price to have paid for U.S. and international security.

Such an immense task would be difficult to accomplish in the best of international moments, with common cause openly felt and pursued by key international powers with the backing or compliance of their domestic constituents. But unlike in the Cold War, today's pervasive anti-American environment throws into the mix an element of uncertainty, instability, and plain old bad blood among our allies, potential partners, and their electorates that may well undermine our immediate security objectives and the world's efforts to bring a measure of health and prosperity to its inhabitants. Although U.S. leadership during the Cold War seldom received unequivocal applause even from those within the Western camp, and as much as Cold War policies and alliances also planted the seeds for today's backlash, paradoxically the era does offer a reference for the degree of anti-Americanism the United States can tolerate.

Even before we can know whether Islamist terrorist groups have been neutralized, whether the gamble in Iraq will pay off, or whether behind the clumsiness, orthodoxy, or contradictory measures on nuclear proliferation lay an effective disarmament strategy, we can reach a preliminary judgment on the question of whether the anti-American cloud holds any silver lining. Despite all of the negative consequences, there are two ways in which the opposition and alienation the United States is experiencing are positive.

First, the new anti-American dissonance provides an opportunity for America and Americans to see ourselves as others see us. It has revealed the gap between U.S. power and U.S. influence. The deliberations of the 9/11 Commission, the reports of numerous congressional committees, the confirmation hearings of the president's nominee for ambassador to the United Nations, John Bolton, and the overwhelming vote in the Senate against the threat of a White House veto to ban the practice of cruel, inhuman, or degrading treatment of prisoners held by U.S. government agencies, for example, revealed that both Republicans and Democrats are thinking seriously about the style and substance best suited to manage and project U.S. power and promote U.S. interests. Still, the instant the United States is attacked again by terrorists, or Iraq dissolves into civil war, or negotiations definitively fail with Iran or North Korea, or U.S. service personnel in some conflict zone somewhere are denied Geneva Convention protections and are tortured, such reflection will be of little consolation without significant course corrections.

Second, by exposing the limits of U.S. influence, the new anti-American international political culture has encouraged the independence and autonomy of countries within and beyond the traditional U.S. domain. Although the obstacles are many—debate continues over whether China's diplomatic and economic weight in Asia or at the UN Security Council is a net positive for the United States and for international security; decided pique remains over the German and French opposition to the Iraq war; hurt feelings and surprise persist over the Mexican, Chilean, and Brazilian challenge to the United States on Iraq, trade, and Hugo Chavez—the emergence of counterweights to U.S. power ultimately points in the direction the United States and global politics were already heading. America will not always be the single superpower, and as the current backlash suggests, we should not desire that status. The global landscape now emerging is one in which the United States, China, the European Union, and perhaps Japan, India, Russia, and Brazil will by nature and necessity face a choice over when to cooperate, when to compete, and how to share power. As recent years suggest, it is not at all clear that the United States will take well to sharing in a new global distribution of power. If the rise of Anti-America has jump-started what is a necessary accommodation internationally, it has also created an opportunity for Americans to see that they have a choice in whether the twenty-first century really will turn out to be the Anti-American Century.

CHAPTER SIXTEEN

History and the Legacy of the Cold War

It is time to declare the death of American exceptionalism, the penchant for displaying "exceptional leadership in promoting international human rights" while at the same time resisting "complying with human rights standards at home or aligning its foreign policy with these standards abroad."[5] For much of its history, U.S. exceptionalism served as a powerful myth—an occasional excuse for double standards and an overarching ideology that explained the domestic and international success of the United States as a combination of geography, industriousness, tolerance, intolerance, and sheer political will. But with Iraq, the detainee abuse scandals, and then hurricane Katrina drawing back the curtains on America's fallibility abroad and at home, exceptionalism can no longer serve as a viable legend for the future.

Other powers that commit trespasses analogous to those now accumulated at America's feet do not face the kind of entrenched distrust the United States now confronts, not only because they do not have as much power as it does but also because no power—great, middle, or small, not even France—has established a national and international discourse of specialness, generosity, and moral authority that remotely approaches the American rhetorical embrace of these qualities. This affect of specialness places the United States on the horns of a permanent dilemma. To preserve U.S. legitimacy and credibility in the world, we have to be regarded as taking concrete action to live up to those standards we have collectively set for ourselves. And yet because for now we remain the sole superpower, by claiming to embrace a universal array of values wed to interests but lacking the financial resources or domestic political will to sustain such a blend, we risk "psychological exhaustion and physical overextension . . . along with a global coalition of the resentful."[6] The question we then face is, under what circumstances can the United States retain its specialness and continue to reap the benefits of its power and place in the international community?

Breaking out of the exceptionalist mind-set will not be easy, but both U.S. and foreign audiences will benefit. However enormous, even preposterous-sounding the goal of shedding this myth, small steps can over time make a difference. How we talk about American history to domestic and foreign audiences, the resources we make available for the teaching of history, and a realistic expectation of the meaning of alliances can alter the sum and substance of how the United States projects itself internationally and the reception it receives. Invoking noble chapters of U.S. history to explain the rationale for current and prospective foreign ventures may be good domestic politics. Americans need to think historically and see themselves in a larger international and historical context. But discourse that has a shrinking shelf life, even for American audiences—photo ops on the decks of aircraft carriers declaring "mission accomplished" or invoking FDR's fight for freedom in World War II to shore up support for the war on terror from foreign audiences fearful of U.S. power and distrustful of U.S. motives—comes off as patronizing, even dangerous happy talk. Nothing is wrong with invoking U.S. greatness during World War II when the analogy holds up, but the United States has not waged a war since with that kind of universal moral appeal, in which the United States is unequivocally seen as the good guy. To retain the evocative value of great American moments in world history, presidential speechwriters of every political stripe would do well to express the commander in chief's confidence by allowing the White House honestly to reference unpopular and unsuccessful chapters in the history of U.S. foreign policy. This honesty is not a sign of weakness but of humility, empathy, and self-reflection and can help shed the unreality that only a failure of public diplomacy can possibly explain the rejection by foreign governments and publics of U.S. military interventions and occupations. The war in Iraq is a failure of policy and strategy, not a failure of communications.

American publics, starting with schoolkids, would also benefit from a nonpartisan, honest view of the history of U.S. foreign policy. For all the attention the United States has called to the accurate telling of history by Japan, China, Saudi Arabia, Israel, or the Palestinian Authority, the teaching of American history at home risks a plague of ideological constraints, one often imposed by federal or state funding vulnerable to politically conservative organizations seeking to cast U.S. history in only the most laudatory of frames.[7] Funding for public television has also become the province of ideological federal litmus tests; under the guise of balance and values, programs about history, current events, national security, and even kids with gay parents have been subjected to censorious scrutiny.[8]

Likewise, the penchant for secrecy in government, which deepened significantly during the Bush II administration, will prevent American and international scholars from obtaining a comprehensive understanding of the decisionmaking process behind the very foreign policies that have so backfired against the United States in recent years. For example, in November 2001 President Bush issued an executive order overturning the Presidential Records Act, thereby stripping the National Archives of control over the release to the public of presidential records and eliminating the deadline that has customarily governed declassification, turning over such decisions to former presidents, vice presidents, and their heirs.[9] It may seem a facile bromide, but after Vietnam and now Iraq, without a public debate that derives from fact-based analysis of how major policy failures unfold, we are apt to remain trapped in self-congratulation or denial and stumble or be led, again, into unwinnable wars. Secrecy damages open societies. The end of the Cold War began to open a crack in the government's secrecy reflexes—these can again be felt in full force. Reversing this trend by respecting the laws governing declassification of documents recording internal U.S. foreign policy debates is part of shedding the unreality that secrecy will somehow shield the executive branch from public accountability and learning for the future.

Although the United States would do well to take a less triumphalist view of its role in the Cold War, the nation cannot unmake this history: neither the lasting political and social cost of proxy wars in the periphery nor the desire by dependent allies in the developed world to break free of America's unforgiving expectations of deference. Precisely because of the ambivalence that lies beneath the surface of alliances, the new ties we are now forging may eventually yield some of the same consequences we watched unfold recently in Germany, Turkey, and South Korea, for example. To protect ourselves from the perils of harboring overheated expectations of prolonged gratitude for U.S. largesse or reciprocity with new allies or partners, we might take the advice of Alexander Hamilton, who cautioned that gratitude can never replace interests and has no real place in international relations.[10] Likewise, as the alliances with Uzbekistan, Egypt, and Saudi Arabia illustrate, we should proceed with our eyes wide open about the consequences for believability of our democratic values of closely associating financially, politically, or militarily with autocrats who are all too eager to embrace America's security paradigm of the day in order to justify killing or suppressing their domestic foes.

The Cold War also showed that paradigms can be straitjackets. As an ingredient in the rise of Anti-America, much of the ambivalence over the Cold War's legacy—its dark side—rests in the zeal with which Americans carried the anticommunist flame in the Third World. In Asia, Africa, and Latin America, the black and white of the U.S.-Soviet contest frequently had the effect of alienating the gray—of weakening moderate forces perhaps philosophically predisposed toward the United States but acutely jealous of their independence and autonomy. Despite the Bush administration's strenuous efforts, neither preemption nor the war on terror will fully dominate America's strategic vision in the coming years. The 2005 natural disasters on the U.S. Gulf Coast, in Pakistan, and in Central America exposed deeply rooted problems shared by wildly disparate countries that a war-footing, whether against terrorists, WMD, or regimes that support or proliferate them, simply cannot alleviate. But the mind-set and resource demands of preemptive war and the priorities and excesses of the war on terror have crowded out the White House's capacity to deal with the pressing needs revealed by suffering on a massive scale. This myopia has had the counterproductive effect of alienating moderate forces in the greater Arab and Islamic world, moderate heads of state, and government bureaucracies, national elites, and populations inclined to see the United States positively but that, for political and policy reasons, will not subordinate their entire international agenda or identities to U.S. preemption and counterterror priorities. Although the Soviet Union has disappeared as an alternative to America, other major powers—the European Union, China, Japan, Russia, India, South Africa, Brazil—in some way can offer benefits and alternatives to countries, elites, and populations in their respective regions and subregions plainly repelled by America.

Having voluntarily given up its exclusive patent to the values and practices once associated with the West, the United States must now contend with the consequences of the emerging diffusion of power internationally and within countries. Neutralizing al-Qaeda and other terrorist groups is of course critical to U.S. security. But persisting in the promotion of a single or vague idea—negatively phrased as a war against terror and evil regimes—harnessing distorted historical analogies to do so as the dominant core of America's projection in the world, and preventing the American public from a fully informed debate about the nation's role in the world has isolated the United States in the international community. This has left it unprepared to tend to the most vulnerable in its own communities at home, while leaving much of the world doubtful of the U.S. commitment to other important goals such as alleviating poverty, slowing climate change, or containing the production and spread of weapons of mass destruction. Lest the United States plant and fertilize the seeds today for a new generation of anti-Americans reacting to a myopic foreign policy agenda organized around fear, we would do well to avoid the intellectual, diplomatic, and public-image constraints of fastening such a straitjacket too tight. Shedding the psychological crutches of U.S. exceptionalism is not an invitation to the United States to relinquish the characteristics that make it appealing or special. It is a suggestion that as a society we become a great deal more honest about what U.S. power can and cannot deliver to our own citizens and to the international community that, however ambivalently, will want or need something from us for the foreseeable future.

|

CHAPTER SEVENTEEN

|

Power and Powerlessness

Whether the United States is the sole or declining super-power or both at this stage of the twenty-first century, these past few years have unambiguously demonstrated that power without constructive influence is not power at all. Big rhetorical flour-ishes about globalization, democracy, or fighting terrorists will not recover America's power or appeal until the United States is viewed as signaling that its interests coincide with those of the wider world, whether in working constructively on global issues or taking steps to cross the 80/20 divide abroad and at home.

It was not one single event that drove world opinion against the United States beginning in 2002. A host of global issues of dissonance had already created serious policy clashes that an-gered electorates and governments inclined to see the United States as an obstacle rather than as part of the solution. The United States is widely perceived less as a leader and more as an outlier to be worked around, dodged, managed, constrained, manipulated, or outsmarted. However one sorts through the causes of such dissonance, it now constitutes a political reality that will not evaporate merely by laying blame on a clash of values or civilizations.

Taken in isolation from one another, no single issue has the potential to drive the almost universal polarization caused by Iraq. But taken together, the whole the issues comprise is much larger than the sum of their parts. Iraq is not the last place on earth where the United States will choose to deploy force without the robust international consensus that existed for the 1991 Gulf War. But to regain the political capital to deploy force on its own, without a grand consensus of the Cold War or immediate post–Cold War era, the United States must rebuild the stock of goodwill it has lost. The international community sees the United States as holding itself outside of the international consensus or imposing inflexible ideological litmus tests on virtually all of the major global issues that publics around the world hold dear—global warming, poverty and development, proliferation. Even regarding democracy, a global issue on which the United States ought to retain an especially deep well of credibility, the unsustainable contradiction embedded in the use of overwhelming firepower to reshape Iraqi society into a democratic country, the gutting of federal funds to promote democracy, the hostility toward democratically elected leaders with whom we disagree—the prime minister of Spain, the president of Venezuela—and the continued alliances with tyrants old and new have dramatically diminished America's international legitimacy.

Rebuilding international capital among governments and populations to draw upon when the United States next deploys force is not the only reason the United States should demonstrate seriousness, consistency, and positive leadership on global issues. Their resolution in and of itself requires pragmatism, not ideology, from the largest power in the world. If seen to be not only engaged but also setting and achieving concrete goals—the

0.7 percent of GDP dedicated to foreign assistance to the Millennium Challenge Goals committed to at the Monterrey (Mexico) summit, for example, or dropping the spin that scientific proof eludes claims that global warming results from carbon dioxide emissions, and joining the Kyoto Protocol if not in word at least in deed—America can recover from its image as a spoiler in world affairs.

To some extent this recovery has begun, albeit tentatively. It may have taken the humility born of prolonged insurgency in Iraq and a pair of devastating natural disasters to foster a return to diplomacy under the second term of the Bush II administration, but by deferring to China in negotiations on North Korean nuclear proliferation and allowing France, Germany, and the United Kingdom to take the lead in holding Iran accountable to the IAEA, the United States has begun to counter domestic claims and international fears that U.S. interests can only be served unilaterally, while signaling a tacit recognition that regime change is not a viable counterproliferation strategy. On debt relief, the United States agreed in the Group of 8 (G-8) Gleneagles Communiqué to cancel 100 percent of the multilateral debts of at least eighteen "highly indebted poor countries." Even though the U.S. commitment stopped well short of the objectives set forward by the Blair Africa Commission, which sought to cancel multilateral and bilateral debt stock and debt service by up to 100 percent, the substance and symbolism of the gesture surprised skeptics and began to regain some diplomatic appeal for the Bush administration in the early months of its second term.

In trade negotiations, the laudable U.S. offer to reduce agricultural subsidies by 60 percent was weakened by the decision to tie such a move to a more significant reduction by Europe and Japan. In that case, a bit of unilateralism—taking the steps at home to reduce subsidies without waiting for the domestic politics of other countries to catch up—could regain for the United States the moral high ground it has lost in recent years in the developing world while having the political effect of jump-starting the stalled international trade talks convened by the World Trade Organization. And in Israel, despite no indication that an Israeli withdrawal from the West Bank is a near-term prospect, the United States has put its diplomatic energy behind Israeli withdrawal from the smaller Gaza Strip, helped organize international resources for the post-Arafat Palestinian Authority, and reiterated its commitment at numerous international forums to a Palestinian state and to Israeli security. With respect to climate change, the United States has flouted Kyoto but forged a potentially constructive climate-change partnership with five countries that collectively emit about half of all global greenhouse gases; moreover, some American states, quite apart from the federal government's lackadaisical response, have devised cap-and-trade carbon dioxide programs to reduce greenhouse gas emissions and also sought to force the Environmental Protection Agency to properly regulate carbon dioxide emissions.[11] Although many of these signs may not reflect a fundamental change of heart in Washington, they nevertheless indicate a growing U.S. recognition of the need to revisit diplomacy and to try to contribute positively, even at times in a multilateral context, to the resolution of global challenges.

Redressing the penchant for reproducing the 80/20 dynamic, one that was forged over centuries in a far less democratic international environment than today's, offers a second area for the United States to lighten the international footprint left by its power. At its core, the 80/20 split is fundamentally about an international class divide. Whether delineated by professional degree or raw economic wealth and interests, the 20 the world over from whom the U.S. political class garners its sense of what is happening abroad tend, by and large, to have analogous professional perspectives or economic standing to that of their U.S. counterparts. Trapped by a "green zone" mentality that extends far beyond the so-named U.S. embassy compound in Baghdad, official U.S. foreign policy is at once driven by a belief that it is possible to transform societies in our own image and, paradoxically given the scale of U.S. ambitions and the proliferation of information in a 24/7 age, distorted by information about the world that derives from a persistently narrow set of interlocutors.

Some basic remedies to cross the 80/20 divide could be easily adapted by government circles. Congressional delegations are notorious for zooming in and out of countries in the blink of an eye, limiting their visits to a few hours of meetings with heads of state, their cabinet, and maybe a handful of representatives from the private sector. To the extent that their staffs check the "civil society" or "NGO" box in organizing the trips, these meetings, especially in the heavily ideological era of the twenty-first century, are too often filled by groups or individuals whose perspective largely reinforces the worldview of the visitor. Executive-branch delegations repeat this pattern, leaving the cumulative impression that Americans are either uninterested in or afraid of stepping over the divide or too convinced of their own correctness to bother. Reversing this impression by abandoning the old Rolodexes, taking the time to take the pulse, however briefly, of the lives and perspectives of the 80, can gradually peel back the layers that allow Americans to embrace the conceit that technology, globalization, rhetoric about democracy, and a bit of brute force can bridge these divides. Crossing the 80/20 divide can help demonstrate that despite its power, the United States is not preternaturally destined to reinforce the power and powerlessness dynamics within other societies. The long-term implication of U.S. international goals around which there is a rough domestic consensus—leveling the economic playing field through genuinely free and fair trade and advancing human rights and democratic political practices—is precisely to transfer power to those who have historically had less or none of it. Signaling that the United States encourages and applauds the dispersal of power within societies by the choice of individuals U.S. officials see and do not see on their visits may seem a small gesture. But precisely because Americans have much more power than they tend to recognize, the symbolism of such choices can offset the green-zoning of U.S. foreign policy while teaching the visitors and the visited something along the way.

One critical reason public diplomacy cannot be expected to shoulder the burden of recovering trust in the United States is that Anti-America is also an unanticipated and paradoxical result of the public expression of dissent that accompanies open societies. For nearly a quarter century, it has been an article of faith in the West that quite apart from all of democracy's inherent benefits to individuals and to societies, democracy is a source of stability in international relations. By comparison with other forms of regimes, it is argued, democracies tend not to go to war with one another. Therefore, as Immanuel Kant hypothesized in the eighteenth century, more democracies would mean more peace and security for the world and for the United States.[12]

Yet in the cases of Latin America, parts of Asia, and increasingly in the Middle East, giving a voice to those long suppressed by authoritarian rulers who were allied with America has also opened political space within societies for anti-American sentiment to be expressed—whether over unpopular past or present U.S. policies or fomented by local politicians or both—by the very populations the United States once sought or now seeks to liberate. Greater democracy within societies may well bolster public appreciation for America's own democratic institutions over time; in the short and medium term, the line between democratic reform and a more nuanced appreciation for the United States will not necessarily be as direct as America's democracy promoters, soft or hard, might hope.

Our willingness to tolerate these democratic growing pains, to cross over and even help attenuate those power divides within societies, will have to be echoed by a tolerance for dissent between societies. New players on the international scene are challenging the United States—not yet in terms of sheer power but on the substance of many international issues that encompass and extend well beyond bilateral ties. To regain the credibility it has lost as a democratic member of the international community, the United States has to be seen as genuinely entertaining dissenting ideas even as it forcefully and fairly argues its own views.

In every region of the world, and of course at the United Nations, multilateral institutions have become more important and more valued by their members in the face of U.S. unilateralism. It is in these venues that the United States can muster its capacity for graciousness and manners to recover some of its credibility, without necessarily abdicating its voice. Whether at the UN, EU, OAS, APEC, WTO, IMF, or NATO, rather than being seen as preoccupied primarily with using power to divide these institutions or member countries to accomplish narrowly construed American ends, the United States must be viewed as explicitly recognizing the value of these institutions and the policies that may emanate from them even while disagreeing with specific policies that may result. There are few corners of the earth today where Americans—in or out of government— can sincerely be said to have the only if not the best answer. Sharing the public dialogue, leaving a lighter footprint, does not mean conceding the national interest but rather will enhance it.

The United States cannot tenably advocate the merits of global integration and democracy, or attendant policies that portend to break down the barriers within and between societies abroad, while erecting new barriers to those who for lack of livable wages in their own countries, driven by war and social conflict, or simply still seeking the American dream will persist in efforts to make it to our shores. Part of America's appeal remains its capacity to absorb new immigrants. As much as gripes about U.S. power may season the salons of the 20, the working poor and aspiring strivers among the 80 worldwide continue to risk their lives to get a toehold on the American opportunity, especially as the economic prescriptions advanced by the United States or local elites fail to produce jobs in their countries. How America treats those who want to live and work here on a temporary or permanent basis will be a critical and visible barometer of America's choice about how it wishes to be seen in this century. Yet the terror-security-fear discourse that has gripped U.S. society since the September 2001 attacks has delivered politicians of both parties easy slogans that allow them to avoid difficult discussions about the negative consequences of significantly proscribing legal access to the United States. Despite manpower, walls, and high-tech surveillance to keep people out, U.S. borders remain as penetrable as ever: Legal immigration has declined since 2000, but illegal immigration has increased.[13]

America's construction boom and growing low-skilled service sector are made possible by workers from Mexico, Central America, and Brazil, for example, many of whom live and work here illegally, unable to derive the social and economic benefits that legal status would otherwise bestow upon them. Beyond the traditional coastal states where new migrants have historically settled, now the Midwest, the South, and even Alaska have Spanish-speaking communities setting down roots. The government of Mexico by 2005 had opened forty-six consulates around the country from Portland, Oregon, to Saint Paul, Minnesota, to Little Rock, Arkansas; Charlotte, North Carolina; and Salt Lake City, Utah. Even as the new migrants fill vacant and necessary, if underpaid, jobs left open by the rise in high school graduates among the U.S.-born labor force, their presence has reinforced the fearfulness of U.S. communities that many of their politicians have exploited since the terrorist attacks.[14]

Neither laws in the 1980s nor new bills currently in Congress that are intended to limit immigration and perhaps give legal status to those already here will substantially reduce the pull of the U.S. economy and family ties or the push that the lack of livable wages in the developing world exerts on people to try their fortunes here. Driving poor foreign workers underground is no disincentive for other people trying to make it to the United States, nor will it stop their efforts to send cash back to families. But along with the squeeze on professional and student visas that has coincided with the militarization of America's southern border, these signs of inhospitality tell the world that Americans are choosing insularity, even while our economy depends upon openness to the world for innovation, solvency, basic services, exports, and cultural renovation. The course we now are on—of clamping down on legal access for the 80 or criminalizing those already here, and erecting humiliating and byzantine security checks that alienate the professionals, scientists, and students (the 20 who historically seek out U.S. jobs, universities, and labs)—instead tells the world that the very qualities that once made America a place of possibility for both the 80 and the 20 are now a thing of the past.

National and local leaders have a responsibility to help shed the myth that the United States can prosper while shutting its borders. They need to speak frankly to their constituents about why keeping the welcome mat out not only makes good economic sense but also substantiates one of the country's greatest assets: the endlessly adaptive and absorptive nature of the country itself. The alternative is to allow Anti-America to consolidate under the guise of a fear-and-security agenda.

|

|

CHAPTER EIGHTEEN

Economic Globalization

As the single superpower after the Cold War, the United States set itself up to reap the benefits, or to pay the price, of globalization's successes or failures. Globalization and Americanization became synonymous over the course of the 1990s. Despite the protests over a farrago of dynamics associated with globalization but often symbolized by the fights over trade agreements, outside of Indonesia or Argentina, the American face of globalization did not become a full-blown and more widespread liability for the United States until world opinion soured in the lead-up to the war in Iraq. In turn, as U.S. workers and their congressional representatives came to feel increasingly vulnerable to what has been somewhat fatalistically called "millennial capitalism," both political parties began to acknowledge that building and sustaining strong middle classes in the developing world as well as in the United States will require much more than trade agreements.[15]

Two elements of how the United States manages its public

discourse and public policy with respect to economic globalization reinforce Anti-America's impulses at home and abroad and are thus ripe for change: The first relates to how Americans think of themselves in the world; the second speaks to how the United States projects its expectations onto others. America's well-being is irreversibly dependent on the connections the country, its citizens, and its economy have to the world. Yet the domestic electorate sees these global ties largely as negative—foreigners come here to take American jobs, companies send even our professional jobs offshore, bureaucrats of other countries' central banks hold our debt, terrorists take advantage of our freedoms to kill us. Yet seeking foreign monsters to destroy creates new enemies. The impulse to isolate ourselves from the other, and to protect what is ours, is no less a product of human nature than the complementary drive to seek sustenance from interacting with others. But the United States cannot have it both ways, picking and choosing which aspects of global life to welcome, which to expunge. Political leadership and public policies must openly address the permanence of change and devise strategies—and there is a wealth of them: meaningful job retraining, cross-cultural educational programs, foreign study and language training—that can socialize the American electorate into seeing the country's ties to the world as a net positive.[16]

Adapting to the myriad and often wrenching challenges of globalization does not mean throwing up our hands and leaving the country's fate to grand historical forces, as if these were fixed and impervious to human agency, as the nearly idolatrous reverence for globalization among the U.S. political class often implies. But it does mean accepting that other countries will inevitably step in with innovation, technology, and answers to the great human, scientific, and moral challenges of the century. This trend is already under way, although too often not as a result of an affirmative U.S. choice deliberately to cede preeminence but as a result of neglect or worse, of ideological policy decisions. For example, by proscribing virtually all federal funds from use by laboratories involved in stem cell research, the United States has opened the door for other countries to achieve related scientific breakthroughs and to attract top-notch scientists—Americans included—who might otherwise be working in U.S. labs. Internationalists will applaud the globi-lization of scientific innovation, but that such success comes not only as a result of globalization but of America's skeptical conservatism toward science diminishes the nation's appeal and strength as a font of opportunity and innovation. It is one thing for the United States to lose preeminence but quite another to lose our eminence, a process well under way in scientific research.[17]

Similarly, the United States is losing its edge in Latin America. For example, China's increasing economic presence in that region is a manifestation of China's global strategy to expand its access to resources and markets. But having focused so tenaciously on an ideologically driven security-first foreign policy agenda, the United States by its own choice has left a vacuum in Latin America that feeds a reflex to view China's presence as a calculated threat to U.S. power. To critics of globalization, competitiveness is often understood mainly as a buzzword favored by corporations seeking to shave costs, generally by seeking tax breaks and cutting wages and benefits to rank-and-file workers and middle-class professionals, in order to boost shareholder earnings. But a quality that has kept the United States both productive and competitive is its innovative spirit. To sustain that, our doors, both literal and intellectual, must remain open. In turn, fostering conditions for America's own working poor and middle class to grow and thrive, including livable wages, strong, accountable unions, affordable healthcare, and superior educational systems, will undercut Anti-America at home, breaking down the fearful, xenophobic impulse to see outsiders and the outside primarily as a threat.

The self-assuredness and exuberance that color how America projects itself internationally—as an unquestioning promoter and beneficiary of economic globalization—reinforce Anti-America. One of the myths that emerged with the collapse of the Soviet bloc was that America had won the Cold War not only with smart geopolitical strategy—the arms race and dragging the Soviets into Afghanistan—but also because the purity of America's free market had exercised a psychological demonstration effect that helped derail the sustainability of state socialism, quite apart from the latter's inherent failures. Collective amnesia set in about the myriad ways in which America's market economy had developed and prospered with, not in spite of, the state, as if it were somehow a zone free of government intervention. Forgotten were regulations, corporate and agricultural subsidies, tariffs, tax collection or loopholes, price supports, federal management of natural resources and job creation, infrastructure development, and the provision of health and education. Free-market triumphalism translated internationally into a phobic, even hostile attitude toward other models of capitalism—social democracies in Europe, land reform and state support for the creation of new industries especially in Asia—capitalist alternatives that the United States had once tolerated, even supported, during the Cold War when undercutting any possible Soviet appeal made logical such flexibility and pragmatism.

After welfare reform of the 1990s and under assault from the conservative idea industry, the U.S. political class had largely abandoned to the left and the right the public debate about the role of the state. As European anti-Americanism became acute in the early twenty-first century, its converse, American anti-Europeanism, seemed to imply that the Continent's rejection of America's war in Iraq was related to a deeper flaccidity and malaise reflected in Germany's and France's nostalgic insistence that social welfare and the common good remain the province of government.[18] State resources may be vital for guns, but too much butter could make entire nations go soft on the use of force, the anti-Europeanists seemed to suggest. Fundamental arguments about employment, productivity, the workweek, and quality of life—issues about which neither Europe nor the United States could claim to have perfect answers—fed nationalistic antagonism on both sides of the Atlantic.

On balance, these disputes reflected the concerns of the most privileged of the world's population. But in the anti-American momentum of the early twenty-first century, for the developing world it was the United States, not Europe or Japan, whose insistence on rapid privatization and preachiness about governance and corruption, in tandem with the gap between its free-trade rhetoric and doggedness on protecting its own industries, that came off as replete with self-interested hypocrisy. Underdeveloped economies cannot simply be thrown to the free-market maelstrom, where the deck is stacked in favor of advanced, industrialized, and postindustrialized economies, and be expected to compete successfully. Shielding industries from such raw competition is not, as the prevailing ideology would have it, diabolically illiberal but rather a recognition that as with the U.S., European, and successful Asian economies, a certain amount of growth, nurtured by government investment in infrastructure, progressive tax systems, human capital, and other smart state policies to narrow inequality, is required before the benefits of new industry can be harvested through international competition.[19]

The task of delivering education, health, and jobs to workers and consumers cannot be met by weak states alone or be handled solely by the private sector. Without substantial tax revenues to support government programs geared toward training, educating, and nurturing generations of working people who are the core of a thriving middle class, neither the United States nor substantially poorer countries stand a chance to compete globally over a sustained period. In that sense, the American private sector and the U.S. government share a common objective, which is to demonstrate, in words and in deeds, that their orthodox advocacy of open trade and liberal investment climates is not, in fact, the starting gun in the "race to the bottom" that so many in the developing world and increasingly at home fear from increased economic integration.

One consequence of President Bush's rhetorical and legislative emphasis on the United States as the ownership society and on the merits of individual entrepreneurship is that the U.S. private sector now bears an increasingly large burden in crafting and sustaining the public good. Some of the most far-reaching and courageous corporate social responsibility initiatives—such as that of General Electric's "Ecoimagination" program, with GE's commitment of $1.5 billion to research on environmentally friendly technologies by 2010 and of doubling sales of such products to $20 billion; Nike's decision to make public its list of global suppliers; or the Las Vegas hotel industry's health, benefits, training, and mortgage financing programs for employees— indicate that the private sector is in many respects leading government in recognizing that its long-term profits require accountability, not only to shareholders but also to an increasingly diverse set of constituents, including the natural environment.

Corporate social responsibility is not a one-size-fits-all answer to redress disappointment and frustration with globalization or to head off the potential effects on American brands of anti-Americanism. Nor does pointing to the value of corporate citizenship efforts suggest that the private sector suffers directly from, or should take the lead in recovering, some of the lost credibility the United States has suffered in recent years. But to the extent that American companies are seen as consciously responsive to a public good broader than just the dividends of their shareholders, they can directly inoculate themselves against punishment by consumers angered over U.S. policies and indirectly help neutralize anger at the United States for having oversold the benefits of economic globalization.[20]

Congress and the executive branch can likewise play an important role in defusing anti-Americanism associated with economic globalization in the developing world by phasing out U.S. barriers to trade while assuring that all stakeholders regard trade agreements as fairly addressing and protecting rights, whether of workers, investment and intellectual property, or the natural environment. Politically, the American public and the U.S. Congress are too evenly divided for trade agreements to reflect disproportionately the interests of one set of rights over another, not least because without representing a broad domestic consensus, such trade agreements will be less sustainable, as the narrow vote over the Central America trade agreement and opposition from the region demonstrated. As long as the rewards of economic globalization are perceived in the developing world especially to come only if countries can offer foreign (read American) investors the lowest wage and most unobtrusive regulatory environment, the challenges of economic globalization will continue to reinforce the foundations of Anti-America.

Surviving, never mind prospering, in the global economy is a task the 2.8 billion world citizens living on less than two dollars a day now face. But is the U.S. economy the model to which they will aspire? America is seen today less as the meritorious beneficiary of a free market but of a rigged market, in which crony capitalism increasingly and unfairly benefits those who are already in the game.[21] Are globalization and capitalism inherently unfair, preordained to swallow the weak and reward the strong? The American temptation may well be to answer yes to this question and set sights on China's or Asia's wage earners and skilled workers for cheap manufactured goods and technology; on India's emerging and English-speaking professional class for technical inputs and services; and on reserving the Middle East, Africa, and Latin America largely as sources of imported energy supplies or other commodities.[22] Carving up the world in this way reinforces the sense among our critics abroad that the United States is no different in its pursuits from the empires that preceded it.

By the time he took his life, Ralph Nickleby, Charles Dickens's excruciatingly cruel and highly successful Victorian capitalist, had revealed himself to have no real friends, only those that feared him, depended upon him, begged him for charity, exploited his weaknesses, or endeavored to make the best of life in his shadow. Almost until his suicide, the elder Nickleby had convinced himself that his financial success was due entirely to his intelligence and strategic good sense. Sparked by the discovery of his neglected child, his entire world eventually stopped indulging these conceits. With his web of denial dissolved, he could not sustain his life.

Like Ralph Nickleby, the United States has lost the immutability cultivated after the 1989 Soviet collapse that it alone possesses an honorable monopoly on the path to economic prosperity and social peace. The heart of Anti-America's disaffection over economic globalization is not a rejection of the U.S. brand of capitalism per se but of the relentlessly broadcast but transparently fictional notion that the United States has succeeded only through a combination of fairness and good sportsmanship that others can—and must— emulate. Just as U.S. leaders must level with Americans themselves about the kinds of choices the country faces in order to prosper as a solvent nation in the twenty-first century, Anti-America's identification of the United States as the party most responsible for the significant dislocations caused by economic globalization can be tempered by clearing the fog that envelops American discourse abroad about the sanctity of one kind of capitalism over another.

.   .   .

An argument can be made that a little anti-Americanism is no more than a nuisance coming from countries and populations that are by and large favorably disposed to the United States (if only for lack of an alternative), as in the Cold War, but that this sentiment does not pose the dangers akin to those we may face from radical terrorists bent on the destruction of modern life. But drawing too sharp a distinction between anti-Americanism that is an uncomfortable nuisance and that which poses a direct danger in the context of such an entrenched anti-American international political culture would be delusional. And that is because the line that separates the nuisance from the danger is political will—of governments and populations. In the newly globalized and increasingly democratic international context, the United States faces a map of political will in which some countries have friendly governments and hostile populations, some have hostile governments and more friendly populations (Iran comes to mind here), and some, though far fewer, have friendly governments and friendly populations. It is precisely political will—from allies whether democratic or not—that the United States will need to draw upon when the next security crisis strikes—in Iran, North Korea, the Taiwan Strait, or elsewhere. But it is also this critical ingredient of political will that is now substantially eroded by the widely held conviction that the United States pursues its interests in a zero-sum power vacuum, dismissing international law, institutions, and the views of others unless they support the U.S. policy objective at hand.

Anti-America at home is nurtured and sustained by the new political strength of socially conservative forces within the

United States, just as Anti-America abroad is fed by the domestic politics and direct actions of elites and populations of foreign countries. That identity politics—who we are and who they are—is part of the anti-American mix is both a source of frustration and consolation: frustration, because there is no straight line that connects the evolving character of U.S. identity or of its detractors with possible ways to deflate Anti-America; consolation, because we have no way of scientifically predicting whether the legislative, judicial, and cultural projects of the religious right in the United States will fundamentally change the small-l liberal character of the American social contract. Besides, anti-Americans found plenty to hate about the United States well before the Bush presidency and the new social forces of the religious right found common cause. Long before September 11, 2001, the answer to why they hate us always has been a little bit of who we are and a little bit of who they are.[23] Nor do we know whether more democracy and greater economic opportunity, along with a diffusion of international power, will alleviate the tendency of the United States to get under the world's skin.

Knowing that the line between domestic politics and foreign policies is increasingly brittle, those preoccupied with improving America's image in the world should be mindful that their job abroad will be substantially more difficult if at home the domestic political forces of the conservative right successfully undermine the aspects of America's open, egalitarian society responsible for reinforcing the success of its twentieth-century internationalism abroad. While America's competing domestic political and cultural forces fight it out, precisely because of its democratic nature, the United States can temper those sources of anti-Americanism on which we can exert some measure of restraint, in the short and intermediate term, by leapfrogging over the structural foundations of Anti-America into policy, the realm of actions the United States can indeed control.

CHAPTER NINETEEN

One Hand Clapping: Anti-Anti-America After Iraq

The United States rightly has taken considerable criticism for myriad aspects of the Iraq war. Yet, with anti-Americanism entrenched in Europe, Latin America, and parts of Asia and Africa, a U.S. withdrawal from Iraq is unlikely to unhinge substantially the congenital distrust of the United States that has crept into the global body politic. No matter how U.S. forces withdraw—flexibly, abruptly, with or without a time line—it is hard to imagine applause in the capitals of Anti-America for steps taken to remedy a policy that from its inception was so widely reviled. The United States will be criticized for staying too long, for not staying long enough, for leaving the country in poor shape, or for not achieving the kind of democracy President Bush set his sights on establishing. However the withdrawal transpires and whatever condition Iraq is in during the immediate aftermath, the United States should expect little international credit as or after it leaves.

The sound of one hand clapping—the absence of global kudos for leaving Iraq—will reinforce the gut sense among many Americans that we are damned if we do and damned if we don't, an attitude that once also pervaded much of Washington's frustration with Latin America when the region provided an earlier laboratory for offshore experiments with U.S. power. This skepticism will reinforce a reluctance in the future to consider seriously the fundamental importance of seeing ourselves as others see us, and of anticipating the impact of our policies not only on our own narrowly conceived national interest but on the interests of others as well. The United States may get little psychological or diplomatic credit for withdrawing from Iraq. But with the right leadership, the American ego can withstand the inevitability that someone somehow will gloat over the bad or choose not to credit successful U.S. policies in the twenty-first century.

What does the permanence of this tension suggest about how America's friends, whose interests also are negatively affected by an embattled, isolated, and isolationist United States, manage their relationships with us? Is it realistic to expect that any country outside the Anglo-Saxon brotherhood could effectively replicate the visceral if also calculated fidelity of Tony Blair's keep-them-close approach? To overcome the cumulative frustrations that today derive from the perception that the United States does not reciprocate the loyalty it expects of others, we will need to recast ourselves to the world as the open and welcoming society we were in the twentieth century. It doesn't take a Tony Blair to adopt a conscious political discourse that shuns the temptation to pander to electorates, in this case with red, anti-American meat. Bringing out the best of America will be better served by framing the participation of the United States as a major actor in world and domestic affairs neither as a foil, enemy, or excuse nor as the great white hope that can solve all the world's problems. It is tempting to scorn such an admonition as impossible to expect from elected officials, media that feed on scandal and caricature, or populations that are increasingly fearful of the future and of change. But the heart of the challenge, as for Americans tempted by xenophobia, is for those countries, populations, and leaders that best know the United States to foster a domestic discourse about America that also forces a shedding of the unreality that has fogged and inflated expectations of what can result, good and bad, of purported U.S. ubiquity and omniscience.

Despite our flaws, the same countries that have sought to profit from complaints about U.S. power continue to have a stake in working with—or at least not against—the United States, whether in diffusing major security threats or seeing that as China emerges into a world power, it does so within an institutional framework. Partnership with the United States can still yield tangible benefits, as countries such as Colombia and India, or even still, Turkey, South Korea, and Germany, can attest. The strategic challenge for countries bristling over but still aspiring to benefit from U.S. power is to decide whether allowing Anti-America to fester and grow can really enhance their own prosperity, security, or power over the long term. From the perspective of those countries that by and large still count themselves as America's friends or partners, and even among those that see the United States largely as an obstacle, it is hard to imagine a scenario in which an isolated, reactive, and hostile United States would represent a net international gain. Just as the nation will have to manage a chronic perception problem by answering fundamental questions about how Americans wish to be received abroad, America's international interlocutors need to ask themselves what kind of United States they would like to contend with and how best to elicit those qualities from it.

The twenty-first century is already characterized by a multipolarity that will prevent the United States from ordering the world or benefiting from such efforts as it once did. Americans will thus need to accommodate to the sound of one hand clapping, not only over Iraq but over the entire U.S. international agenda. Counterintuitive, yes, but the best antidote to Anti-America may well come not from how we fight (or prevent) the next war but from the degree to which we keep intact the social contract and international appeal of American society. Withdrawing from Iraq may not temper Anti-America abroad, but it will free us to pursue an international agenda that includes dealing with terrorism but also safeguards the commons from the other sources of twenty-first-century insecurity that damage lives and nations.

With the invasion of Iraq, the United States tested its power to overturn the existing order not only in Iraq but in the entire Middle East. Because of the virulence and human and economic toll of the insurgency, the experiment of bringing democracy to Iraq cannot be described as a success. Just as enthusiasts of free trade frequently remind skeptics (or the "losers" and their advocates) that in the long term, economic growth will benefit not only the short-term "winners" but all trade partners, the macro-historical time frame the Bush administration has chosen for judging the merits of its ambitious Iraq policy does not adequately account for its human, political, financial, and diplomatic costs in the short and medium term. And it is in the short and medium term, over the next ten years or so, when the United States and the international community will be forced to grapple with a number of daunting global issues outside of Iraq.

The balance of power in the world is now such that, measured by the capacity of the United States to influence other countries or populations to support it on a range of international issues, its power is waning just as a number of contenders for global weight are emerging to contest the gravitational pull of the single superpower. America's isolation in and over Iraq has given cause to rising powers—as well as to recruitment capacities of terrorist groups—to resist America just as U.S. leadership, credibility, and financial heft are needed to address the challenges of nuclear proliferation, the global or regional reach of China's economic, environmental, and military might, failing states, terrorism, infectious disease, environmental degradation, poverty, and illiteracy.

The spillover from Iraq did not have to be so pronounced. Despite his alliance with the United States in Iraq and the loss of parliamentary seats in the 2005 elections, Prime Minister Tony Blair managed to insulate and even enhance his and the United Kingdom's international credibility by simultaneously advancing serious proposals to deal with major global issues such as climate change, debt and poverty relief, and the Middle East. To be sure, Blair avoided some anti-UK backlash by not bearing the cross of being the world's superpower and by responding to his own domestic political pressures to lead on global issues. Despite its isolation in and over Iraq, the White House could, but has chosen not to, draw upon American power and the ample but untapped domestic political support to offer viable alternatives and compromises to global issues and thereby, like Blair, help to contain and compartmentalize the political spillover from Iraq.

The United States cannot lead in a vacuum, with fewer and fewer followers, reliant on power, GDP, and throw weight to have its way. The critical component the country needs to give the international community cause to desire and respect its leadership is legitimacy.[24] In the absence of solid evidence that the United States genuinely understands and ratifies the importance of being seen as a member, not an outsider, of the international community, progress on global issues will remain painfully slow.

One answer for the United States is to contemplate some dramatic policy reversals: joining the Kyoto Protocol, embracing the International Criminal Court, immediately dropping agricultural subsidies and other barriers to trade, and plowing unconditioned

billions into debt relief, poverty alleviation, and programs to prevent the spread of infectious diseases. Whatever the domestic political calculus, economic feasibility, or philosophical objections to
such policy directions, a course correction on these issues will help
defuse anti-Americanism among U.S. allies. Moreover, flexibility
on these global issues falls well within the range of the acceptable
for substantial numbers of Americans in both parties: In response
to a question about whether U.S. interests should be put first, 63
percent said America should cooperate with other countries, even
if that means occasionally compromising.[25] Because Anti-America
abroad is reinforced by specific and fundamental policy clashes,
even a demonstration, short of a full-court policy reversal, that the
United States respects and is willing to engage the perspective of
others on global issues or can offer credible alternatives will help
recover some of the political will and credibility we have lost in recent years.

    If Anti-America is in part a reaction to policies that derive
from a fundamental misreading of U.S. power, reducing anti-
American dissonance will require a course correction beyond
Iraq in the manner in which the United States is seen by others
to understand and use its power.

    Manners. First and foremost a sign of empathy toward others
and an awareness of cultural norms, manners have the effect of
allowing those with less or equal power to feel fully (even if
largely symbolically) respected. Manners, which include the ad-
mission of error, also give those with power a great deal more
latitude to increase, keep, share, or use power to achieve their interests.

    The decency, respect, and reciprocity associated with the idea
of good manners do not mean being nice for the sake of niceness:
These qualities embody a commonsense, pragmatic approach
that is critical to recovering U.S. credibility so that we can find
willing partners to pursue our priorities—whether controlling

proliferation and neutralizing terrorists, strengthening democracy, or integrating the world economy—and so that, whatever the outcome, the United States can be seen as plausibly interested in breaking the policy stalemate now impinging on so many critical global issues.

Rules and Fairness. The United States may never be a "permission slip" society, but there will come a day when it will need the help of the international community.[26] Because the world is increasingly transparent, governments from which the United States will need cooperation, especially regarding the use of force to deal with transnational security threats, will need to demonstrate to their populations that such military action is grounded in legality and thus is legitimate. Likewise, to the extent that the war on terror remains one long-term feature of the U.S. and international community's focus, the United States will need to ground its treatment of suspected terrorists in international law, not only to protect our own service personnel and those of other countries involved in such efforts but also to reduce the recruitment capacity of terrorist organizations. New stories circulating the globe about death or torture or sexual or psychological humiliation of Muslims and their symbols at the hands of U.S. soldiers may be less a deterrent than a call to arms against the United States and against the governments and political forces that are seen as working on America's behalf.

Rules and laws are never an end in themselves—they are tools that can inoculate the United States against its own temptations and empower others to regard U.S. power as legitimate, fair, and even necessary. Following the rules, respecting the institutions of others, obeying the law, and participating fairly in the reform of existing rules, laws, and international institutions provide a path to follow that will speak for itself, long before we figure out how to spend (or more likely waste) hundreds of millions of dollars on public diplomacy programs.

Empathy. In the half dozen major studies on public diplomacy that U.S. organizations have produced since the 9/11 attacks, a great deal of attention has been paid to the challenge the United States faces in getting its message heard above the din of the 24/7 satellite news/propaganda environment. It is time to recognize the obvious: Public diplomacy hasn't failed to remedy the U.S. image problem for lack of talented, well-meaning people. Public diplomacy alone simply cannot be expected to fix a problem that America's "communications" strategy, however flawed, poorly funded, and out-of-date, was not principally responsible for creating. It is high time we stop thinking about public diplomacy as mainly a mix of communications, messaging, branding, or explaining what America is about to skeptical and angry populations in the greater Muslim world and beyond. In the same vein as the value of expressing U.S. power within rather than outside of laws and institutions, in public diplomacy too much of America may not, on the surface, be a good thing. A long-term strategy for rebuilding trust might well reside not in financing still more programs to tell the world about ourselves and our good intentions but in expanding the level of education and thus the American public's comfort zone with the benefits to U.S. interests of engaging in multilateral institutions.

Government-funded public diplomacy programs can make some headway, but only when they complement the fundamentals of structure and policy outlined here. In the interim, people-to-people diplomacy, as quaint as it sounds, whether in the form of journalistic, cultural, educational, entrepreneurial, or humanitarian exchanges, is nothing to mock. Nor does educating an internationalist American public require hundreds of millions of dollars. Private-public partnerships can finance college- and university-based educational programs designed to send the up-and-coming generations of American scholars and analysts abroad to develop deep knowledge of foreign countries and cultures. As part of their corporate social responsibility initiatives, the American private sector and the American chambers of commerce can launch and sponsor internship programs that send Americans to companies overseas and that bring young people to American companies. Likewise, border-tightening security concerns that have overreached and kept foreign students out of American universities must be redressed, lest American universities lose their appeal against other English-speaking countries with less onerous visa requirements. And when law-abiding, opportunity-seeking foreign residents come to our consulates abroad to apply for visas to work in or visit the United States, an effort should be made to greet them not with concertina wire and thick glass but with enthusiasm, dignity, and respect.

Much hand-wringing over the lack of human intelligence about America's jihadist enemies followed the September 11 attacks. We still have not educated and trained enough Americans to help meet this demand. But for all the world's flatness, for all of globalization's expansion of the American "brand," the American people remain woefully detached from the motivations and worldviews of the countries—allies or rivals—upon whose cooperation American and international security, prosperity, and public health may very well depend.

There is something inherently humdrum—either naively American, or decidedly un-American even—about concluding a passionate depiction of the rise of Anti-America with an earnest lecture about the golden rule, manners, rules, fairness, empathy, foreign exchange programs, and the discourse of political leaders—the very standards many American communities, large and small, rural and urban, hold dear. That is because as deeply rooted as the foundations of Anti-America are, the "fixes" are not particularly complicated. For all of our foibles and quirks, Americans are problem solvers: We love to fix what's broken and generally have an optimistic "let's have an early breakfast and solve it" approach to even the toughest of problems. We want everything to come out okay in the end—to wake up one day and find that we are again liked, respected, and followed, not derided, feared, and dismissed.

Anti-America was not built overnight. Deflating it won't happen only with a withdrawal of U.S. troops from Iraq, a fat public diplomacy budget, or a convoluted bureaucratic reorganization. But the answer does not depend only on us. However respectful of others and their institutions the United States may eventually become, reducing the anti-American dissonance will also depend on our allies and partners allowing the United States to save face. I imagine that one reason George W. Bush hates to apologize or admit an error is because he suspects that acknowledging any crack in the American armor will uncork a cascade of self-congratulatory finger-wagging. To be sure, a certain amount of perversely delighted anti-Americanism will always color the context in which the United States functions, just as it always has.

But unlike during the Cold War when fits and starts of hardcore anti-Americanism arose over specific policies, this time it's different. And the risk of doing nothing to contain the friendly fire pales in comparison with the benefits for the United States and the world of our demonstrably, even democratically showing that our ears and eyes are open, no longer only to those who tell us what we want to hear but precisely to those who do not.

Anti-America, Latin America, and the Symbolism of Guantánamo

The United States obtained rights to the coaling station at Guantánamo Bay, Cuba, in 1903 through a lease agreement signed by President Theodore Roosevelt and pushed onto the Cuban government (whose president at the time was a U.S. citizen) by the passage of the Platt amendment. This amendment to the Cuban constitution gave Washington the right to intervene in Cuba in order to preserve Cuban independence; maintain "a government adequate for the protection of life, property, and individual liberty"; and uphold U.S. obligations under the Treaty of Paris ending the Spanish Civil War. Although Franklin Roosevelt abrogated the Platt amendment in 1934 as part of the Good Neighbor policy, the United States held on to the base, paying a nominal annual fee under the original terms that required the consent of both parties for termination but not for continuation.

Even before the 1959 revolution, Guantánamo became a symbol for Cubans of U.S. imperialism and violation of Cuban sovereignty. Over the course of the decades after the revolution, the Castro government demanded that the United States return the base to Cuba, and Fidel Castro stopped cashing the U.S. rent checks. Lore has it that Treasury Department payments accumulate each year, uncashed, in one of his desk drawers. During the Cold War, nationalists in Cuba and throughout Latin America on occasion cited America's retention of the base as a pernicious symbol of U.S. hegemony. But over the years, Guantánamo's symbolism lost its pungency both for Latin Americans and even within Cuba, where more pressing domestic and bilateral matters topped the government's agenda.

After the Cold War, planners at the Pentagon found little use for the base, and debates popped up in and out of government over whether to mothball it or otherwise reduce U.S. responsibilities and expenditures there. The United States had returned Subic Bay to Philippine sovereignty in 1992—why, many argued, not Guantánamo? The answer? Such a concession to a communist government was plainly unthinkable. And by the middle of the decade, after the Cuban economy crashed with the withdrawal of Soviet subsidies, and political upheaval roiled Haiti, the base came to serve an extremely practical, even humanitarian function by housing thousands of Cuban and Haitian refugees picked up at sea by the U.S. coast guard. By the end of the decade, military officers from the United States and Cuba met monthly to monitor safety and security procedures implemented by both countries at the gate separating the U.S. base from Cuban territory. Both countries routinely cited this cooperation as evidence of what might be possible should they broaden cooperation beyond the Guantánamo gate to other mutual security interests. By the beginning of the twenty-first century, the base had become less a symbol of U.S. imperialism or a cause to stir Cuban nationalism than an opportunity for the United States and Cuba to forge a more pragmatic relationship.

When the United States began to use Guantánamo in 2002 to interrogate and jail suspected terrorists who had been picked up by U.S. and allied forces in Afghanistan and Pakistan, the Cuban government was intent on demonstrating its law-and-order bona fides to the new Bush administration. Defense Minister Raúl Castro went so far as to hold a press conference on the Cuban side of the gate, declaring that the government of Cuba would cooperate in returning to U.S. custody any detainee caught attempting to escape to Cuban jurisdiction. This display of realpolitik was a far cry from the revolutionary anti-imperialist diatribes of the Cold War or the holier-than-thou resistance to U.S. resolutions condemning Cuba for prison and human rights abuse at annual gatherings of the United Nations Human Rights Commission. Indeed, until the war in Iraq, and especially until revelations of prisoner abuse at Abu Ghraib and the Cuban base came to light, neither the Cuban government nor many in Latin America made much of a peep about the new use of the Guantánamo facility.

But with America's image in shambles, the base—retained over the objection of the host nation and used for the indefinite detention of suspects in the war on terror, many of whom are citizens of countries closely allied with the United States—again emerged as a symbol of malignant U.S. power not only in Latin America but well beyond America's historic sphere. In a chapter of history pregnant with irony and meaning that even the most anti-American of observers could not have hoped to invent, a strategically useless military base on a strategically insignificant island in a region of the world that only a handful of years ago was poised to embrace U.S. leadership and values has become, for Latin Americans, the international community, and increasingly U.S. citizens themselves, a Jungian archetype of what has gone wrong with America. Yet, that the significance of Guantánamo could morph over time from negative to neutral to positive and back again to negative also suggests that although am-bivalence toward U.S. power and policies may well remain a part of the international landscape, the anti-American default need not become the defining feature of the twenty-first century. Pre-cisely because of Guantánamo's global symbolism and its negli-gible strategic utility, the United States would do well to begin the rest of the century by simply giving it back.

|

ACKNOWLEDGMENTS

|

At the Council on Foreign Relations where I have the good fortune of working, I am grateful to Richard N. Haass, the Council's president, and James M. Lindsay, vice president and director of studies, for their constructive and enthusiastic endorsement of this book and of my work. The Council's vice president for the Washington program, Nancy E. Roman, chaired my study group and cheered me on with careful and time-consuming reading, thoughtful counsel, and true friendship. My Council colleagues Rachel Bronson, Steven A. Cook, Elizabeth C. Economy, Lee Feinstein, Laurie Garrett, Lilita V. Gusts, Eric Heginbotham, Edward J. Lincoln, Walter Russell Mead, and William L. Nash offered me valuable and much appreciated feedback, insights, and friendship. Michael Marx McCarthy, Alex Sarly, and Sean Kimball provided crucial research assistance at different junctures of the project. Amanda Raymond worked tirelessly on this project from beginning to end: Her research, editing, and organizational skills were superb, for which I am truly grateful. In addition, my thanks go to Janine Hill, Jan Hughes, Jan Murray, Irina Faskianos, Lisa Shields, Patricia Dorff, Ashle Baxter, Charles Day, the library staff at the Council on Foreign Relations, and Linda Carlson and the library staff at the Johns Hopkins School of Advanced International Studies.

I am especially indebted to the members of my study group for their thoughtful comments: Elizabeth Frawley Bagley, Warren Bass, Robin Broad, Karen J. DeYoung, Joseph D. Duffey, Amitai Etzioni, Craig I. Fields, Bennett Freeman, Tom Gjelten, Roya Hakakian, Alexander S. Jutkowitz, Judith Kipper, Charles A. Kupchan, William M. LeoGrande, Carl E. Meacham, Theodore J. Piccone, Susan E. Rice, Tara Sonenshine, Alisa Stack-O'Connor, and Ray Takeyh. John G. Heimann, Jeffrey Goldberg, Erika Raskin, Marcus Raskin, Saul Landau, Fulton Armstrong, Kishore Mahbubani, Bernard W. Aronson, Nelson W. Cunningham, Jeffrey E. Garten, Rabbi Danny Zemel, Cari Eggspuehler, Keith Reinhard, Riordan Roett, Daniel William Christman, Peter Kornbluh, Robert O. Keohane, Richard Lapper, and Peter Katzenstein provided valuable insights as well. Carol Sweig and James Lawry read and edited numerous drafts with love and care.

Anne Petersen, of the William K. Kellogg Foundation, generously supported this project; Cristina Eguizabal of the Ford Foundation embraced this endeavor as she has others on previous occasions. Thanks go also to the Carnegie Corporation of New York.

Although writing a book is a solitary process, it would not have been possible without the intellectual support and loyal friendship of several individuals. The idea for this book arose in early 2003 from a series of conversations with two close friends, Leslie H. Gelb and Richard L. Plepler. Their enthusiasm gave me a real boost at the beginning; they helped me think through the argument and remained steadfast, thoughtful, and generous critics throughout. I am especially indebted to Les for his enduring support while president of the Council on Foreign Relations and since, his generous presence on the other end of the phone: His advice as a reader and as a mentor remains an unexpected and treasured gift. Marianne Szegedy-Maszak again saved the day with her genius ability to conceptualize even vaguely formed ideas. William A. Arkin came to my side in countless ways, whether in decoding war debates or as a virtuoso sounding board. At PublicAffairs, Peter L. W. Osnos and Susan Weinberg have my thanks for their endorsement of this effort and for their patience. My editor there, Clive Priddle, offered his exceptionally insightful advice and friendship at every turn. The guidance and friendship of my agent, Esther R. Newberg, have been invaluable.

Friendship and support of a different nature came from Heidi Bourne, Carol Sweig, James V. Lawry, Fritzie Seidler, Naomi Blumberg, Michael Sweig, Mary Thompson, Sara Thompson, Marisa de Andres, Jaimie Sanford, Jamin Raskin, Sarah Bloom Raskin, Janet Shenk, Janice O'Connell, Marcy Wilder, Aurie Hall, Edith Roberts, Mathea Falco, Joe Miller, Suzie Hurley, Marion Griffin, Bunny Kolodner, Richard Parker, Craig Faulks, Carole Horn, Daniel Gross, Steven Goldstein, and Jingyuan Gao—my gratitude goes to each of them.

I am blessed by the abundant humor, strength, and love of my husband, Reed Thompson, whose understanding, prodding, and endless patience make everything possible, including this book. And for the sunny love and remarkable forbearance of our children Isabel and Alexander, I am forever grateful.

Julia E. Sweig
Washington, D.C., January 2006

NOTES

INTRODUCTION

1. Dafna Linzer, "Nuclear Arms Inspectors Get Peace Prize: Nobel Committee Honors Work of Director and Staff of U.N. Agency," *Washington Post*, October 8, 2005.
2. "Pause for Thought," *The Times of London*, October 14, 2005.
3. *Lidove Noviny* (Czech Republic), cited by "Perception of America: International Media Response to Hurricane Katrina," Business for Diplomatic Action and Echo Research Group, September 2005, http://businessfordiplomaticaction.org/learn/articles/international_katrina_study_101905_final.ppt.
4. *Transatlantic Trends 2005* (Washington: German Marshall Fund, 2005); Standard Eurobarometer 63 / Spring 2005, TNS Opinion and Social, http://europa.eu.int/comm/public_opinion/inde_en.htm; "American Character Gets Mixed Reviews; U.S. Image Up Slightly, But Still Negative," Pew Global Attitudes Project, June 23, 2005; "What the World Thinks of America," *The Guardian* and others, October 15, 2004; Latinobarómetro, "The Image of the United States in Latin America," presented at *The Miami Herald*'s Americas Conference, September 2004.
5. Peter J. Katzenstein and Robert O. Keohane, eds., *Anti-Americanism in World Politics* (Ithaca, N.Y.: Cornell University Press, 2006). The authors correctly point out the difficulty of measuring intensity of anti-American views.
6. Barry Rubin, "The Real Roots of Arab Anti-Americanism," *Foreign Affairs*, November/December 2002, p. 73.
7. See also Fouad Ajami, "The Falseness of Anti-Americanism," *Foreign Policy*, September/October 2003. Writing before and during the war in Iraq, Fouad Ajami has been among the most ardent critics of the hypocrisy of anti-Americanism in the Arab world.

PART ONE

1. Alan McPherson, *Yankee No!: Anti-Americanism in U.S.–Latin American Relations* (Cambridge: Harvard University Press, 2003).
2. José Enrique Rodó, *Ariel* (Austin: University of Texas Press, 1988); José Martí, *Our America: Writings on Latin America and the Struggle for Cuban Independence* (New York: Monthly Press Review, 1977); José Martí, *Inside the Monster: Writ-*

ings on the United States and American Imperialism (New York: Monthly Review Press, 1975).

3. Piero Gleijeses, *Shattered Hope: The Guatemalan Revolution and the United States, 1944–1954* (Princeton, N.J.: Princeton University Press, 1991).

4. Douglas Farah, "War Study Censures Military in Guatemala; Panel Blames Army for Most Atrocities," *Washington Post,* February 26, 1999, p. A19.

5. Roger Morris, *Uncertain Greatness: Henry Kissinger and American Foreign Policy* (New York: Harper and Row, 1977), p. 241.

6. Eduardo H. Galeano and Cedric Belfrage, *Open Veins of Latin America: Five Centuries of the Pillage of a Continent* (New York: Monthly Review Press, 1973); Fernando Henrique Cardoso and Enzo Faletto, *Desarrollo y Dependencia en América Latina: Ensayo de Interpretación Sociológica* (Mexico City: Siglo Veintiuno Editores, 1969).

7. For evidence of international hostility not just toward the U.S. government but also the American people, see "In 18 of 21 Countries Polled, Most See Bush's Reelection as Negative for World Security," BBC World Service, January 19, 2005; "American Character Gets Mixed Reviews; U.S. Image Up Slightly, But Still Negative," Pew Global Attitudes Project, June 23, 2005.

8. Walter Lippman, "Today and Tomorrow: The Agitated Alliance," *Washington Post,* December 20, 1962. British intelligence sources believed for decades that the UK had helped diffuse the crisis by sending information to the White House suggesting only a limited Soviet missile presence in Cuba. But in 1992, retired Soviet generals revealed the opposite: that by October 1962, not only were missiles deployed on the island but thirty-six warheads intended for medium-range nuclear missiles, with the ability to reach U.S. territory, had already been armed and pointed toward the United States.

9. Kai Bird, *The Chairman* (New York: Simon and Schuster, 1992), p. 312.

10. John Lewis Gaddis, *We Now Know: Rethinking the Cold War* (New York: Oxford University Press, 1997).

11. The Hughes-Ryan amendment to the Foreign Assistance Act of 1974 (PL No. 93–559) states that "no funds may be expended by the Central Intelligence Agency for operations in foreign countries, other than those intended solely for obtaining necessary intelligence, unless the President makes specified findings and reports to specified Congressional committees." The Clark amendment reaffirmed the ban on military and other U.S. assistance to any armed group in Angola.

12. Richard B. Cheney: "Twenty years ago we had a similar situation in El Salvador. We had—guerrilla insurgency controlled roughly a third of the country, 75,000 people dead, and we held free elections. I was there as an observer on behalf of the Congress. The human drive for freedom, the determination of these people to vote, was unbelievable. And the terrorists would come in and shoot up polling places; as soon as they left, the voters would come back and get in line and would not be denied the right to vote. And today El Salvador is a whale of a lot better because we held free elections. The power of that concept is enormous. And it will apply in Afghanistan, and it will apply as well in Iraq." "The Cheney-Edwards Vice Presidential Debate," Case Western Reserve University, Cleve-

land, October 5, 2004, http://www.debates.org/pages/trans2004b.html; Jonathan D. Tepperman, "Flash Back: Salvador in Iraq," *New Republic*, April 11, 2005.

13. Timothy Garton Ash, *Free World: America, Europe, and the Surprising Future of the West* (New York: Random House, 2004); Niall Ferguson, "A World Without Power," *Foreign Policy Magazine*, July/August 2004; Richard Haass, "By Invitation: Richard Haass on American Foreign Policy Agenda," *The Economist*, November 4, 2004; Charles A. Kupchan, "Rethinking the Western Alliance?" Salon.com, November 13, 2004; Fareed Zakaria, "Hating America," *Foreign Policy Magazine*, September/October 2004.

14. "American Character Gets Mixed Reviews; U.S. Image Up Slightly, But Still Negative," Pew Global Attitudes Project, June 23, 2005.

15. David W. Ellwood, "The American Challenge Renewed: U.S. Cultural Power and Europe's Identity Debates," *Brown Journal of World Affairs*, Winter/Spring 1997; David W. Ellwood, "Anti-Americanism in Western Europe: A Comparative Perspective," Occasional paper no. 3, European Studies Seminar Series, Johns Hopkins University Bologna Center, April 1999.

16. Latinobarómetro, "The Image of the United States in Latin America," presented at *The Miami Herald*'s Americas Conference, September 2004; University of Miami School of Business Administration and Zogby International, Latin America Elite Poll, 2003–2005, http://www.zogby.com; Pablo Bachelet, "Latin America's Elites Embrace Chilean Leader; Groups in Six Latin American Nations Admire Chilean President Lagos, Dislike President Bush and Back Free Trade," *Miami Herald*, September 25, 2005.

17. See, for example, Barry Lynn, *End of the Line: The Rise and Coming Fall of the Global Corporation* (New York: Doubleday, 2005); and Jeff Faux, *The Global Class War: How America's Bipartisan Elite Lost Our Future* (New York: Wiley, 2005).

18. Walden Bello, "What Is the IMF's Agenda for Asia?" Focus on the Global South, 1998, http://www.focusweb.org; Walden Bello, testimony before the House Banking and Financial Services Committee, Banking Oversight Subcommittee, April 21, 1998.

19. United Nations Online Network in Public Administration and Finance (UN-PAN), Statistical Database: Basic Data on Government Expenditure and Taxation, 1990–2002.

20. For a flavor of the debate over economic globalization, poverty, and America's role, see, for example, David Dollar and Aart Kraay, "Growth *Is* Good for the Poor," World Bank Development Research Group, 2000; Mark Weisbrot et al., "Growth May Be Good for the Poor—But are IMF and World Bank Policies Good for Growth? A Closer Look at the World Bank's Recent Defense of Its Policies," Center for Economic and Policy Research, May 2001; Dani Rodrik, *Has Globalization Gone Too Far?* (Washington, D.C.: Institute for International Economics, 1997). For a recent collection with contributions from Dollar, Rodrik, and Joseph Stiglitz, among others, see Michael Weinstein, ed., *Globalization: What's New?* (New York: Columbia University Press, 2005).

21. Jeff Faux, "Rethinking the Global Political Economy," speech, Asia-Europe-

U.S. Scholar's Forum: "Globalization and Innovation of Politics," Japan, April 11–13, 2002.

22. William Jefferson Clinton, "Remarks by the US President Clinton to the Joint Session of Indian Parliament," New Delhi, March 22, 2000, http://www.indianembassy.org/indusrel/clinton_india/clinton_parliament_march_22_2000. htm.

23. "American Character Gets Mixed Reviews; U.S. Image Up Slightly, But Still Negative," Pew Global Attitudes Project, June 23, 2005; "In 18 of 21 Countries Polled, Most See Bush's Reelection as Negative for World Security," BBC World Service, January 19, 2005; "La Opinión Pública Argentina sobre Política Exterior y Defensa," Consejo Argentino para las Relaciones Internacionales (CARI), 2002; Latinobarómetro, "The Image of the United States in Latin America," presented at *The Miami Herald*'s Americas Conference, September 2004; Mario Osava, "Latam: Anti-'Yanqui' Feelings Spurred by Unpopular War," Inter-Press Service, March 27, 2003.

24. Peter Waldman, "Power and Peril: America's Supremacy and Its Limits. Heavy Hand: Washington's Tilt to Business Stirs a Backlash in Indonesia," *Wall Street Journal*, February 11, 2004.

25. Paul Blustein, *The Chastening: Inside the Crisis That Rocked the Global Financial System and Humbled the IMF* (New York: Public Affairs, 2001); Paul Blustein, *And the Money Kept Rolling In (and Out)* (New York: Public Affairs, 2005); Kishore Mahbubani, *Beyond the Age of Innocence: A Worldly View of America* (New York: Perseus Books, 2005). Only the concrete evidence of U.S. assistance after the 2005 tsunami began to soften Indonesian public opinion, even though of the official U.S. commitment of $350 million, only $100 million had been disbursed by fall 2005, according to USAID's Web page on tsunami assistance, http://www.usaid.gov/locations/asia_near_east/tsunami.

26. Richard J. Barnet, *Global Reach: The Power of the Multinational Corporations* (New York: Simon and Schuster, 1974); John Cavanagh and Richard J. Barnet, *Global Dreams: Imperial Corporations and the New World Order* (New York: Simon and Schuster, 1994).

27. Robin Broad, ed., *Global Backlash: Citizen Initiatives for a Just World Economy* (New York: Rowman and Littlefield, 2002).

28. Nancy Birdsall and Augusto de la Torre, *Washington Contentious: Economic Policies for Social Equity in Latin America* (Washington, D.C.: Carnegie Endowment for International Peace and the Inter-American Dialogue, 2001); Jagdish Bhagwati, *In Defense of Globalization* (New York: Oxford Press, 2004).

29. Walden Bello, "Implications of Cancun," September 23, 2003, http://www.zmag.org; see also opinions posted at http://ftaaresistance.org/Mambo and http://www.citizen.org/trade.

30. *Freedom in the World 2005: Civic Power and Electoral Politics* (Washington: Freedom House, 2005).

31. According to Timothy Naftali in *Blind Spot*, at the beginning of the Clinton administration "half of the members of the [National Security Council] staff who covered terrorism were let go." Vice President Gore's National Security Adviser Leon Fuerth told Naftali in an interview that "terrorism was a prob-

lem elsewhere in the world." And Winston Wiley, the deputy chief of the Counterterrorism Center at the CIA in the early 1990s, also told Naftali that "terrorism was considered a dead issue" during his tenure. See Timothy Naftali, *Blind Spot: The Secret History of American Counterterrorism* (New York: Basic Books, 2005), p. 228; author interview with William Arkin, author of *Code Names: Deciphering U.S. Military Plans, Programs, and Operations in the 9/11 World* (Hanover, N.H.: Steerforth, 2005), October 17, 2005; Michael Sheuer, *Imperial Hubris: Why the West Is Losing the War on Terror* (Dulles, Va.: Potomac Books, 2004).

32. President Theodore Roosevelt's Annual Message to Congress, December 6, 1904; "The National Security Strategy of the United States of America," September 2002, http://www.whitehouse.gov/nsc/nss.html.

33. See the U.S. Senate Committee on Foreign Relations website, http://foreign. senate.gov, for the posted testimony from current and former government officials during April 2005 hearings, which suggested government analysts were subjected to political pressures. See also Richard A. Clarke, *Against All Enemies: Inside America's War on Terror* (New York: Free Press, 2004); Ron Suskind, *The Price of Loyalty: George W. Bush, the White House, and the Education of Paul O'Neill* (New York: Simon and Schuster, 2004).

34. The Iraq Resolution (Public Law 107–243) passed by a 77–23 vote in the Senate and a 296–133 vote in the House and was signed into law by President Bush on October 16, 2002.

35. For polling data on international public opinion of the United States and Americans since the reelection of George W. Bush, see "In 18 of 21 Countries Polled, Most See Bush's Reelection as Negative for World Security," BBC World Service, January 19, 2005; polling conducted by the Program on International Policy Attitudes at the University of Maryland and Globescan; Security and Peace Institute and Marttila Communications Group, "American Attitudes Toward National Security, Foreign Policy, and the War on Terror," April 13, 2005. For information on the lack of trust in U.S. companies, see Edelman, "Sixth Annual Edelman Trust Barometer: A Global Study of Opinion Leaders," January 24, 2005, http://www.edelman.com/news/ShowOne. asp?ID=57.

36. For examples, see World Press Review, http://www.worldpress.org; WatchingAmerica.com, www.watchingamerica.com; Middle East Media Research Institute, www.memri.org; Foreign Broadcast Information Service, LexisNexis, http://www.lexisnexis.com; U.S. Department of State's International Information Programs Foreign Media Reaction, http://usinfo.state. gov/products/medreac.htm; and Jefferson Morley's World Opinion Columns in the *Washington Post*'s online editions, www.washingtonpost.com.

37. David Cole, *Enemy Aliens: Double Standards and Constitutional Freedoms in the War on Terrorism* (New York: New Press, 2003).

38. Barton Gellman and Walter Pincus, "Depiction of Threat Outgrew Supporting Evidence," *Washington Post*, August 10, 2003, p. A1; Frank Rich, "It's Bush-Cheney, Not Rove-Libby," *New York Times*, October 16, 2005; Secretary Condoleezza Rice, interview on *Meet the Press* with Tim Russert, October 16,

2005, http://www.state.gov/secretary/rm/2005/55171.htm; White House, "President Discusses War on Terror at National Endowment for Democracy," Ronald Reagan Building and International Trade Center, Washington, D.C., October 6, 2005, http://www.whitehouse.gov/news/releases/2005/10/20051006 –3.html.

39. Michael Lind, "The Weird Men Behind George W. Bush's War," *New Statesman*, April 7, 2003; White House, "Remarks by the President at the 20th Anniversary of the National Endowment for Democracy," United States Chamber of Commerce, November 6, 2003, http://www.whitehouse.gov/news/releases/2003/11/20031106–3.html.

40. White House, "President Discusses War on Terror and Upcoming Iraqi Elections," Park Hyatt Philadelphia, Philadelphia, Pa., December 12, 2005, http://whitehouse.gov/news/releases/2005/12/20051212–4.html.

41. "Americans on Promoting Democracy," Chicago Council on Foreign Relations and Program on International Policy Attitudes (PIPA), September 29, 2005; Better World Campaign and Public Opinion Strategies, "Presentation of Key Findings from a National Survey of 800 Registered Voters, with 514 Well Informed Voters Conducted July 6–11, 2004," on the Image of the United Nations; Security and Peace Institute and Marttila Communications Group, "American Attitudes Toward National Security, Foreign Policy, and the War on Terror," April 13, 2005.

42. Pew Center for the People and the Press and the Council on Foreign Relations, "Foreign Policy Attitudes Now Driven by 9/11 and Iraq; Eroding Respect for America Seen as Major Problem," August 18, 2004.

43. Gary Langer, "Poll: Bush Approval Hits New Low," ABC News, November 3, 2005.

44. Michael Lind, *Made in Texas: George W. Bush and the Southern Takeover of American Politics* (New York: New America and Basic Books, 2003). For information on the Christian evangelical mission to spread its message abroad, see the National Association of Evangelicals Web site, http://www.nae.net/index.cfm?FUSEACTION=nae.valuesl; "Event Transcript: Ministering to Those in Need: The Rights and Wrongs of Missions and Humanitarian Assistance in Iraq," Pew Forum on Religion and Public Life, Washington, D.C., June 4, 2003, http://pewforum.org/events/index.php?EventID=46.

45. For a discussion on the relation of Christian evangelical thinking to market orthodoxy, see Gordon Bigelow, "Let There Be Markets: The Evangelical Roots of Economics," *Harper's Magazine* 310, no. 1860, May 1, 2005; William E. Connolly, "The Evangelical-Capitalist Resonance Machine," *Political Theory* 33, no. 6 (December 2005).

46. "American Character Gets Mixed Reviews; U.S. Image Up Slightly, But Still Negative," Pew Global Attitudes Project, June 23, 2005.

47. White House, "President Commemorates 60th Anniversary of V-J Day," Naval Air Station North Island, San Diego, Calif., August 30, 2005, http://www.whitehouse.gov/news/releases/2005/08/20050830–1.html.

48. The United States has not signed or ratified the "Protocol against the Illicit Manufacturing of and Trafficking in Firearms, Their Parts and Components

and Ammunition, supplementing the United Nations Convention against Transnational Organized Crime," and has not ratified the Inter-American Convention Against Illicit Manufacturing of and Trafficking in Firearms, Ammunitions, Explosives, and Other Related Materials (CIFTA).

49. For examples of foreign press commentary on the U.S. gun culture and gun laws, see "Shame of the U.S. Gun Lobby," *Scottish Daily Record*, January 17, 2005, p. 8; Alex Contreras Baspineiro, "Eduardo Galeano: 'La guerra antidrogas es una gran hipocresía del imperio,'" *Narco News Bulletin*, November 8, 2004, http://narconews.com/Issue35/articulo1122.html.

50. Jagdish Bhagwati et al., "The Muddles over Outsourcing," *Journal of Economic Perspectives*, Fall 2004; Paul A. Samuelson, "Where Ricardo and Mill Rebut and Confirm Arguments of Mainstream Economists Supporting Globalization," *Journal of Economic Perspectives*, Summer 2004; Aaron Bernstein, "Shaking up Trade Theory," *Business Week*, December 6, 2004.

51. "Meritocracy in America: Ever Higher Society, Ever Harder to Ascend," *The Economist*, January 5, 2005; Janny Scott and David Leonhardt, "Class in America: Shadowy Lines that Still Divide," *New York Times*, May 15, 2005.

52. Mark Leonard, *Why Europe Will Run the Twenty-first Century* (New York: Public Affairs, 2005), pp. 71–74.

53. Gary Younge, "Left to Sink or Swim: Tragic Events in New Orleans Have Laid Bare America's Bigotry and Exposed the Lie of Equal Opportunity," *The Guardian*, September 5, 2005; Arvind Sivaramakrishnan, "America's Shame: The Aftermath of Katrina," *The Hindu*, September 7, 2005; "Katrina Reveals Political Failure and Citizen Heroes," *Der Spiegel Online*, trans. by World News Connection, September 8, 2005; "More Powerful Than a Superpower," *Milliyet* (Turkey), trans. by World News Connection, September 3, 2005.

54. "Two-in-Three Critical of Bush's Relief Efforts; Huge Racial Divide over Katrina and Its Consequences," Pew Center for the People and the Press, September 8, 2005; "Katrina Relief Effort Raises Concern over Excessive Spending, Waste; Growing Number Sees U.S. Divided Between 'Haves' and 'Have-Nots,'" Pew Center for the People and the Press, October 19, 2005.

55. Pew Center for the People and the Press and the Council on Foreign Relations, "Foreign Policy Attitudes Now Driven by 9/11 and Iraq; Eroding Respect for America Seen as Major Problem," August 18, 2004; Pew Center for the People and the Press and the Council on Foreign Relations, "America's Place in the World 2005," November 17, 2005.

56. Neil A. Lewis, "U.S. Court Asserts Authority over American in Saudi Jail," *New York Times*, December 17, 2004; Jane Mayer, "Outsourcing Torture; Annals of Justice," *New Yorker*, February 14, 2005.

57. David Cole, *Enemy Aliens: Double Standards and Constitutional Freedoms in the War on Terrorism* (New York: New Press, 2003).

PART TWO

1. Yongshik Bong, "Yongmi: Pragmatic Anti-Americanism in South Korea," Brown Journal of World Affairs 10, no. 2, Winter/Spring 2004, pp. 153–165.
2. For surveys of international media coverage, see Media Tenor International, http://www.mediatenor.com; World News Coverage, http://wnc.dialog.com; World Press, http://www.worldpress.org; Newseum, http://www.newseum. org; and the Middle East Media Research Institute, http://www.memri.org.
3. Chris Giles, "Central Banks Shift Funds Away from US," *Financial Times*, January 24, 2005.
4. *Views of a Changing World*, Pew Global Attitudes Project, June 2003.
5. *Transatlantic Trends 2004* (Washington: German Marshall Fund, 2004); Globescan and the Program on International Policy Attitudes (PIPA) of the University of Maryland, "In 20 of 23 Countries Polled Citizens Want Europe to Be More Influential Than US," April 2005.
6. For Jordan, see *Views of a Changing World*, Pew Global Attitudes Project, June 2003; for Egypt and Saudi Arabia, see *Impressions of America [or] Americans 2004*, Zogby International and the Arab American Institute, 2004.
7. For other polling data, see Pew Global Attitudes Project; Globescan and the Program on International Policy Attitudes (PIPA) of the University of Maryland, "In 20 of 23 Countries Polled Citizens Want Europe to Be More Influential Than US," April 2005; Globescan, "World Public Opinion Says World Not Going in Right Direction," June 4, 2004; "What the World Thinks of America," *The Guardian* and others, October 15, 2004; Latinobarómetro, "The Image of the United States in Latin America," presented at *The Miami Herald*'s Americas Conference, September 2004; Centro de Investigación y Docencia Económicas y el Consejo Mexicano de Asuntos Internacionales, *Global Views 2004: Mexican Public Opinion and Foreign Policy*, September 2004; Eric V. Larson et al., "Ambivalent Allies? A Study of South Korean Attitudes Toward the U.S.," Rand Corporation, March 2004; German Marshall Fund, *Transatlantic Trends 2004, World Views 2002, Transatlantic Trends 2003*; Standard Eurobarometer 62 / Autumn 2004—TNS Opinion and Social, http://europa.eu.int/comm/public opinion/index en.htm.
8. For Germany and Great Britain, see "A Year After Iraq War: Mistrust of America in Europe Ever Higher, Muslim Anger Persists," Pew Global Attitudes Project, March 16, 2004; for Indonesia, see: *Views of a Changing World*, Pew Global Attitudes Project, 2003.
9. "In 18 of 21 Countries Polled, Most See Bush's Reelection as Negative for World Security," BBC World Service, January 19, 2005.
10. *Daily Mirror*, November 4, 2004.
11. *Being American* (Chicago: Research International, 2004); "Half of European Consumers Distrust American Companies," GMI Poll, December 27, 2004; "European Backlash: International Consumers Shun American Brands," Global Market Insite, November 22, 2004; NOP World polls, http://www.nopworld.com.
12. I have Keith Reinhard, president of Business for Diplomatic Action and chairman of DDB Worldwide, to thank for this observation.

13. NOP World polling, 2003–2004, http://www.nopworld.com; for citations of NOP data, see Ruth Mortimer, "Yankee Doodle Branding," *Brand Strategy,* December/January 2005, http://www.nopworld.com/content/hottopics/hot_19.pdf.

14. *Nation Brands Index,* Anholt-GMI, 2005 Q2, http://www.nationbrandindex.com.

15. "Half of European Consumers Distrust American Companies," GMI Poll, December 27, 2004.

16. *Being American* (Chicago: Research International, 2004).

17. Douglas B. Holt, John A. Quelch, and Earl L. Taylor, "How Global Brands Compete," *Harvard Business Review,* September 2004. See, for example, proceedings of the *2005 Partnership Conference: Corporate Citizenship and the Global Economy,* U.S. Chamber of Commerce, Washington D.C., May 19–20, 2005, http://www.uschamber.com/events/ViewEvent.htm?eventID=352. For attitudes of American corporate leaders, see "Zogby International Business for Diplomatic Action Global Listening Research Project, Phase I: Report on Corporate and Foreign Policy Opinion Leaders' Views on Anti-American Sentiment," Zogby International, Fall 2005, http://businessfordiplomaticaction.org/index.php.

18. NOP World polls, 2003 and 2004; "Half of European Consumers Distrust American Companies," GMI Poll, December 27, 2004; Edelman, "Sixth Annual Edelman Trust Barometer: A Global Study of Opinion Leaders," January 24, 2005, http://www.edelman.com/news/ShowOne.asp?ID=57.

19. White House Office of the Press Secretary, "Press Briefing by Ari Fleischer," March 20, 2003, http://www.whitehouse.gov/news/releases/2003/03/200303 20–3.html.

20. "Country Reports on Human Rights Practices," U.S. Department of State, Bureau of Democracy, Human Rights, and Labor, 2002; "Annual Freedom in the World Country Scores 2001–2002," Freedom House, 2002.

21. Thirty-six countries sent troops, medical teams, and/or military equipment during the first Gulf War, including ten countries that made significant troop contributions of more than 1,000 troops each. In total, more than 160,000 non-U.S. troops participated in Operation Desert Storm. In addition, more than $270 billion in cash and in-kind donations was contributed by non-U.S. partners. See GlobalSecurity.org, "Operation Desert Storm."

22. "Iraq Involvement, Bad Economic News Hits Australian Leader's Popularity," *Agence France Presse,* March 15, 2005; Ivan Cook, *Australians Speak 2005: Public Opinion and Foreign Policy* (Sydney: Lowy Institute for International Policy, March 2005).

23. The Paris Club agreement with Iraq was signed on November 21, 2004, by members Australia, Austria, Belgium, Canada, Denmark, Finland, France, Germany, Italy, Japan, the Netherlands, the Republic of Korea, the Russian Federation, Spain, Sweden, Switzerland, the United Kingdom, and the United States. The Paris Club is an informal group of official creditors who have sought since 1956 to find sustainable solutions to the payment difficulties experienced by debtor nations through rescheduling debt. See www.clubdeparis.org/en.

24. Globescan and the Program on International Policy Attitudes (PIPA) of the University of Maryland, "In 20 of 23 Countries Polled Citizens Want Europe to Be More Influential Than US," April 2005.

25. Ivan Krastev, "Anti-Americanism in Eastern and Central Europe Before and After 1989," paper presented at a Central European University Conference, "Past and Present: Is There Anything New with Anti-Americanism Today?" December 11, 2004.

26. According to the most recent Pew polling data, only India, Poland, Canada, Great Britain, and Russia of the sixteen countries polled showed majorities rating the United States favorably. See "American Character Gets Mixed Reviews; U.S. Image Up Slightly, But Still Negative," Pew Global Attitudes Project, June 23, 2005.

27. On the postwar U.S.-Japanese relationship, see Glenn D. Hook et al., *Japan's International Relations: Politics, Economics, and Security* (New York: Routledge, 2001).

28. My thanks go to my colleagues Eric Heginbotham and Edward J. Lincoln for sharing with me their insights on Japan.

29. Philippe Roger, *The American Enemy: The History of French Anti-Americanism*, trans. Sharon Bowman (Chicago: University of Chicago Press, 2005).

30. Clive Davis, "The Very British Broadcasting Corporation," *In the National Interest*, February 25, 2004.

31. John Dumbrell, *A Special Relationship: Anglo-American Relations in the Cold War and After* (New York: St. Martin's Press, 2001), p. 14.

32. Clement R. Attlee, "Britain and America; Common Aims, Different Opinions," *Foreign Affairs*, January 1954, p. 200–201.

33. Jonathan Freedland, *Bring Home the Revolution: The Case for a British Republic* (London: Fourth Estate, 1999).

34. Harold Pinter, "The American Administration Is a Bloodthirsty Wild Animal," speech at the University of Turin, published in the *Daily Telegraph*, December 11, 2002.

35. Tony Blair, speech on the Doctrine of the International Community at the Economic Club, Chicago, April 13, 1999, http://www.number–10.gov.uk/output/Page1297.asp.

36. Tony Blair, speech on the threat of global terrorism, March 5, 2004, http://www.number–10.gov.uk/output/Page5461.asp.

37. *Views of a Changing World*, Pew Global Attitudes Project, June 2003.

38. Alan Travis and Patrick Wintour, "Votes Reject Tory Hopefuls," *The Guardian*, October 21, 2003; Guardian Opinion Poll, *The Guardian*-ICM Research Limited, April 2003, http://politics.guardian.co.uk/polls.

39. Margaret Drabble, "I Loathe America, and What It Has Done to the Rest of the World," *Daily Telegraph*, August 5, 2003.

40. "In 18 of 21 Countries Polled, Most See Bush's Reelection as Negative for World Security," BBC World Service, January 19, 2005; "MORI Political Monitor February," Market and Opinion Research International, February 24, 2005, http://www.mori.com/polls/2005/mpm050221.shtml.

41. "American Character Gets Mixed Reviews; U.S. Image Up Slightly, But Still Negative," Pew Global Attitudes Project, June 23, 2005; "MORI Political

Monitor," Market and Opinion Research International, August and September 2005, http://www.mori.com/polls/index.shtml.

42. William Shawcross, "Stop This Racism," *The Guardian*, September 17, 2001, http://www.netribution.co.uk/news/industry_buzz/84/2.html.

43. Confidential minutes from July 23, 2002, meeting, available from the *Times* at http://www.timesonline.co.uk/article/0,,2087-1593607,00.html; Attorney General's Confidential Memo, March 7, 2003, available from *BBC News* at http://news.bbc.co.uk/1/shared/bsp/hi/pdfs/28_04_05_attorney_general.pdf.

44. "Methode Wild-West," *Stern*, October 20, 2004.

45. Martin Walser and Zvi Rex, quoted in Stephen F. Szabo, *Parting Ways: The Crisis in German-American Relations* (Washington, D.C.: Brookings Institution, 2004), p. 111, 114.

46. During her tenure as national security adviser, Condoleezza Rice advised that the United States "punish France, ignore Germany, and forgive Russia" in response to their stances at the United Nations over going to war in Iraq. See Anne Applebaum, "Memo to Bush: Europe Is Listening," *Washington Post*, May 28, 2003, p. A19.

47. For an analysis of this generation's perspective on the use of force, see Paul Berman, *Power and the Idealists: Or, The Passion of Joschka Fischer and Its Aftermath* (Brooklyn, N.Y.: Soft Skull Press, 2005).

48. Stephen F. Szabo, *Parting Ways: The Crisis in German-American Relations* (Washington, D.C.: Brookings Institution, 2004), p. 114.

49. Ibid., pp. 123–130.

50. "In 18 of 21 Countries Polled, Most See Bush's Reelection as Negative for World Security," BBC World Service, January 19, 2005.

51. "Ocalan: Greeks Supplied Kurdish Rebels," *BBC News*, June 2, 1999, http://news.bbc.co.uk/1/hi/world/europe/358115.stm; "Terrorism Questions and Answers: Kurdistan Workers' Party," Council on Foreign Relations, http://cfr terrorism.org/groups/kurdistan2.html.

52. "Report on Allegations of Human Rights Abuses by the Turkish Military and on the Situation in Cyprus," U.S. Department of State, 1995.

53. Kemal Kirisci, "Post–Cold War Turkish Security and the Middle East," *Middle East Review of International Affairs*, July 1997.

54. *Views of a Changing World*, Pew Global Attitudes Project, June 2003.

55. For information on anti-Americanism in the Turkish media, see the website of the Middle East Media Research Institute, http://memri.org.

56. Robert L. Pollock, "The Sick Man of Europe—Again," *Wall Street Journal*, February 16, 2005.

57. The award-winning novelist Orhan Pamuk, author of *Snow*, *My Name Is Red*, and *Istanbul*, faces three years in jail for charges of "public denigration" of Turkish identity over comments critical of these episodes in Turkish history. "The Turkish Identity," *New York Times*, September 10, 2005, p. A26.

58. Don Oberdorfer, *Two Koreas: A Contemporary History* (Reading, Pa.: Addison-Wesley, 1997), p. 6.

59. John Kie-chiang Oh, "Anti-Americanism and Anti-Authoritarian Politics in Korea," in Ilpyong J. Kim, ed., *Two Koreas in Transition: Implications for U.S. Policy* (Rockville, Md.: InDepth Books, 1998), p. 250.

Notes

60. USAID Overseas Loans and Grants [Greenbook], available at http://qesdb. cdie.org/gbk/home.html.
61. Kim Hyung-jin, "Parliamentary Session Paralyzed After MDP Lawmaker Lambasted Opposition Leader Lee," *Korea Herald*, February 19, 2002.
62. Aidan Foster Carter, "Roh Gets a Second Chance in South Korea," *Financial Times*, April 19, 2004.
63. "International Public Concern About North Korea: But Growing Anti-Americanism in South Korea," Pew Research Center for the People and Press, August 22, 2003.
64. "Sino–South Korea Trade to Top US$100 Bln in 2005," *Asia Pulse*, September 7, 2005.
65. Poll carried out by Research and Research (Seoul), cited by Jong-Heon Lee, "Analysis: S. Korea's Dual Image," United Press International, January 23, 2004.
66. Eric V. Larson et al., "Ambivalent Allies? A Study of South Korean Attitudes Toward the U.S.," Rand Corporation, March 2004; Lee Sook-jong, "Generational Change in South Korea: Implications for the U.S.-ROK Alliance," in Derek J. Mitchell, ed., *Strategy and Sentiment: South Korean Views of the United States and the U.S.-ROK Alliance* (Washington, D.C.: Center for Strategic and International Studies, 2004).
67. Paul Blustein, *And the Money Kept Rolling In (and Out)* (New York: Public Affairs, 2005), p. 4.
68. White House, "Press Briefing with Ari Fleischer," April 12, 2002, http://www. whitehouse.gov/news/releases/2002/04/20020412–1.html; Philip T. Reeker, Press Statement, U.S. Department of State, Washington, D.C., April 12, 2002, http://www.state.gov/r/pa/prs/ps/2002/9316.htm; "IRI President Folsom Praises Venezuelan Civil Society's Defense of Democracy," PR Newswire, April 12, 2002.
69. Peter Kornbluh, *The Pinochet File: A Declassified Dossier on Atrocity and Accountability* (New York: New Press, 2003); John Dinges, *The Condor Years: How Pinochet and His Allies Brought Terrorism to Three Continents* (New York: New Press, 2004).

PART THREE

1. Many such studies have been released in the years since 9/11. See *Report of the Defense Science Board Task Force on Strategic Communication*, September 2004, http://www.acq.osd.mil/dsb; U.S. Government Accountability Office Report, "U.S. Public Diplomacy: Interagency Coordination Efforts Hampered by the Lack of a National Communication Strategy," April 2005; Report of the U.S. Advisory Group on Public Diplomacy for the Arab and Muslim World, "Changing Minds, Winning Peace: A New Direction for U.S. Public Diplomacy in the Arab and Muslim World," chaired by Edward Djerejian, October 2003; *Public Diplomacy: How to Think About and Improve It*, Rand Corporation, October 2004; Report of the Subcommittee on Public-Private Partnerships and Public Diplomacy to the State Department Advisory Committee on In-

ternational Economic Policy, June 2003; *Finding America's Voice: A Strategy for Reinvigorating U.S. Public Diplomacy*, Council on Foreign Relations, 2003; Craig Charney and Nicole Yakatan, *A New Beginning: Strategies for a More Fruitful Dialogue with the Muslim World*, Council on Foreign Relations, May 2005.

2. Steven R. Weisman, "Turkish Women, Too, Have Words with U.S. Envoy (on Iraq War)," *New York Times*, September 29, 2005, p. A10; Glenn Kessler, "Turks Challenge Hughes on Iraq: Female Activists Decry U.S. Policy," *Washington Post*, September 29, 2004, p. A16.

3. *Report of the Defense Science Board Task Force on Strategic Communication*, September 2004, http://www.acq.osd.mil/dsb.

4. *The 9/11 Commission Report: Final Report of the National Commission on Terrorist Attacks upon the United States*, Report of the National Commission on Terrorist Attacks (New York: W. W. Norton, 2004), see especially pp. 375–379.

5. Michael Ignatieff, *American Exceptionalism and Human Rights* (Princeton, N.J.: Princeton University Press, 2005), p. 1.

6. Henry A. Kissinger, "Implementing Bush's Vision," *Washington Post*, May 16, 2005.

7. Edmund S. Morgan, "The Other Founders," *New York Review of Books*, September 22, 2005; Lynne V. Cheney, "The End of History," *Wall Street Journal*, October 20, 1994, p. A22; Gary B. Nash, Charlotte Crabtree, and Ross E. Dunn, *History on Trial: Culture Wars and the Teaching of the Past* (New York: Knopf, 1997); Edward T. Linenthal and Tom Engelhardt, eds., *History Wars: The Enola Gay and Other Battles for the American Past* (New York: Metropolitan Books, 1996); James W. Loewen, *Lies My Teacher Told Me* (New York: Simon and Schuster, 1995).

8. Ben Feller, "Education Secretary Condemns Public Show with Gay Characters," Associated Press, January 25, 2005; Kaitlin Bell, "Funding for PBS Hinging on War of Ideology; Senate Panel to Tackle Budget as Partisan Debate Heightens," *Boston Globe*, July 11, 2005, p. A3.

9. E-mail to author, Thomas S. Blanton, Director, National Security Archive, George Washington University, September 26, 2005.

10. For a fuller discussion, see John L. Harper, *American Machiavelli: Alexander Hamilton and the Origins of U.S. Foreign Policy* (New York: Cambridge University Press, 2004), from Pacificus no. 4, July 10, 1793, in Harold C. Syrett and Jacob C. Cooke, eds., *The Papers of Alexander Hamilton* (New York: Columbia University Press, 1961–1987), Vol. 15, 82–86.

11. Richard Black, "Climate Pact: For Good or Bad?" *BBC News Online*, July 28, 2005, http://news.bbc.co.uk/1/hi/sci/tech/4725681.htm; "Asia-Pacific Partnership for Clean Development and Climate (APP)," U.S. Department of State, http://www.state.gov/g/oes/climate/c16054.htm; "Innovative Policy Solutions to Global Climate Change," *In Brief*, no. 8, Pew Center on Global Climate Change, http://www.pewclimate.org/docUploads/InBrief04%2Epdf.

12. Immanuel Kant, *Perpetual Peace* (New York: Liberal Arts Press, 1957). For a contemporary exposition of the theory of democratic peace, see Dean Babst, "Elective Governments: A Force for Peace," *Wisconsin Sociologist*, 1964;

Rudolph J. Rummel, *Understanding Conflict and War*, Vol. 4: *War, Power, Peace* (Beverly Hills, Calif.: Sage Publications, 1979); Michael W. Doyle, "Kant, Liberal Legacies, and Foreign Affairs," *Philosophy and Public Affairs* 12, no. 3 (1983), pp. 202–235; no. 4 (1983), pp. 323–353.

13. "Rise, Peak, and Decline: Trends in U.S. Immigration 1992–2004," Pew Hispanic Center, September 27, 2005.

14. Eduardo Porter and Elisabeth Malkin, "In Minnesota, a Community of Mexican Immigrants Takes Root," *New York Times*, September 30, 2005, p. C1.

15. Walter Russell Mead, *Power, Terror, Peace, and War: America's Grand Strategy in a World at Risk* (New York: Knopf, 2004).

16. Gene Sperling, *The Pro-Growth Progressive: An Economic Strategy for Shared Prosperity* (New York: Simon and Schuster, 2005); *A Fair Globalization: Creating Opportunities for All* (Geneva: International Labor Organization, 2004); *U.S. In the World: Talking Global Issues With Americans: A Practical Guide*, Rockefeller Brothers Fund and the Aspen Institute, 2004.

17. Sharon Begley, "U.S. Science Research Is in Danger of Losing Place on Cutting Edge," *Wall Street Journal*, August 12, 2005, p. B1; David J. Skorton and Robin Davisson, "No Foreign Exchange Devalues Our Universities," *Wall Street Journal*, August 2, 2005, p. B2; also Pankaj Mishra, "How India Reconciles Hindu Values and Biotech," *New York Times*, August 21, 2005.

18. Tony Judt, "Europe vs. America," *New York Review of Books*, February 10, 2005; Tony Judt, "America and the World," *New York Review of Books*, April 10, 2003.

19. Stephen Haggard, *Pathways from the Periphery: The Politics of Growth in the Newly Industrializing Countries* (Ithaca, N.Y.: Cornell University Press, 1990); Nancy Birdsall and Frederick Jaspersen, eds., *Pathways to Growth: Comparing East Asia and Latin America* (Washington, D.C.: Inter-American Development Bank, 1997); Jong H. Park, "The East Asian Model of Economic Development and Developing Countries," *Journal of Developing Societies* 18, no. 4 (2002), pp. 330–353.

20. Interviews with corporate leaders bear this out. See "Zogby International Business for Diplomatic Action Global Listening Research Project, Phase I: Report on Corporate and Foreign Policy Opinion Leaders Views on Anti-American Sentiment," Zogby International, Fall 2005, http://businessfordiplomaticaction.org/index.php; Douglas B. Holt, John A. Quelch, and Earl L. Taylor, "How Global Brands Compete," *Harvard Business Review*, September 2004.

21. For articles and resources that demonstrate skepticism that the U.S. economic model thrives primarily on a transparent rewards system, see the Web sites of the World Social Forum, http://www.forumsocialmundial.org.br; and Focus on the Global South, http://www.focusweb.org/main/html.

22. Barry C. Lynn, *End of the Line: The Rise and Coming Fall of the Global Corporation* (New York: Doubleday, 2005).

23. As Rubin and Rubin have shown, anti-Americanism predates the founding of the American republic; it was triggered by the perception of an uncivilized and classless American frontier, perpetuated by European ignorance and self-interest, and strengthened by jealousy of the American Revolution. See, for

example, comments by French figures Comte de Buffon; Cornelius de Pauw; Thomas Francois Raynal; and German philosophers Kant, Hegel, von Schlegel, and Schoppenhauer, in Barry Rubin and Judith Colp Rubin, *Hating America: A History* (New York: Oxford University Press, 2004), pp. 5–19; see also Frances Trollope, *Domestic Manners of the Americans*, 1827 (Reprint Services Corp., 1993).

24. In 1918 the sociologist Thorsten Veblen defined legitimacy in institutions as the "usages and conventions that have by habit become embedded in the received scheme of use and wont, and so have been found to be good and right." See Thorsten Veblen, *The Higher Learning in America: A Memorandum on the Conduct of Universities by Businessmen* (New York: Sagamore, 1957). More recently, Robert Kagan, a supporter of the Iraq war, invoked the importance of legitimacy in the use of American power in *Of Paradise and Power* (New York: Vintage, 2004).

25. Security and Peace Institute and Marttila Communications Group, "American Attitudes Toward National Security, Foreign Policy, and the War on Terror," Century Foundation and Center for American Progress, April 13, 2005. See also *Global Views 2004*, Chicago Council on Foreign Relations, September 2004; Pew Center for the People and the Press and the Council on Foreign Relations, "Foreign Policy Attitudes Now Driven by 9/11 and Iraq; Eroding Respect for America Seen as Major Problem," August 18, 2004.

26. Richard Haass, *The Opportunity* (New York: Public Affairs, 2005).

I

ADDITIONAL READING

I

SUGGESTED ADDITIONAL READING

Appleby, R. Scott, and Martin E. Marty, eds. *The Fundamentalism Project*. Chicago: University of Chicago Press, 1991.

Barber, Benjamin. *Jihad Versus McWorld: How Globalism and Tribalism Are Reshaping the World*. New York: Ballantine, 1996.

Berman, Paul. *Power and the Idealists: Or, The Passion of Joschka Fischer and Its Aftermath*. Brooklyn, N.Y.: Soft Skull Press, 2005.

Buruma, Ian, and Avishai Margalit. *Occidentalism: The West in the Eyes of Its Enemies*. New York: Penguin, 2004.

Crockatt, Richard. *America Embattled: September 11, Anti-Americanism, and the Global Order*. New York: Routledge, 2003.

Gaddis, John Lewis. *We Now Know: Rethinking Cold War History*. New York: Oxford University Press, 1998.

Gibson, John. *Hating America: The New World Sport*. New York: Regan Books, 2004.

Granta. "Over There: How America Sees the World." *Granta* 84 (January 1, 2004).

———. "What We Think of America." *Granta* 77 (March 28, 2002).

Greene, Graham. *The Quiet American*, 1955. New York: Penguin Books, 1996.

Hardt, Michael, and Antonio Negri. *Empire*. Cambridge: Harvard University Press, 2000.

Hertsgaard, Mark. *The Eagle's Shadow: Why America Fascinates and Infuriates the World*. New York: Picador/Farrar, Straus and Giroux, 2002.

Hodgson, Godfrey. *More Equal Than Others: America from Nixon to the New Century*. Princeton, N.J.: Century Foundation and Princeton University Press, 2004.

Hoffman, Stanley. "America Goes Backward." *New York Review of Books* 50, no. 10 (June 12, 2003): 74.

Hollander, Paul. *Understanding Anti-Americanism: Its Origins and Impact at Home and Abroad*. Chicago: Ivan R. Dee, 2004.

———. *Anti-Americanism: Critiques at Home and Abroad 1965–1990*. New York: Oxford University Press, 1992.

Huntington, Samuel. *Who Are We: The Challenges to America's National Identity*. New York: Simon and Schuster, 2004.

Joffe, Josef. "A World Without Israel." *Foreign Policy* 146 (January/February 2005): 36.

———. "Who's Afraid of Mr. Big?" *National Interest* 64 (Summer 2001): 43–52.

Johansson, Johny K. *In Your Face: How American Marketing Excess Fuels Anti-Americanism*. New York: Financial Times/Prentice Hall, 2004.

Joseph, Franz M., ed. *As Others See Us: The United States Through Foreign Eyes.* Princeton, N.J.: Princeton University Press, 1959.

Judt, Tony. "Anti-Americans Abroad." *New York Review of Books* 50, no. 7 (May 1, 2003): 24–27.

Katzenstein, Peter J., and Robert O. Keohane, eds. *Anti-Americanism in World Politics.* Ithaca, N.Y.: Cornell University Press, 2006.

Kroes, Rob. *If You've Seen One, You've Seen the Mall: European and American Mass Culture.* Chicago: University of Illinois Press, 1996.

Kuisel, Richard. *Seducing the French: The Dilemma of Americanization.* Berkeley: University of California Press, 1993.

Lieven, Anatol. *America, Right or Wrong.* New York: Oxford University Press, 2004.

Lind, Michael. *Made in Texas: George W. Bush and the Southern Takeover of American Politics.* New York: New America and Basic Books, 2003.

Mahbubani, Kishore. *Beyond the Age of Innocence: A Worldly View of America.* New York: Perseus Books, 2005.

Markovits, Andrei S. "European Anti-Americanism (and Anti-Semitism): Ever Present Though Always Denied." Center for European Studies Working Paper Series no. 108, Harvard University. January 2004.

Martí, José. *Inside the Monster: Writings on the United States and American Imperialism.* New York: Monthly Review Press, 1975.

Micklethwait, John, and Adrian Wooldridge. *The Right Nation: Conservative Power in America.* New York: Penguin, 2004.

Naughtie, James. *The Accidental American: Tony Blair and the Presidency.* New York: Public Affairs, 2004.

Pamuk, Orhan. *Snow.* New York: Knopf, 2004.

Pells, Richard. *Not Like Us: How Europeans Have Loved, Hated, and Transformed American Culture Since World War II.* New York: Basic Books, 1997.

Pfaff, William. Columns. *International Herald Tribune* 2002–2004.

Pollack, Kenneth. *The Persian Puzzle: The Conflict Between Iran and America.* New York: Random House, 2004.

Prestowitz, Clyde. *Rogue Nation: American Unilateralism and the Failure of Good Intentions.* New York: Basic Books, 2003.

Priest, Dana. *The Mission: Waging War and Keeping Peace with America's Military.* New York: W. W. Norton, 2003.

Reid, T.R. *The United States of Europe: The New Superpower and the End of American Supremacy.* New York: Penguin Press, 2004.

Remnick, David. "Letter from Cairo: Going Nowhere." *New Yorker* 80, no. 19 (July 12, 2004): 74.

Revel, Jean François. *Anti-Americanism.* San Francisco: Encounter Books, 2003.

Rinder, Lawrence et al. *The American Effect: Global Perspectives on the United States 1990–2003.* New York: Whitney Museum of American Art, 2003.

Rodó, José Enrique. *Ariel.* Trans. Margaret Sayers Peden. 1900. Reprint. Austin: University of Texas Press, 1988.

Roger, Philippe. *The American Enemy: The History of French Anti-Americanism.* Trans. Sharon Bowman. Chicago: University of Chicago Press, 2005.

Ross, Andrew, and Kristin Ross, eds. *Anti-Americanism.* New York: New York University Press, 2004.

Rubinstein, Alvin Z., and Donald E. Smith, eds. *Anti-Americanism in the Third World: Implications for U.S. Foreign Policy*. New York: Praeger, 1985.

Sardar, Ziauddin, and Merry Wyn Davies. *Why Do People Hate America?* New York: Disinformation Company, 2003.

Schoultz, Lars. *Beneath the United States: A History of U.S. Policy Toward Latin America*. Cambridge: Harvard University Press, 1998.

Shawcross, William. *Allies: The United States, Britain, Europe, and the War in Iraq*. New York: Public Affairs, 2004.

Shorrock, Tim. "The Struggle for Democracy in South Korea in the 1980s and the Rise of Anti-Americanism." *Third World Quarterly* 8, no. 4 (October 1986): 1198–1199.

Sim, Stuart. *Fundamentalist World: The New Dark Age of Dogma*. (Cambridge: Icon Books), 2004.

Soros, George. *The Bubble of American Supremacy: Correcting the Misuse of American Power*. New York: Public Affairs, 2003.

Steinberg, David I. *Korean Attitudes Toward the United States: Changing Dynamics*. Armonk, N.Y.: M. E. Sharpe, 2005.

Stiglitz, Joseph E. *Globalization and Its Discontents*. New York: W. W. Norton, 2003.

Thornton, Thomas Perry, ed. *Anti-Americanism: Origins and Contexts*. Newbury Park, Calif.: Sage Publications, 1998.

Tocqueville, Alexis de. *Democracy in America*, 1835. New York: Vintage Books, 1954.

Van Ham, Peter. *Improving America's Image After 9/11: The Role of Public Diplomacy*. Madrid: Real Instituto Elcano, 2003.

Zakaria, Fareed. "The World's Most Dangerous Ideas: Hating America." *Foreign Policy* 144 (September/October 2004): 47–49.

———. "Why Do They Hate Us? The Politics of Rage." *Newsweek* 138, no. 16 (October 15, 2001): 22–25.

Zaldívar, Carlos Alonso. *Miradas torcidas. Percepciones mutuas entre España y Estados Unidos*. Madrid: Real Instituto Elcano, 2003.

PUBLIC OPINION AND POLLS

Anti-Defamation League
Arab American Institute
BBC World Service
Better World Campaign
Business for Diplomatic Action
Chicago Council on Foreign Relations
Consejo Argentino Para Las Relaciones Internacionales
Consejo Mexicano de Asuntos Internacionales
Eurobarometer (European Commission Public Opinion Analysis)
Foreign Policy Association
Gallup Poll
German Marshall Fund of the United States
Global Market Insite
GlobeScan

Guardian Opinion Polls
Latinobarómetro
Lowy Institute for International Policy (Australia)
Market and Opinion Research International (MORI) (Britain)
Nation Brands Index (Anholt-GMI)
Pew Global Attitudes Project
Pew Research Center for the People and the Press
Program on International Policy Attitudes (PIPA), University of Maryland
Research International
Terror Free Tomorrow (Indonesia)
University of Miami Business School
Zogby International

FOREIGN PRESS SURVEY

ABC (Spain)
Acanefe
Africa News
Agence France Presse
Al-Ahram Weekly (Egypt)
AllAfrica.com
Anatolia News Agency
Arab News
Asahi Shimbun (Japan)
Asia Week
Asian Age
Australian
Bangkok Post (Thailand)
Bitterlemons International
   (Middle East)
Business Times (Malaysia)
Canberra Times
Chatham House (RIAA)
Clarín (Argentina)
Copenhagen Politiken (Denmark)
Corriere della Serra (Italy)
Daily Star (UK)
Daily Telegraph (UK)
Daily Times (Pakistan)
Dawn (Pakistan)
Der Spiegel (Germany)
Deutsche Welle (Germany)
Die Welt (Germany)
Economist
Egypt Today

Egyptian Gazette
El Cronista (Argentina)
El Mercurio (Chile)
El Mundo (Spain)
El País (Spain)
El Tiempo (Colombia)
El Universal (Mexico)
El Universal (Venezuela)
EUObserver.com
Europe Information Service—
   European Report
Financial Times
Folha de São Paulo (Brazil)
Frankfurter Allgemeine Zeitung
   (Germany)
Frankfurter Rundschau (Germany)
Gazeta Mercantil Intl Ed (Brazil)
Guardian (UK)
Gulf News
Ha'arezt (Israel)
Handelsblatt (Germany)
Helsingin Sanomat (Finland)
Hina (Croatia)
Hurriyet (Istanbul)
Independent (UK)
InfoBae (Argentina)
Jakarta Post
Jerusalem Post
Jordan Times
Jornal do Brasil
Korea Herald
Korea Times

La Jornada (Mexico)
La Libération (France)
La Libre Belgique (Belgium)
La Nacíon (Argentina)
La Razón (Argentina)
La Repubblica (Italy)
La República (Peru)
La Stampa (Italy)
Le Figaro (France)
Le Monde (France)
Le Monde Diplomatique (France)
Le Soir (France)
Liberation (Morocco)
Magyar Hirlap (Hungary)
Mail and Guardian (South Africa)
Malaysia General News
Manila Bulletin
Manila Times
Middle East Mirror
Middle East News Agency
Middle East Reporter
Nation (Kenya)
Nation (Pakistan)
Nation (Thailand)
Natural Resources Defense Council
New Statesman (UK)
New Straits Times (Malaysia)
Notimex (Mexico)
O Globo Online (Brazil)

Observer (UK)
Página/12 (Argentina)
Philippine Daily Inquirer
PolitixGroup:
   http://www.politixgroup.com
Polityka (Poland)
Reforma (Mexico)
Rompres (Romania)
SBC
Scotsman
Sme (Slovakia)
South China Morning Post
Spectator (UK)
Standard (Kenya)
Sueddeutsche Zeitung (Germany)
Sydney Morning Herald
Tageblatt (Luxembourg)
Taipei Times
This Day (Nigeria)
Times (London)
Times of India
Turkish Daily News
Vjesnik (Croatia)
Warsaw Voice
World Health Organization
Wuppertal Institute for Climate,
   Environment, and Energy
Xinhua General News Service (China)

INDEX